OBJECTIVITY

THE OBLIGATIONS OF IMPERSONAL REASON

OBJECTIVITY

THE OBLIGATIONS OF
IMPERSONAL REASON

Nicholas Rescher

University of Notre Dame Press

NOTRE DAME AND LONDON

Manufactured in the United States of America

Book design by Wendy McMillen
Set in 10.5/13 Bembo by Books International
Printed and bound by Braun-Brumfield

Library of Congress Cataloging-in-Publication Data
Rescher, Nicholas.
    Objectivity : the obligations of impersonal reason / Nicholas
Rescher.
        p.   cm.
    Includes bibliographical references and index.
    ISBN 0-268-03701-9 (alk. paper). —ISBN 0-268-03703-5 (alk.
paper)
    1. Objectivity.   I. Title.
BD220.R49   1997
149'.7—dc20   96-26431
                                                    CIP

∞ The paper used in this publication meets the minimum
requirements of the American National Standard for Information Sciences
Permanence of Paper for Printed Library Materials,
ANSI Z39.48-1984

FOR AXEL WÜSTEHUBE

Dedicated Philosopher and Good Friend

CONTENTS

PREFACE

This book was written between November 1994 and October 1995, drawing upon work done over the preceding two decades in a wide variety of contexts. It appeared to me on reflection that many threads of this work ran together to tell a unified story about objectivity that defends this traditional desideratum against a wide variety of fashionably modern and "postmodern" objections.

I am grateful to Estelle Burris for the patience and competence with which she has turned my hen scratches into an elegantly word-processed text.

Nicholas Rescher
Pittsburgh

INTRODUCTION

Why should I not just go my own way in matters of belief, decision, and evaluation without worrying about what others may or may not do? Why should I seek to be objective—to proceed as other intelligent people would do in my place? Why should not an all-pervasive relativism of "to each his own" prevail, instead of an endeavor to assess what people do by impersonal standards of rationality and good sense? These questions set the problem-agenda to which this book addresses itself.

Objectivity has fallen on hard days. Among some because of a failure to understand its linkage to rationality. Among others, who understand this linkage all too well, because rationality itself is an object of repugnance. To be sure, objectivity has not fallen from philosophical view—various influential philosophers of the day have a good deal to say *about* it. It is just that they generally do not have much good to say *for* it.[1] Feminists see it as a male fetish, new-agers reject it as mere left-brain thinking, radicals dismiss it as a cover for bourgeois self-interest. Most of the fashionable tendencies of the day agree in wanting to topple objectivity from its traditional pedestal. We live in an era where the spirit of the times favors the siren call of subjectivism, relativism, skepticism. In particular, our era is witnessing the influences of three tendencies that undermine objectivity:

- A cultural relativism that has diffused from anthropology into much of the social science and the social theory of the day, urging that each culture and subculture has its own set of standards somehow extracted from its contingent historical vicissitudes—and any one of which is as vital and appropriate as any other. To maintain the primacy of our view one against others is a matter of imperialistic ethnocentrism.
- A liberalistic political correctness that presses the questions: Who are we to insist that our standards are superior to theirs?—and which goes on to insist on a live-and-let-live open-mindedness that takes the line: To each his own (presumably recast as: "To all their own").
- A postmodern aversion to the normative, denying that there are any inherently cogent standards. The very idea of the true, the right, the

1

just, etc. is discussed as part of an obsolete dogmatism. There are no general, parochialism-transcending standards. Sense vs. nonsense, truth vs. fiction, and all such normative distinctions simply lie in the eye of the beholder.

These widely current tendencies of thought, and others like them, all conjoin to undermine a traditionalistic prizing of objectivity and to consign its claims to the trash-heap of the obsolete, unfashionable, and untenable.

Against all such negativistic tendencies, the present discussion will seek to rehabilitate the case from a commitment to objectivity. And there is good reason for such a venture. For what a relativistic indifferentism to truth and rightness in effect achieves is to destroy the very conception it presumably elucidates. Where a factual question is at issue ("Was there indeed a Nazi holocaust that killed more than six million people in execution camps?") an answer that is supposed to hold true for X but not for Y is not an answer at all. And the same situation obtains where a moral question is concerned ("Is it morally acceptable to foster an ideological program by killing people?"). A physics, a history, a morality that abandons its claims to impersonal cogency is simply no physics, no history, no morality at all.

The deliberations of the book propose to locate objectivity's reason for being deep in our nature as "rational animals" by tracing its source back into the very core of rationality itself. Admittedly, all that one can do on objectivity's behalf is to indicate the flaws and fallacies at work in the deliberations of those who recommend its dismissal. The point of such an exercise is to show that a rejection of objectivity is in fact unreasonable— and to accomplish this in the only way worth following, that of reasoned argumentation. Of course, the logophobes to whom rationality itself means little or nothing will themselves doubtless reject any such argumentation with disdain. There is no point in trying to convert them by a rationality they explicitly abandon. All one can reasonably expect to achieve is to reach people who are not as yet among those converted to the cause of unreason. My hope is that this book will make some small contribution to this very large task.

—one—

OBJECTIVITY
AND RATIONALITY

Synopsis

(1) Objectivity calls for putting one's idiosyncratic predilections and parochial preferences aside in forming one's beliefs, evaluations, and choices. It is a matter of proceeding in line not with one's inclinations but with the dictates of impartial reason. (2) The universality of reason must be recognized: What it is rational for one person to do, to believe, or to value will thereby also of necessity be equally rational for the rest of us who might find ourselves in the same circumstances. For rationality is inherently "objective": it does not reconfigure itself to meet the idiosyncratic predilections of particular individuals. To be sure, objectivity will have to take context into account, seeing that different individuals and groups confront very different objective situations. Rationality is universal, but it is circumstantially universal—and objectivity with it. It is a matter of what "any of us" would do in one's place. (3) The "us" at issue in that formula's reach for generality can in theory involve a lesser or a larger group. For present purposes, however, it will have to be seen as the group of rational beings in general. On this basis, objectivity is coordinate with the universalized concern for the modus operandi of rational beings at large. (4) The contextuality of good reasons can be reconciled with the universality of rationality itself by taking a hierarchical view of the process through which the absolutistic (and uniform) conception of ideal rationality is brought to bear context-differentially on the resolution of concrete cases and particular situations. (5) By way of post-script, it may be noted that K. R. Popper's idea that objectivity calls for leaving agents out of it is not only eccentric but inappropriate.

1. WHAT OBJECTIVITY IS ALL ABOUT

The issue of the objectivity of claims and contentions has two principal sides or aspects. One is object-oriented. It relates to an aspect of subject matter, namely, whether the claims at issue deal with actual *existents*—with concretely realized objects in the real world rather than with mere phe-

3

nomena or impressions or speculative possibilities and comparable things of the mind. This sort of *ontological* objectivity turns on the pivotal contrast between that which is in some way connected with existing things and that which is somehow ideational and mind-bound. The salient distinction here is that between real things and mere appearances.

However, the second, presently more relevant mode of "objectivity" is something rather different. It relates to the appropriateness of *claims or contentions*, addressing the question of whether a claim is impersonally and generically cogent rather than personal and idiosyncratic—whether it holds not just for me (egocentric subjectivity) or for some of us (parochial subjectivity) but for all of us (impersonal or interpersonal objectivity). It is this *epistemic* mode of objectivity that primarily concerns us here. Objectivity in this sense has to do not with the *subject matter* of a claim but with its *justification*. It pivots on the way the claim is substantiated and supported—namely without the introduction of any personal biases or otherwise distortive individual idiosyncrasies, preferences, predilections, etc. It is this sort of probative "objectivity"—one that stands coordinate with rational cogency—that will be our primary focus of concern.[1]

Objectivity is related to reality in a rather complex way. Emotions, illusions, and delusions are in a way *real* enough—we have real fears of ghosts and real experiences of mirages. But while such of-oriented experiences are real enough, those ghosts and mirages that they purport are not. They are figments of our own imagination. And this fact of their inaccessibility to others precludes their qualifying as objective.

Objectivity calls for not allowing the indications of reason, reasonableness, and good common sense to be deflected by "purely subjective" whims, biases, prejudices, preferences, etc. Accordingly, objectivity always strives for the sensible resolution, while subjectivity gives rein to temper and lets personal inclination have its way. This does not require excluding personal values as such (how could humans ever achieve that?), but rather insists on not being deflected from the path of reason by rationally inappropriate or prejudicial influences. The juror who gives credence to the defendant's pretty sister that he denies to a less attractive prosecution witness is a traitor to objectivity. And so is the laboratory investigator who admits to the record a reading favorable to his expectations but dismisses an unfavorable one as a mere observation error. What matters in this regard is not reality versus appearance, but generalized impersonal cogency as opposed to an indulgence of potentially idiosyncratic subjectivity. Epistemic objectivity is thus tantamount to rational appropriateness. It consists in proceeding in such a way that people at large—or at any rate the reasonable ones among them—will see the sense of it because any sensible person possessed of the relevant information would do the same.[2]

The tendencies and pressures that deflect people from being objective—from heeding the call of reason and reasonableness in matters of belief, action, and evaluation—will preeminently include:

- prejudices and "passions": hatred, fear, envy, greed, etc.
- conformity: just "going with the flow" to do the popularly done thing rather than thinking things through
- personal affinity, loyalty and affective involvement with particular individuals and cliques
- ideological or political allegiances
- personal bias: giving credit or discredit by appreciation or "symbolic" connection rather than on merit
- "wishful thinking": being guided by our own desires and conveniences rather than by evidence and argument

Failures of objectivity are at work in all such ways of yielding to the pull of personal or group idiosyncrasies so as to depart from rationality's call to be guided by the impersonally telling realities of the situation. Objectivity wears its meaning on its sleeve for all to see; with subjectivity we must inquire into the idiosyncratic predilections of the individual.

Epistemic objectivity is sometimes said to turn on the appearance/reality contrast: objectivity gets at the reality of things, while subjectivity coordinates with mere appearances. But this is misleading. Objectivity is not necessarily detached from the issue of appearance. A perfectly viable way to objectivity proceeds by the consideration of how things *should* appear to me, how they *would* appear to me if matters went well—if conditions were right in terms of external circumstances and personal reactions. The salient contrast is not between objectivity and appearance as such; rather it is between actual appearance, no-questions-asked, and the normatively geared issue of what sorts of appearances would count as appropriate in given circumstances.

To get a better grasp on objectivity, it is thus useful to examine its contrast, subjectivity. In one sense, of course, any human experience is "subjective"—by its very nature it belongs to some subject or other (as any *thought* of course also must). But this is not really the point at issue: what matters here is the difference between what pertains to persons at large and what pertains to a particular person individually, between what is generi-

cally cogent for people in general and what is individual-specific. And
once this key difference is taken into account, it emerges that human experiences—and indeed even human *feelings*—can be objective, that is, can
be cut loose from the idiosyncratic peculiarities of individuals by being
of such a nature that any normal person whatsoever could reasonably
be expected to have the same experience (or the same feeling) in the
circumstances at issue. It is a matter of universality of access, of being
within reach of all.

Objectivity can helpfully be viewed in terms of a pictographic analogy,
that of scenery painting. There is, of course, no feasible way of a painting's
depicting a scene except from a particular vantage point. Pictographic objectivity cannot in principle consist in attempting the depiction of "a view
from nowhere." And so what is at issue with objectivity is not point-
of-view-lessness but what might be characterized as photographic accuracy—trying to represent pretty much what any normal observer would
recognize as a depiction of that scene from that point of view. An eccentric, highly personalized treatment of a scene—that of a dadaist, say,
or of a cubist, or of a Picasso—lacks (no doubt for good and sufficient
artistic reasons) the sort of objectivity that is at issue with trying to depict
what "is actually there for anyone to see," rather than seeking to present a
strictly personalized response to it.

It is also instructive to consider the subject/object from the angle of
the poet. For the poet wishes to communicate personal, private, idiosyncratic vision in the generally accessible linguistic medium of his society.
He seeks to formulate his own reaction to things and does not care if the
rest of us *share* it as long as we *understand* it. While the poem's words,
framed with an unrestricted communicative intent in this way, have a certain objective aspect, nevertheless the *content* of the poem—the vision of
things that it presents—is something personalized and subjective. The poet
accordingly does not, in general, care a fig for "what another would say in
his place." A poem is a public and generally accessible vehicle for a private
and potentially idiosyncratic message. In this way, poetry differs crucially
from science where the message deliberately seeks to be universal not only
in accessibility but in purport. While both the poet and the scientist
may seek universality of access, the scientist alone wants to present an objective, impartial, and even in some degree impersonal vision of the facts.

Physicists see objectivity as a matter of the invariance of results under
changes of an observer-correlative coordinate system. Analogously, we
may regard cognitive objectivity in general as a matter of an invariance

of result under changes of a opinion-correlative system of personal or communally held prejudices, preferences, biases, or the like. An objective judgment is one that abstracts from personal idiosyncrasies or group parochialisms. It is a judgment made without the influence of individual or communal preferences and predilections, a judgment in line with generic standards of rationality that can plausibly be seen as abstracting from the personal or communal inclinations or allegiances. Objective judgments are those that have a cogency compelling for everyone alike (or at least all normal and sensible people), independently of idiosyncratic tendencies and inclinations. Those agents who resolve the issues at hand by doing everything that can reasonably be expected of them to honor the demands of rationality are being objective.

Objectivity, then, is a matter of universality (or at least generality) of recognition access, unrestricted availability to the community of standard respondents—in the cognitive case *rational thinkers*, in the photographic case *normal observers*. Such objectivity calls for seeking to eliminate the distorting influence of personal or parochial eccentricities. The crucial thing for objective comportment is that another sensible person, presented with what is essentially the same problem situation, would then say: "Yes I can see why he resolved the issue that way. In the circumstances, I would have done much the same thing myself."

To be sure, there is, as this account indicates, a significant difference between the objectivity of thought (of conception) and the objectivity of feeling (of perception). With the former, conception, it is a matter of what any *rational* (intellectually idealized) person could reasonably be expected to think in the circumstances; with the latter, perception, it is a matter of what any *normal* (perceptually idealized) person could reasonably be expected to experience in the circumstances. But in both cases the fundamental contrast is the same: that between the individual-differential personally idiosyncratic on the one hand, and the individual-indifferent generically available on the other.

One potentially effective means of achieving objectivity is "to put oneself in another's place" and to proceed by taking into view some paradigmatically reasonable person and asking what they would do if confronted by a situation of the sort that one is facing oneself. And of course there is always the prospect of actually asking them. Seeking good advice from others is thus one of the most effective means of cultivating objectivity. Objectivity is "impersonal" and "impartial" not by way of dehumanization but by way of abstracting from those idiosyncrasies that stand in the way of someone's doing what "any of us"—any rational, reasonable, sensible, normal person—would do in one's place. (Committees are generally more objective than individuals.)

Objectivity thus contrasts both with subjectivity and with parochialism. It aims at a standardized result, so to speak; while its contrary brings fragmentation through the idiosyncratically personal elements of individual bias, prejudice, and predisposition, that derogate from the publicly available indications of reason. The distinction is not that between a personal vision of things and an impersonal vision of them, but between those aspects of personal views that are (or should be) compelling for rational people in general and those which are shaped by the particular biases, preferences, and loyalties of particular individuals or groups. To strive for objectivity is to seek to put things in such a way that not just kindred spirits but virtually *anyone* can see the sense of it. It is not so much a matter of being impersonal as impartial—of putting aside one's idiosyncratic predilections and parochial preferences in forming one's beliefs, evaluations, and choices.

2. OBJECTIVITY AND THE CIRCUMSTANTIAL UNIVERSALITY OF REASON

It must, of course, be granted that, as William James insisted, "There is no point of view absolutely public and universal."[3] The "God's eye view" on things is unavailable—at any rate to us. Whatever we can judge we must judge from the vantage point of a position in space, time, and cultural context. But it is not the absoluteness of an unrealizable point of view from nowhere or from everywhere-at-once or from God's vantage point that is at issue with objectivity. Objectivity is a matter of how we *should*— and how otherwise reasonable people *would*—proceed if they were in our shoes in the relevant regards. It is a matter of doing not what is impossible but what is appropriate.

Reason is (circumstantially) universal, and it is objectivity's coordination with rationality that links it to universality. That which (as best one can tell) is the sensible thing for us to do in the circumstances is thereby the reasonable thing for ANYBODY—any rational individual—to do *in those circumstances*. The objectivity at issue accordingly comes down to rationality. If it is reasonable for you to *A* in circumstance *X*, then it is so for anybody else—and conversely. Reason is agent-indifferent. It involves Kantian universalization: the issue of appropriateness for agents-in-general.

What can those others bring and what of mine are they allowed to displace? Clearly what they are bringing is their rationality and reasonableness, their common sense and good judgment. But my circumstances and conditions, my commitments and interests are things they have to leave in place. Clearly they are not to substitute their predilections and preferences, their values and affinities, for mine, their beliefs and desires for mine. *Everything* must remain as was except for those characteristics that go against the dictates of reason: phobias, groundless anxieties, delusions, senseless antipathies, and irrationalities of all sorts. These must be erased, so to speak—and left blank. In making that suppositional transfer, one has to factor out all those psychic aberrations that stand in the way of a person's being sensible or reasonable.

Rational belief, action, and evaluation are possible only in situations where there are *cogent grounds* (not just compelling personal motives) for what one does. And the cogency of grounds is a matter of objective standards. The idea of rationality is in principle inapplicable where one is at liberty to make up one's rules as one goes along—effectively to have no predetermined rules at all. For a belief, action, or evaluation to qualify as rational, the agent must (in theory at least) be in a position to "give an account" of it on whose basis others can see that "it is only right and proper" for him to resolve the issue in that way. An intelligent, detached observer, apprised of the facts of the case, must be in a position to say: "While I myself do not believe or value these things, I can see that it is appropriate that sensible people placed in the agent's circumstances should do so, and in consequence it was altogether sensible for the agent to have proceeded as he did."

Objectivity thus pivots on rationality. But the rationality at issue involves more than mere logical coherence. It is a matter of the intelligent pursuit of circumstantially appropriate objectives.[4] Accordingly its demands are few in type but elaborate in extent:

- aligning one's beliefs with the available evidence
- making one's evaluations appropriately (valuing things in line with their true worth: getting one's prizings and priorities right)
- adopting meritorious goals
- maintaining consistency within one's beliefs and within one's evaluations
- keeping one's goals in proper alignment with one's beliefs and evaluations
- pursuing one's goals intelligently (i.e., effectively and efficiently)

Innumerable precepts of rational economy follow from these demands: "Don't set unworthy goals for yourself," "Don't expend more effort on pursuing a goal than it is worth," "Don't expend more resources on pursuing your aims than you need to," and so on. And this whole business of rational comportment wears its objectivity on its sleeve. For there is nothing idiosyncratic about any of the principles at work. What is evidence for one will have to count as evidence for another, what is an ignoble goal for you is an ignoble goal for me, and so on.[5] The principles operative in the rational economy of things are all objective and universal—though of course their application will bear differently on differently situated individuals.

The generality of access at issue with objectivity becomes crucial here. If something makes good rational sense, it must be possible in principle for anyone and everyone to see that this is so. This matter of good reasons is not something subjective or idiosyncratic; it is objective and lies in the public domain. There is no exclusively personalized rational cogency: what is cogent for me would be equally cogent for anyone in the same circumstances. Both the appropriateness of ends (for a person of particular make-up, talents, tastes, and the like) and the suitability of particular means for pursuing those particular ends pose objective issues that are open to others every bit as much as to the agent herself. Indeed, with respect both to somebody's needs and to his best interests, other informed people (his doctor, his lawyer, his tax advisor, and so on) may well be in a position to make better and wiser—that is, more rational—judgments than the individual himself. Robinson Crusoe may well act in a perfectly rational way. But he can do so only by doing what would make sense for others in similar circumstances. He must in principle be in a position to persuade others to adopt his course of action by an appeal to general principles that will show them that his actions were appropriate in the circumstances. Rationality is thus inherently general and objective in its operations, endeavoring to deal with issues in an objective manner—in such a way that anyone can see the sense of it.

However, rational resolutions, while indeed universal, are only *contextually and circumstantially* universal in a way that makes room for the variation of times, places, and the thousands of details encountered with each individual and situation. This circumstantiality of reason makes for an unavoidable aspect of person-relativity. What was rational for Galen to believe—given the cognitive "state of the art" of his day regarding medical matters—is in general no longer rational for us to believe today. The routines of diet and exercise that a young "natural athlete" can rationally set for himself may not make sense for a young cripple or an active septuagenarian. To be objective in one's proceedings is to do what any sensible person would do in one's place. The resolution of an issue is objective if it is arrived at without the introduction of any resources (be they substantive or methodological) that would not be deemed as acceptable *in the circumstances* by any rational and reasonable individual. An objective resolution is one that is independent of "extraneous factors" above and beyond the resources of abstract reason and circumstantial reasonableness. Obviously, what it is rational for someone to do or to think *hinges on the particular details of how this individual is circumstanced*—and the prevailing circumstances of course differ from person to person and group to group. The rulings of rationality are indeed universal, but conditionally universal, subject to a person-relativity geared to the prevailing circumstances.

Consider an example. I am hungry; I go to a restaurant; I order a meal. Have I acted rationally? Of course. But why, exactly? Well—because a long story can correctly be told about what I have done, a story in which all of the following play a significant role: my well-evidentiated beliefs that eating food alleviates hunger and that restaurants provide food; my sensible preference for the comfort of satiation over the discomfort of hunger; my custom of doing what I effectively can to alleviate discomfort. The whole chain—"alleviate discomfort, proceed to secure food, go to a food supplier, order food"—is part and parcel of a sound rationale for my action. If the chain were severed at any point (if, for example, I realized that the restaurant had run out of food last week), then my action (ordering that meal) would cease to be rational in the circumstances.

In deliberating about objectivity in the context of rationality, it is useful to consider the following apory:

(1) Rationality is homogeneous: it calls for uniformity and objectivity, demanding that different people judge issues in the same way.
(2) It is eminently rational to form one's judgments on the basis of one's experience.
(3) Different people (eras, cultures) have different experiences.

These three plausible-looking theses are, clearly, collectively inconsistent, seeing that (2) and (3) together entail the negation of (1).

The resolution lies in the consideration that, while (3) is unproblematic, both (1) and (2) need to be qualified. As follows:

(1') Rationality demands that different people judge issues in the same way in *the same circumstances*. (Circumstantiality)

(2') It is eminently rational to form one's judgment on the basis of *the available experience*, including that of other individuals and cultures insofar as this is vicariously accessible. (Urbanity*)*

As far as objectivity is concerned, principles (1') and (2')—circumstantiality and urbanity—are crucial aspects of the situation.

Objectivity is accordingly not at odds with having particular commitments. It is, above all, rationally realistic, and on this basis is prepared to recognize that one has to work with the tools at hand and the materials that one can obtain. If I live in the Arctic I cannot grow tropical fruit. If I am a contemporary of Ptolemy, I cannot use telescopes. We cannot escape our destiny, cannot extract ourselves from our position in the world's scheme of things. The fact of contextuality is an objective fact. And because different contexts call for different problem-resolutions we cannot escape pluralism, cannot avert the diversity of product that the diversity of process engenders in the cognitive domain. Physicians could not practice Pasteur's medicine in Galen's day. Problem solutions are situation-determined, even as inferential conclusions are premiss-relative. This sort of contextualism does not engender corrosive do-as-you-please "relativism" but represents a deep central fact about our procedural situation. To reemphasize: rationality is universal, but it is *circumstantially* universal.

To be sure, a yet different construal of "objectivity" can also be contemplated: fairness or impartiality. This is based on the idea of proceeding towards another as we would treat anyone else, and thus specifically not allowing our personal relationship to influence our treatment. The issue here is one of excluding bias, nepotism, favoritism, as with the just ruler, the righteous judge, the honest policeman. This fairness-objectivity at issue with impartiality is something rather different from the reasonableness-objectivity that concerns us here, namely, doing what other reasonable people would do in our place. The two modes of objectivity are not only distant but involve very different sorts of issues. The operative principle of the one is "Treat the person X as you would anybody else in their place." The operative principle of the other is "Judge of the issue Y as anybody else would in your place." Apart from the difference in object there is also the difference in substitutional perspective to be reckoned with.

The fairness-objectivity at issue with impartiality represents a moral approach that is largely beside the point of the present discussion. Here we have been concerned with objectivity only in the former mode of agent generalization. And its appropriateness is not undermined by the problematic nature of its cousin. For we must, in this context, distinguish between:

- *Agent generalization* or *impersonality:* Do in this situation what any other agent would do in your place.
- *Patient generalization* or *impartiality:* Do to this party what you would do to any other in its place.

The sort of agent generalization that is at issue with impersonal reason is altogether proper and appropriate. But patient generalization is something else again. It calls for a mixed reaction because its appropriateness is relationship-dependent. It is clearly appropriate for judges and those acting ex officio as implementers of impartial justice. But it is clearly inappropriate for parents, guardians, teachers, and anyone with a particular special obligation to particular individuals.

Because we know all too well that actual flesh-and-blood people are not always impersonally rational, through having personal involvements with one another, we do not, in actual practice, expect impartiality of them. And so when his own brother is on trial, we expect a judge to take himself out of the picture. When a reporter's sister is in the news, we expect an editor to send someone else to cover the story. To be strictly impartial is to proceed without any bias, but this is more than we can generally expect of flesh-and-blood mortals. Nor does a rationality that does not ask for the impossible demand it of us. What it does do is to ask that these subjective commitments not be allowed to intrude into matters where they have no place—rational inquiry and moral action among them.

Objectivity in its impersonal mode is generally advisable. It is in many or most sorts of situations in our best interest to proceed objectively. But is it not just advantageous but somehow obligatory? Its bonding to rationality shows that this is indeed so. For insofar as we reason-capable agents have an obligation to exercise this capacity—as we indeed do—we are involved in a venture that carries the obligation to objectivity in its wake. Let us see how this is so.[6]

3. OBJECTIVITY AND THE COMPLEXITY OF THE FIRST-PERSON PLURAL

The subjectivity/objectivity contrast turns on the distinction between what is *accepted by me*—and quite possibly by me alone—over against that which is *acceptable for us* in general. This issue of a range of cogency pivots on the I/WE contrast. The crucial distinction is that between what simply holds for oneself versus what is to be seen as holding for all of us. Objectivity is coordinate with generality: what is objectively so holds independently of the vagaries, contingencies, and idiosyncrasies of particular individuals.

But just what is that generalization group at issue? Who are those "we"? Exactly how is that first-person we-us group constituted—that FPP or *first-person plural* group, as one may call it.

Clearly this is in a way a matter of degree. One can be more or less inclusive about it. For it is clear that a FPP group can be more or less narrowly delimited; it is something that requires further specification along the lines of such qualifications as we Americans, or we lawyers, or we humans-in-general, or perhaps even we mammals. Those FPP affiliation groups can vary in scope, in their range of inclusiveness. This poses the question of who we are, and the resultant issue of parochialism vs. urbanity, between how it stands with a narrowly defined us/we group and how it stands at a higher level of generality.[7]

In particular, it is important to observe that there are two principal sorts of FPP affiliation groups. There are those about which we have no choice: fate, or at least circumstances beyond our control, place us into one (we males, we denizens of the twentieth century, etc.) And there are those which we join under the impetus of our own initiative: we lawyers, we members of the Vegetarian Party, we believers who accept that this or that proposition. Again, some very natural and important FPP groups are those whose members constitute a community. But this is not always and necessarily so. For community requires "identification" and "mutual recognizance"; it requires that members identify themselves with others and recognize those others as suitably coordinated with themselves. Such recognition demands a certain reciprocity and the extension of "professional courtesy" as it were. And such a mere FPP grouping can be one-sided: a human being can recognize a chimpanzee or a lioness as a "fellow parent." Some FPP groups (we right-minded thinkers, we perceptive judges of character, we mammals), unlike others (we physicians, we Americans, we humans), fail to constitute such a mutual recognizance society. The crux of community lies in reciprocity: in the expectation by oneself—and by group members in general—that we will recognize one another as such and treat one another accordingly. In communities people "identify" with one another in certain determinate ways. This too is an important feature that must guide our search for an objectivity-determinative FPP group.

When one looks beyond *me* to *we* and *us* how far is one to go? What is the range of first-person plurality that is appropriate for our understanding of objectivity?

The crux is to go as far as is reasonably possible subject to maintaining the prospect of reciprocity and mutual recognizance. And it is this consideration that leads us to the pivotal case where the FPP group at issue consists of rational/intelligent beings in general—anyone who is in a position to effect deliberate choices in matters of belief, action, and evaluation; anyone who can take the matter at hand into due deliberate consideration. Thus when I say that "Two plus two is four" or "'Cat' in English means *cat*" I do not mean to say that this holds merely for us Americans or us college-educated sophisticates, but that it holds for anybody and everybody who is a duly informed rational being.

The idea of an FPP group sets the stage for an important contrast. For over against the WE/US group stand THEY, the rest, the other, the residue at issue with the us-vs.-them contrast. Any community is defined as such through its contrast with outsiders; in virtue of being inclusive it is also exclusive. To be sure, exclusion need not (should not!) involve antagonism. But nevertheless an element of distancing and estrangement is nevertheless involved in it. We cannot have the benefits of community without the negativity of division. This, if you will, is simply an aspect of original sin, of our expulsion from the Garden of Eden and impulsion to the Tower of Babel with its fragmentation of the human family. Nevertheless, there is one maximally inclusive FPP group that includes not only *homo sapiens* but also whichever high-powered extraterrestrial and even celestial intelligences there may be in the world, embracing the totality of *rational* beings. Accordingly, the WE/US group in question consists of rational beings/agents in general: those who function at the cognitive level of having beliefs, the evaluative level of having needs and wants (and thus wishes-preferences-goals), and at the decisional stance of choosing courses of action. In sum, the group at issue consists of all who can in principle act intelligently in the world in the light of beliefs and values, that is, all rational agents.

In matters where claims to knowledge are at issue, one automatically assumes a "public responsibility," as it were. When responsible individuals say "I know" (rather than "I surmise") or "There is good reason to think" (rather than "I would like to believe") they thereby undertake a larger commitment. And all the more emphatically so where they say "It is certain that p" rather than "I am certain that p." They then cease to speak merely for themselves and take on the role of a communal spokesperson, as it were, stating what all members of a certain FPP group—that of specifically rational beings—stand committed to.[8] In contexts of this sort, members of the class of rational beings cease to function as individuals and figure as group representatives. Where normative judgments of correctness, appropriateness, etc., are concerned, being reasonable/rational and proceeding objectively are two sides of the same coin. Here objectivity and rationality stand in coordination.

We are thus led to contemplate what is the largest of possible FPP-reciprocity groups, that of rational (i.e., high-order intelligent) beings, the group $\mathbb{R}$ that consists of all those intelligent beings who have the capacity of saying WE and of entertaining a concern for how it is that we ought to proceed on this basis. And at this point reciprocity and affinity are closely intertwined. We deem them—those others—to be rational exactly when and because we expect them to be able to recognize intelligence in ourselves. In some fashion—however rudimentary—we expect them to be able to communicate with us (something that, after all, even animals can do to some extent). Recognizance, reciprocity, affinity, communication are all bound up with one another in the context of $\mathbb{R}$, seen as a community of beings to whom we attribute a special value on the basis of this membership.

In cultivating objectivity one will, accordingly, care for what is convincing to others—or, rather, would be so convincing if they were suitably situated. If I care for objectivity, then only those things should be convincing to me that would be convincing to others—those things of which I can reasonably say that they would and should be convincing to anybody who would be "in my shoes." We enter (even if merely hypothetically) into a public forum of discussion (of dialectics if you will) where we must see it as incumbent on ourselves to put what we maintain in a way that others (insofar as reasonable) would be hard put to deny. We try, in short, to free what we maintain from our personal idiosyncrasies: from biases, idiosyncrasies, predilections, personal allegiances, and the like. To be objective about it is to speak in the voice of "we"—to say on one's own account only what any one of us would, in the circumstances, be prepared to maintain. It is, in *this* sense, to strive for an us-correlative universality, where the "us" at issue looks to the FPP group $\mathbb{R}$ of reasonable/rational people in general—for all we know, a group that has a wider membership in the cosmos than *Homo sapiens* does here on earth. There is no need to be chauvinistic about it. It is a part of rationality/reasonableness to implement the idea of R-membership in a reasonable and that is to say in a *generous* way: to extend the benefit of doubt to others wherever this can plausibly be done and to err—if need be—on the side of a generous inclusiveness. In refusing to proceed on this basis, one would be undermining one's own claims to R-membership. For this is part and parcel of what R-members are for this very reason called upon to do.

Objectivity keeps us on the straight and narrow path of commitments that are binding on all rational beings alike. But cultivating objectivity is not an exercise in power-projection. It is not a matter of trying to speak for others—to somehow preempt their judgment by a high-handedness that constrains them into alignment with oneself. Quite to the contrary, it works exactly the other way around. The proper pursuit of cognitive objectivity requires trying to put one's own judgment into alignment with what—as best one can determine it—the judgment of those others is going to be. It is not a matter of coordination by an imposition upon others but the very reverse, one of a coordination by self-subordinated submission to the *modus operandi* of the group. Such conformity is a requisite for objectivity, but the matter of how it comes about is pivotal. It is—and must be—a matter of my conforming to them (the generality of reasonable people) as opposed to any megalomaniacal insistence that they conform to me. Objectivity is a policy not of the dictatorial but of the cognitively gregarious who seek to be in cognitive harmony with the rest—at least insofar as they subscribe to the standards of rationality.

But who gets to decide what it is rational for an agent to do? Foolish question! In these factual matters there just is no one who "gets to decide," any more than someone "gets to decide" that $2 + 2$ yields 4 or sunlight is brighter than moonlight. Or, differently put, this is something where everyone must decide for themselves—and are well advised to get all the help they can get, in particular from others in the wider community of rational creatures.

The impetus to rationality, then, has important and immediate implications for our concern with objectivity. For rationality carries objectivity in its wake: the universality and impersonality of reason validate the pursuit of objectivity in direct consequence. Objectivity's insistence on resolutions that are rational and reasonable—that prevent the course of reason from being deflected by wish and willfulness, biases and idiosyncrasies— automatically fosters and implements a commitment to the primacy of reason.

Let us consider, in particular, the objectivity of claims and contentions. An objective truth does not hold *of* everyone; it holds *for* everyone. "Bald men have little or no hair" clearly holds only *of* some—namely, bald men. But it holds *for* everyone: is just as true for you as for me. The questions "who realizes it?" or "who has reason to believe it?" certainly arise—and may well be answered by saying that only some people do so and many others don't. But the question "For whom is it true?" simply does not arise in that form. If that contention is true at all, it is true for everyone. Truths do not need to be *thematically* universal and they do not need to be *evidentially* universal; but they do need to be universal in point of *validity*. And just this is the basis of their objectivity. As truths they will necessarily have that for-everyone aspect.

And as with the objectivity of *truth,* so also with the objectivity of *reason.* If something constitutes a good reason for X to do something (be it in matters of belief or action or evaluation), then it is just as good a reason for Y to do likewise whenever Y's circumstances are the same as X's. Of course X may have a valid reason to do something that Z lacks (say by way of available information). The locution "There is good reason for X to do A but not for Z to do so" generally makes good sense. But the locution "R is a good reason for X to do A but would not be so for someone else in X's circumstances" steps outside the bounds of tenability.

To proceed objectively is, in sum, to render oneself perspicuous to others by doing what any reasonable and normally constituted person would do in one's place, thereby rendering one's proceedings intelligible to anyone. When the members of a group are objective, they secure great advantages thereby: they lay the groundwork for community by paving the way for mutual understanding, communication, collaboration. And in cognitive matters they also sideline sources of error. For the essence of objectivity lies in its factoring out of one's deliberations personal predilections, prejudices, idiosyncrasies, and the like that would stand in the way of intelligent people's reaching the same result. Objectivity follows in rationality's wake because of its effectiveness as a means of averting both isolation and error.

4. FUNCTIONAL HIERARCHIES

But the absolutistic universality of the defining principles of rationality, themselves rooted in the monolithic uniformity of "what rationality is," must be reconciled with the pluralistic diversity of appropriate answers to the question: "What is it rational to do?"

The reconciliation can be effected by insisting that there is a *functional hierarchy* at work here. At the top there are uniform general principles that are inherent in the very nature of the project at issue. But at the lower levels of concrete implementation there is room for variation brought about by the variability of circumstance.

Some things we desire for ourselves ("Mary as a wife"), others we see as universal desiderata that hold generally and for everyone ("having a good spouse if married"). But the crucial fact is that a personal want or preference qualifies as *rational* only insofar as it can be "covered" by something that is an unrestrictedly universal desideratum. Only insofar as I am convinced that Mary will prove to be an instance of something that everyone can acknowledge as desirable (having one's marriage partner be "a good spouse," "a caring helpmeet," "a desirable mate") will my own desire to have her for a wife be a rational one. Only those acts which instantiate in this way something that deserves the rather pompous title of a "universal principle of reason" can qualify as rational. It is not "being the last to cross the bridge to safety before its collapse" but "managing to cross the bridge safely" that would be rationally advisable for anyone and everyone to opt for in relevant circumstances.[9] Only those acts whose *salient* characterization is universally rational are rational at all: what is rational for me must, in like circumstances, be rational for all of us.

One only proceeds rationally when what one does at each step is a particular instance "covered" by a universal principle of rationality that holds good generally and for everyone. I study the menu and order steak. Was it *rational* of me to do so? Of course—because I was hungry, came to eat something at the restaurant, and found steak to be the most appealing entry on the menu. On this last point, for example, it could be (quite appropriately) said that I proceeded on the principle "Presented with various options for food (and other things being equal), select that which one deems the tastiest." (To be sure, other things may not be equal; my choice of beef might deeply offend my dinner guest, who deems cattle sacred.) Here we have a strictly universal principle, one that it makes perfectly good rational sense for *anyone* to act on. Though clearly not every sensible person would order steak, I nevertheless could be said to have done, under the aegis of the indicated covering principle, something that any sensible person would do. And similarly, any rational choice must be "covered" by a universally valid desideratum. It must implement, in its particular context, a principle that is of strictly universal validity, although, to be sure, this universality will be of a conditional and circumstantial nature.

Such a perspective makes it clear that a uniformitarian absolutism at the high-generality level of "what rationality is"[10] is perfectly consonant with a pluralism and relativism at the lower level of concrete resolutions regarding "what is rational" within the contextual setting of particular cases. The ruling principles of rationality never uniquely constrain their more specific circumstantial implementations. At each step along the way we repeat the same basic situation: delimitation, yes; determination, no. The sought-for reconciliation between the universalistic absoluteness of rationality and the variability and relativity of its particular rulings is thus provided for by the consideration that the absolutism of principles operates at the highest level of the hierarchy of rational development, while there is ever more "slack" and variability as one moves towards the lowest level of concrete determinations. The variability and relativity of good reasons at the level of our actual operations can indeed be reconciled with the absolutism of rationality itself by taking a hierarchical view of the process through which the absolutistic conception of ideal rationality is brought to bear on the resolution of concrete circumstances and particular situations.[11]

In being rational, we pursue universal desiderata in person-differential ways, ways that we have good reason to deem effective in the peculiar conditions of our particular case. Not all of us eat what Tom does. But we can, all of us, (1) explain and understand his eating kumquats once we realize that he happens to like them and (responsibly) believes them to be both hunger-removing and healthful, and (2) agree that the modus operandi involved in his case ("eating what one likes and responsibly believes to be nourishing") is one to which we ourselves do and should see as representing (universally appropriate) ends to be pursued by appropriate means—but means that are *individually* appropriate and adjusted to the circumstances of one's personal situation.

And so we pursue common projects by person-differential means. But there can be no rationality at the level of the concrete without supersumptive universality at the level of the general. The overall account (or "rationale") that establishes the rationality of what we do (in action, belief, or evaluation) must be one in which universal needs and universalizable standards play the ultimate determinative role.

People must feed themselves and shelter themselves—what is at issue here are universal human needs. But nature does not dictate any one procedure for meeting them; we must proceed to make the best use we can of the materials that the conditions of place and time put at our disposal. The same holds good for reason. We need to build a cognitive home for ourselves in this world; to create a viable thought-structure for our beliefs, choices, and evaluations. Here too one must simply do the best one can. Neither the project nor its implementation is irrelevant, immaterial, or in-different. The most we can reasonably do in the direction of relativism is to accept a contextualism that is certainly not at odds with the fundamental and altogether absolute demand of rationality: that we pursue our ends intelligently, that we do the best we can with the limited means at our disposal in the restrictive circumstances in which we labor. In heeding these conditions of rationality we put ourselves into a position where what we do can be seen as circumstantially appropriate by anyone, so that the demands of objectivity are fully satisfied.

5. APPENDIX: AGAINST POPPER'S IDEA OF OBJECTIVE KNOWLEDGE

One of the most distinctive theories of objectivity currently available in the marketplace of ideas is that proposed in K. R. Popper's essay on "Epistemology without a Knowing Subject." Envisioning a Platonic realism of objective thought-content, Popper's pivotal thesis is:

> [There is] *knowledge or thought in an objective sense*, consisting of problems, theories and arguments as such. Knowledge in this objective sense is totally independent of anybody's claim to know; it is also independent of anybody's belief or disposition to assent, or to assert, or to act. Knowledge in the objective sense is *knowledge without a knower*: it is *knowledge without a knowing subject.*[12]

This leads to Popper's "third world," a realm populated not by things that are thought-independent in themselves but rather "virtual or possible objects of thought—intelligibilia" (p. 154). These, so it is supposed, are not possible-thought objects but rather available thought-contents. On this basis, Popper goes on to say:

> On this pluralistic philosophy the world consists of at least three ontologically distinct sub-worlds; or, as I shall say, there are three worlds: the first is the physical world or the world of physical states; the

second is the mental world or the world of mental states; and the third is the world of intelligibles, or of *ideas in the objective sense;* it is the world of possible objects or relations; of arguments in themselves; and of problem situations in themselves. (p. 154)

Popper's position involves a decidedly eccentric way of talking, however. Keeping our feet on the ground of common sense, we can recognize four distinguishable items:

(1) The cat and the mat and the spatial relationship between them (cat and mat) as an *objective item* of the physical world.
(2) The *situation or state of affairs*—be it past, present, future, or merely possible—of the cat's being on the mat that may or may not be the subject of some person's belief.
(3) Smith's or someone else's *belief* (be it correct or incorrect, well founded or ill founded) that the cat is on the mat.
(4) The *abstract proposition or thesis* (again, be it correct or incorrect), assertible alike by Smith and Jones, that the cat is on the mat—as formulated in whichever language we ourselves may use to indicate someone's beliefs.

It would be an untenable distortion of sensible usage to call any one of these items *knowledge*. For factual knowledge is inherently relational: it arises only when someone's belief as per (3)—or, if you prefer, their endorsement of a thesis as per (4)—is suitably related to the world's arrangements as per (1) and (2). Knowledge thus involves all four of the indicated factors. To be sure, the facts as such (actual states of affairs) that are known do not require any knower to *exist*. But they do require a knower in order to be apprehended as actually *known*, to acquire the status not of mere items as such but items-of-knowledge. Knowing is something that can be accomplished only by knowers: the idea of knowledge without a knower is an absurdity. Even a Platonic realism of *knowable* facts and propositions does not carry a Platonic realism of *knowledge* in its wake. Because of the relational nature of the issue, knowledge as such cannot be detached from knowing subjects.

Of course, the idea of *objective* knowledge makes perfectly sound sense. But it is not autonomous of knowers, and certainly not a (context-free) "view from nowhere." Nor is it knowledge without a knower (subject-free). Rather, objective knowledge is subject-transcendent. It is knowledge—*personal* knowledge—that obtains in those special circumstances where it arises without the influence of any of the idiosyncratic biases and distinctions to which the operations of particular knowers are otherwise liable. In short, objective knowledge is not knowledge without knowers but knowledge by knowers arising without any formative impact of those issue-irrelevant peculiarities that all too often influence the cognitive operation of frail humans. Objectivity calls for neither extrahuman knowledge nor superhuman knowledge; it calls for human knowledge of the specifically rational sort—acquired and maintained subject to the rules of reason. What objectivity factors out is not the agents themselves but their affective idiosyncrasies.

To be sure, intermediate between "It is *a fact* that *p*" and "It is *a known fact* that *p*" there stands "It is *a knowable fact* that *p*" which comes to:

(1) p & poss $[(\exists x)\ (x$ knows that $p)]$

And it *must* be acknowledged that *this* leaves any and every particular knower out of account, unlike

(2) p & $(\exists x)$ (poss $[x$ knows that $p])$

For by occurring *after* that possibility operator in (1), that existential quantifier comes to be abstracted from any concrete existential involvement. Yet to speak of possibilities for people at large is still not to factor out person-reference altogether. Even the mere abstraction of "knowable fact" does not—and cannot—escape relativization to knowers altogether.

To know a truth is not to enter into an impersonal third world, but merely to come to recognize some actual state of affairs (the cat's being on the mat). Popper's third cognitive world is so much useless (and issue-confusing) baggage. It beclouds the recognition that objective knowledge is simply a matter of the rationally appropriate recognition (of course by knowers) of how matters stand. Admittedly, "it is known" is an impersonal locution. But it is also an ellipsis that supposes that tacit rider: "by relevantly informed people." Thus in speaking of something as "known by the science of the day" we refer to what the bulk of the scientists of the time take themselves to know, not of what exists in some person-demanded realism. It is not that we suppositionally remove people from the scene, just that *particular* people are left out of sight. The "knowledge of the day" is no more a knowledge without knowers than the "vehicle traffic of the moment" consists of cars without drivers. Popper to the contrary notwithstanding, such locutions do not eliminate knowing subjects but merely prescind from their specificity (by way of existential quantification, as in the examples given above).

If we need to refight the medieval battles over universals, then we had best recognize (as the shrewdest intellects then did) that the way out is neither that of an abstraction-denying nominalism nor that of a cognitive realism of world-detached Platonic ideas, but that of a conceptualism which coordinates the status of universals with the possession by ordinary human minds of certain abstractive capabilities.[13]

two

CRITICS OF
OBJECTIVITY

Synopsis

(1) Objectivity has been under attack from many quarters. (2) Anthropologists think that different cultures have different modes of rationality. (3) Historians question the feasibility of achieving objectivity within their domain, (4) and sociologists do so as well. (5) Personalists think that objectivity somehow conflicts with the characteristic nature of the human condition. (6) Feminist epistemologists and (7) Marxists and class-interest theorists question the desirability of objectivity. (8) Post-modernists see all cognitive commitment as a matter of mere opinion and view objectivity as fraud. (9) Social activists, on the other hand, see objectivity as being at odds with an active personal commitment and deny its legitimacy on that basis. However, all these objections rest on some sort of misunderstanding or misappreciation of what objectivity is really about.

1. INTRODUCTION

Objectivity is not exactly popular in the present era. It is under attack from many quarters.[1] Some think that it is unrealistic and unachievable, others that it is undesirable and counterproductive. It is worthwhile to make a brief survey of the sorts of objections with which the proponents of objectivity have to reckon nowadays, and to consider their claims to cogency.

2. AGAINST THE ANTHROPOLOGISTS

Objectivity, as we have seen, stands coordinate with rationality. And no group of inquirers has been more insistent on the idea of alternative

modes of rationality than the anthropologists. But there are deep problems here.

The driving force of anthropological relativism has been the observation of intergroup differences in matters of belief. Its advocates hold that
there are no historically and culturally invariant principles of reason,
seeing that people's (altogether plausible) views about what rationality is
change with changes in place and time. But is this actually so?

What all modes of "rationality" have in common is precisely this—that
they all qualify as "modes of rationality" under *our* conception of the
matter (which, after all, is what we're talking about). At this level of deliberation, "questioner's prerogative" prevails, and our own conception of
the matter becomes determinative. Of course, different people in different places and times conduct their "rational" affairs quite differently. But,
at the level of basics and fundamentals there is bound to be a uniformity.

After all, it is *our conception* of rationality that fixes the "rules of the
game" when we pursue our deliberations about these matters. We have to
play the rationality game by our ground rules because it is exactly those
ground rules that define and determine "the rationality game" that is in
our deliberations. If we were not playing the game on this basis, it would
not be the rationality game that we were engaged in—it would not be *rationality* that is the subject of our concern. It is the determinative role of
our own rationality standards that makes them absolute for us.

But is it reasonable to stake such grand claims for one's position? Emile
Durkheim was perhaps right in insisting that "all that constitutes reason,
its principles and categories, is made [by particular societies operating] in
the course of history."[2] But the fact that everyone's rational knowledge,
standards, and processes are historically and culturally conditioned—our
own of course included—does not preclude their binding stringency for
those to whom they pertain (ourselves preeminently included). In conducting our cognitive, practical, and evaluative affairs in this world—as in
conducting our movements within it—we have no choice but to go on
from where we are. It is the very fact that we take it to be binding on us
that makes an accepted standard *our* standard. If we are rational, then our
standards and criteria of rationality are ours precisely because we deem
them to be (not necessarily the best possible, but at any rate) the best available to us. To be sure, seeing our own standards as the appropriate ones for
us to use, here and now, is not to deny the prospect of a change of standards. But of course our then stance towards those new standards will have
to be identical with our present stance towards the currently prevailing

ones. (As we have seen, a commitment to the appropriateness of his present standards follows the rational man about like his own shadow.)

But are the beliefs of primitive, prescientific cultures indeed less rational than ours? A resounding negative is maintained in Peter Winch's widely cited article on "Understanding a Primitive Society,"[3] which maintains vividly that Azande beliefs about witchcraft and oracles cannot be rejected as rationally inappropriate despite their clear violation of the evidential canons of modern Western scientific culture. Winch maintains that the Azande can quite "rationally" see those occult beliefs to be justifiable in their own (deviant) way. But just here lies the problem. The answer you get depends on the question you ask. If we ask "Do they hold their beliefs rationally?" we, of course, mean "*rationally* on our understanding of the matter." And the answer here is clearly "No," because in fact this sort of rationality does not figure in *their* thinking at all. The fact that they (presumably) deem their beliefs somehow "justified" by some considerations or other that they see as appropriate is going to cut no ice in *our* deliberations regarding the cogency of those beliefs. ("Are they being 'rational' by *their* lights?" is one thing and "Are they being rational by *our* lights?" another.) When *we* ask about the rational acceptability of those beliefs, we mean the issue to be considered from *our* point of view, and not from somebody else's!

The issues that arise at this juncture go back to the quarrel between Evans-Pritchard and Lévy-Bruhl. In his book on *Primitive Mentality*,[4] Lucien Lévy-Bruhl maintained that primitive people have a "pre-logical mentality." Against this view, E. E. Evans-Pritchard argued that primitive people were perfectly "logical" all right, but simply used a logic *different* from ours.[5] When, for example, the Nuer maintain that swamp light *is identical with* spirit, but deny that spirit *is identical with* swamp light, they are not being illogical but simply have in view a logic of "identity" different from that of the identity claims in vogue in Western cultures. The obvious trouble with this sort of thing is that nothing apart from bafflement and confusion can be achieved by translating Nuer talk by use of *our* identity language, if what is at issue in their thought and discourse is simply not reflected by our identity conception. Instead of translating the claim at issue as "Swamp light *is* identical with Spirit" and then going on to explain that "is identical with" does not really mean what it says because the ground rules that govern this idea are not applicable, an anthropologist would do well to paraphrase (if need be) the claim at issue in such a way as to explain what is actually going on. The fact that the Nuer have differ-

ent (and to us strange-seeming) beliefs about "spirits" no more means that
they have a *logic* different from ours than the fact that they eat different
(and to us strange-seeming) foods means that they have a digestive chem-
istry different from ours.[6] To reemphasize: when *we* ask about logical
acceptability, it is logical acceptability by *our* lights that is at issue.

In discussions about "alternative modes of rationality" we do indeed
have a "higher standpoint" available to us, namely, our own. And this is rationally justified by the consideration that no alternative is open to us; we
have to go on from where we are. Accordingly, while one must recognize
the reality of alternative cognitive methodologies, one certainly need not
see them as equally valid with one's own. "You have your standards and I
have mine. There are alternatives." But this fact leaves me unaffected. For
I myself have no real choice about it: I *must* judge matters by my own
lights. (Even if I turn to you as a consultant, I must ultimately appraise the
acceptability of your recommendations on my own terms.)

Anthropologists, and even, alas, philosophers, often say things like "The
Wazonga tribe has a concept of rationality different from ours, seeing
that they deem it rationally appropriate (or even mandatory) to attribute
human illness to the intervention of the rock-spirits."[7] But there are big
problems here; this way of talking betokens lamentably loose thinking.
Compare:

    (1) The Wazonga habitually (customarily) attribute . . .
    (2) The Wazonga think it acceptable (or perhaps even necessary) to at-
           tribute . . .
    (3) The Wazonga think it rationally mandatory to attribute . . .

Now, however true and incontestable the first two contentions may be,
the third is untenable. Compare (3) with

    (4) The Wazonga think it is *mathematically* true that dogs have tails.

No matter how firmly convinced the Wazonga may be that dogs have tails,
thesis (4) taken as a whole remains a thesis *of ours*, and *not* of theirs! Accordingly, it is in deep difficulty unless the (highly implausible) condition
is realized that the Wazonga have an essentially correct conception of what
mathematics is, and, moreover, are convinced that the claim that dogs have
tails belongs among the appropriate contentions of this particular realm.
Analogously, one cannot appropriately maintain (3) unless one is prepared
to claim both that the Wazonga have an essentially correct conception of
what rationality is (correct, that is, by our lights), and furthermore that

they are convinced that the practice in question is acceptable within the framework of this rationality project. And this concatenation is highly implausible in the circumstances.

The anthropological route to a relativism of rationality, is, to say the least, highly problematic. There is no difficulty whatever about the idea of different belief systems, but the idea of different rationalities faces insuperable difficulties. The case is much like that of saying that the tribe whose counting practices are based on the sequence "one, two, many" has a different arithmetic from ourselves. To do anything like justice to the facts one would have to say that they do not have *arithmetic* at all—just a peculiar and very rudimentary way of counting. And similarly with the Wazonga. On the given evidence, they do not have a *different* concept of rationality; rather, their culture has not developed to the stage where they have *any* conception of rationality whatsoever.

When anthropologists say that alien cultures have a different "rationality" from ourselves, what they generally mean (strictly speaking) is (1) that they have different *objectives* (for example, that we seek to control and change our environment to suit our purposes, while they tend to reconstitute their purposes to suit their environment, to endeavor to come into "harmony" with nature); and/or (2) that they use *problem-solving techniques* which are different from ours (for example, that we employ empirical investigation, evidence, science, while they use divination, omens, or oracles). But, if they pursue different sorts of ends by different sorts of means they, perhaps, have a different thought-style and a different intellectual ethos, but not a different *rationality*. The anthropologists' talk of different "rationality" is simply an overly dramatic (and also misleading) way of making a valid point, namely, that they do their intellectual problem-solving business in a way different from ours. But, those different processes of theirs do not mean that they have a different *rationality* any more than those blowguns of theirs mean that they have a different *rifle*.

For the presently contemplated purposes, then, the search by anthropologists and sociologists for cultural universals is beside the point. This sort of spatially distributive universality is not at issue. Our concern with rationality puts us on an unavoidably normative track. The issue is not what people happen to think or do in common, but how they ought to proceed if a claim to rationality is to be made good. (The strictures about consensuality set out in the preceding chapter apply at this point as well.) The supremacy (for us) of our standards lies not in the universality of their de facto acceptance but in their (ex hypothesi) condition as our best estimate of what the demands of rationality are—our conscientiously formed conviction that universality *ought* to obtain.

Anthropologists do often say that a certain society has a conception of rationality that is different from ours. But that is literally nonsense. Those others can no more have a conception of rationality that addresses an object different from ours, than they can have a conception of iron that addresses an object different from ours, or a conception of elephants that addresses objects different from ours. If they are to conceive of *those* particular things at all, then their conception must substantially accord with ours. Iron objects are *by definition* what we take them to be; "elephant" is our word and *elephant* our conception. If you are not talking about *that*, then you are not talking about *elephants* at all. You have simply "changed the subject," and exited from the domain of the discussion. Similarly, if a conception of theirs (whatever it be) is not close to what *we* call rationality, then it just is not a conception of *rationality*—it does not address the topic that *we* are discussing when we put the theme of rationality on the agenda. Rationality, as we ourselves see it, is a matter of striving intelligently for appropriate resolutions—using *relevant* information and *cogent* principles of reasoning in the resolution of one's conjunctive and practical problems. If that is not what those others are after, then it is not *rationality* that concerns them. The issues at stake in *our* deliberations have to be the issues as *we* construe them.

And so, while what is deemed to be rationally appropriate knowledge-claims and rationally appropriate actions and even criteria of appropriateness may vary across times and cultures, the determinative principles of rationality do not. This interesting circumstance does not so much reflect a fact about different times and cultures as the fact that what *counts* as a "standard of rationality" at all is something that rests with us, because we are the arbiters of the conceptual makeup of an issue within the framework of our own discussions of the matter. What sort of thing we ourselves understand by "rationality" becomes determinative for our own deliberations. And this uniform conception of "what rationality is" suffices to establish and render uniform those top-level, metacriteriological standards by whose means each of us can judge the rationality of another's resolutions relative to that other's own basis of appraisal. For those "deeper principles" of reason are inherent in the very conception of what is at issue. If you "violate" certain sorts of rules then—for merely *conceptual* reasons—you simply are not engaged in the rationality enterprise at all. The basic principles of knifehood or evidence or rationality are "culture-dependent" only in the sense that some cultures may not pursue a particular project (the cutting project, the evidence project, the rationality project) at all. It is not that they can pursue it in a different way, that they have learned how to make knives without blades, to evidentiate without grounds, or make rational deliberations without subscription to the fundamental principles we take as definitive of what rationality is all about. In such matters we do—inevitably and quite rightly as well—take our own position to be pivotal. Anthropologists who think that different cultures have different modes of rationality conflate process and product via the mistaken idea that different bodies of justified belief require different concepts of what belief justification is all about. After all, if it were not for objectivity's crucial capacity "to put oneself in another's place," the explanatory mission of such branches of human studies as anthropology and sociology would itself be rendered impracticable.

3. HISTORICISTS

History represents yet another field of serious inquiry where objectivity has been sharply contested. All too often, historical objectivity has been honored by lip service only. And nowadays even this modest benefit is denied to it by a host of skeptical theorists who propose to abandon it altogether, insisting that historical objectivity is simply beyond realistic reach.[8] These historicist objections to objectivity rest on a line of reasoning that runs roughly as follows:

> One cannot escape enmeshment in history. We ourselves—all of us—are inevitably emplaced within a historical context of place, time, and culture. Our own judgment is accordingly bound to be formed and conditioned by its historical setting. And this means that strict objectivity, with its demand for universal cogency, is simply impracticable.

The contextuality of all human endeavor is accordingly taken to excuse and validate a rejection of objectivity. In its place, historians of the "historicist" orientation envision the toleration of an essentially biased "point of view" as something that is not only understandable but inevitable. The only difference here is that between those biases that our set of right-minded congeners approve of and those that it does not.

The flaw with the historicist justification for abandoning historical objectivity is that it mistakenly views objectivity as a matter of extra-contextuality. And this is totally false. Of course historical study must be conducted by people existing within a given state-of-the-art level of information and of ideas. But such contextuality does not preclude objectivity, because objectivity is not a matter of freedom from context. Rather, it is a matter of how reasonably one manages to proceed *within* the context in which one operates: namely, by doing that which any rational person would do in the particular conditions and circumstances at issue. Objectivity in history, as elsewhere, is not a matter of extra-contextuality but of intra-contextual rationality. And it would be distinctly inappropriate to give up on that.

Admittedly, history is, as the dictum has it, generally written by the victors, and often as not historians are—and even see themselves as being—partisans committed to the cause of one particular side of the conflicts that figure in the world's temporal stage. But even if this has, alas too often, been the historical reality, the question of how one is to assess it remains open. Is it to be seen as a lamentable falling off from appropriate standards, or as a condition of things that deserves to be taken in stride and perhaps even welcomed as reflecting the natural order of things?

Traditionally, four principles have been seen as axiomatic for the quality assessment of historical work:

- That any historical account be based on the available evidence—and that the net of available evidence should be spread as widely and inclusively as possible, with no suppressions, exclusions, or distortions made on purely partisan grounds.
- That insofar as the evidence at hand leaves the questions at issue unresolved, and alternative constructions and interpretations are possible, these information-gaps should be explicitly indicated and their indecisiveness as between alternative interpretations specified.
- That where we have to deal in probabilities rather than determinate certainties these should be weighed by the same standards of plausibility and conscientious care that would be expected elsewhere.
- That where a historian's own interests are at stake and her own biases of interpretation operative, these should not be glossed over or concealed but should be made explicit so that readers can assess their possible influence for themselves.

Such standards, and others like them, are surely not too much to ask of a branch of inquiry that lays claim to the proud title of scholarship.

It seems only reasonable that historians should be expected to live up to such standards insofar as the circumstances in which they work permit this. Nobody is perfect, and no reasonable consumer of historical work would expect the practitioners of the field to achieve perfection in these matters. But it is—or rather, should be—clear to all concerned that historians will be open to professional reproach and their work will invite serious complaints insofar as there is any culpable negligence in implementing such standards. Of course, allowance must be made for the time and circumstances—this goes almost (but not quite) without saying.

Interestingly, while historians nowadays often abandon any pretensions to a "scientific history" that describes "what actually happened," they nevertheless almost always want to maintain an objectively defined distinction between competent and incompetent workmanship. There are very good reasons for this. If one way of proceeding were no more rationally cogent than any other—that is, if any and all pretensions to objectivity were abandoned—then no standards could possibly be deployed to differentiate between good and bad historiography. The line between conscientious competence and careless ineptitude would vanish. Few historians would gladly go that far.

The historian who claims a right to be taken seriously by his colleagues and readers here and now must learn to live by the rules of competency as best we can discover them "by our own lights" (for what others would we want to use?). They represent crucial aspects of the quality of work in this domain, a quality doubtless not attainable to perfection but certainly attainable to a significant extent. And what such rules demand is straightforwardly a matter of objectivity of procedure, of due rational cogency, as best the conditions and circumstances of time and place permit.

4. SOCIOLOGISTS OF KNOWLEDGE

Sociologists of knowledge endeavor to extract large consequences from the distinctly prosaic fact that human knowledge is a human artifact. They reason:

> Since knowledge is something which, like everything man-made, is produced by people operating in particular social and cultural conditions, it is bound to reflect the particularities and peculiarities of these circumstances. Objectivity with its need for circumstantial detachment is simply unavailable.

But this position also has its problems. No one denies (how could they?) that everything we include in our canon of accepted knowledge comes to be such as the result of human endeavor proceeding in particular conditions and circumstances. But this circumstantiality of our knowledge does not and should not mean that it cannot escape distorting biases. The idea of what any sensible person would and should do *in the circumstances* is still applicable. There is still the perfectly open possibility and prospect that our circumstance-produced knowledge should be circumstance-transcendently cogent.

The fact is that sociologism's rejection of circumstance-transcendent knowledge runs into trouble because of insufficient care in distinguishing between such contentions as:

- The X's (e.g., Greeks of Plato's time) believed Athens to be Greece's largest city.

and

- The X's correctly believed Athens to be Greece's largest city.

The former is a matter of reportage. But the latter is an evaluation made on our own account. And when we stake such claims that we ourselves propound, very different things come to be at issue. The circumstantiability that any belief is a human artifact (our own included) does nothing to address one way or the other the issue of a belief's correctness (its truth or veracity) or even its warrant (its evidential cogency).

The fact is that it is nowise appropriate to make an inferential leap from

- A belief is a circumstance-produced artifact

to

- A belief is a circumstance-restricted artifact; it is no more than an artifact; its cogency is confined to the conditions and circumstances of its production.

For the artifactual nature of beliefs (their being a matter of human resources derived in settings of space and time and culture, etc.) is something that nowise precludes their truth any more than the artifactuality of a bomb precludes its explosive impact on the real world. In both instances it is the nature of the objective conditions that is the paramount factor.

In particular, and very importantly, the objectivity of science is not something sociological; it does not reside simply and solely in the customs and practices of the community by which scientific work is done. Rather, it lies in the nature of the enterprise as the sort of question-answering endeavor it is. If a scientific question—"What is the melting point of lead?" or "Why do all snowflakes have six points?" or "Why does the sky look blue on clear, sunny days?" or whatever—does not have a uniform and person-indifferent answer, one that is equally available to men and women, to Norwegians and Balinese, then it does not have an answer at all. A correct answer to such questions must be of unrestricted validity; its adequacy is in principle open to check and verification on anyone's part. The repeatability of observations and the verifiability of reasonings are matters of unrestricted access. If there indeed is physics at all, then Jewish physics cannot differ from Catholic physics. The fact—if fact it be—that acquired characteristics are not heritable may be less *welcome* to Marxist agronomists than to the run of bourgeois geneticists. But that clearly does not—or *should* not—warrant either group in proceeding differently in assessing the available evidence for this claim or the cogency of the justificatory reasoning that underlies it.

5. PERSONALISTS

Personalists incline to argue as follows:

> People cannot live by abstract rationality and impersonal objectivity
> alone. There surely is—and must be—a personal space for each of us
> where we are "off duty," so to speak, and can indulge our personal
> whims and idiosyncrasies without caring about how others think or
> feel about it.

And this view has much to be said for it—like many another sort of good objectivity has its limits. But what can be said here really does not go counter to the legitimate demands of objectivity.

The first point to be made is that it is objective reason itself that sets those limits to objectivity. Consider the question: can one be simply too rational in the management of one's life? It is often said that a person's rationality can actually impede that realization of happiness. Assuredly, man does not live by reason alone, and many rewarding human activities make little or no use of reason or reasoning. And so, people often say things like: "Objective rationality is cold, passionless, inhumane. It stands in the way of those many life-enhancing, unreflective, spontaneous activities and interrelationships that have an appropriate place in a full, rewarding, happy human life." Here, however, one must take heed of the important distinction between those actions and activities that are *a-rational* in that they involve little or no use of reason and those that are *irrational* in actually going against reason. Now, reason can and does recognize as wholly proper and legitimate a whole host of useful activities in whose conduct it itself plays little if any part—socializing, diversions, recreation, and so on. Reason itself is altogether willing and able to give them its stamp of approval, recognizing their value and usefulness.

Reason urges the intelligent cultivation of appropriate ends. And insofar as those various a-rational activities do indeed have value for us, reason herself is prepared to recognize and approve this. The life of reason is not all calculating, planning, striving; for us humans, rest, recreation, and enjoyment are very much a part of it. Accordingly, reason is perfectly willing to delegate a proper share of authority to our inclinations and psychic needs. It goes against reason to say that rational calculation should pervade all facets of human life. Reason does not insist on running the whole show by herself, blind to her limitations in being simply one human resource among others.

To be sure, *homo sapiens* is indeed a (potentially) rational being. Yet this is not the whole story; there is more to humanity than rationality. Our natural makeup is complex and many-sided, a thing of many strains and aspects. We have interests over and above those at issue in the cultivation of reason. But there is no reason whatever why our reason should not be able to recognize this fact. To fail to do so would be simply unintelligent and thus contrary to the very nature of rationality. The fact that man is the rational *animal* means that there is a good deal more to us than reason alone, and nothing prevents reason from recognizing that this is so.

Accordingly, one cannot be too rational for one's own good. If, contrary to fact, there were such a defect—if this could be established at all—then reason herself could bring this circumstance to light. Intelligence does not stand as one limited faculty over against others (emotion, affection, and the like). It is an all-pervasive light that can shine through to every endeavor, even those in which reason herself is not involved. Whatever human undertaking is valid and appropriate can be shown to be sound by the use of reason. It is the exercise of rationality that informs us about priorities. For that very reason it takes top priority.

To say that reason is cold, inhumane, bloodless, and indifferent to human values is to *misconceive* rationality as purely a matter of means to arbitrary ends, committed to the approach of "let's get to the goal but never mind how, with no worry about who or what gets hurt along the way." But, such a "mechanical" view of reason, regrettably widespread though it is, is totally inappropriate. It rests on that familiar fallacy of seeing reason as a mere instrument that is in no position to look critically at the goals towards whose realization it is being employed. It refuses to grant reason that which is in fact her definitive characteristic—the use of intelligence.

And a further important point must also be made in this connection. People do indeed need a "personal space" in their lives; they require "a room of one's own" as it were, where they can be off-duty as far as the issue of care for impersonal cogency goes.[9] But for one thing this itself is an objectively validatable "fact of life" whose nature the impersonal use of reason can fully appreciate. And for another it is clear that the appropriate indulgence of our personal preferences and individual idiosyncrasies has its limits. Idiosyncratic aims and preferences certainly deserve to have a place in some departments of personal life, but science (rational inquiry) and human interaction at the social level (moral and ethical comportment) are not among them.

6. FEMINISTS

Feminist cognitive theorists have propounded a position that runs roughly as follows:

> In abstracting from the issue of gender, objectivity is a form of depersonalization—of a detachment from personal involvement that is typical of the "clinical" and "professional" mode of interactions customary among males. It abandons the personalized affective-emotional relationship to the world and one's fellows that is specifically characteristic of females. And for this reason the objective approach distorts and slants the views one takes and the beliefs one holds in any area—science included. There is nothing all that intersubjective about objectivity—it is simply, in actuality, the specifically male slant on things.

Feminist epistemologists accordingly go on to insist that scientific claims reflect a gender orientation—a bias that operates to invalidate such claims.[10] And so, one feminist author speaks approvingly of her fellow travelers' "recent critical protest against the Cartesian notion that reason can and should be a 'pure' realm free from contamination by emotion, in-stinct, will, sentiment, and value."[11]

In assessing the merit of such a position, it is useful to focus on those quintessentially subjective factors of cognitive bearing: emotional re-sponses, instinctive inclinations, idiosyncratic wants and preferences, and sentimental attitudes. What can actually be said for according weight to such matters in the context of rational inquiry? And what can be said against their expulsion from the arena of serious cognitive concern (apart from formulas of derogation denouncing "outmoded Cartesian notions" that are somehow "tied to Descartes' mind-matter dualism"—not to speak of the pineal gland)?

The answer, either way, is: very little. Why we should let our inclina-tions dictate our problem-resolutions in regard to science's characteristic questions about how things stand in the world? What useful work can our emotions and sentiments contribute to our endeavors to resolve problems regarding the nature of physical processes, chemical reactions, historical transactions, economic cycles, or the diffusion of social customs? One can puzzle and wonder long and hard: answer there comes none.

To be sure, gender-specific concerns and interests are perfectly natural and to be expected. Women anthropologists may well take more inter-est than do men in the female bonding behavior of a tribe. But that, of course, is no reason why the findings of such an inquiry—be it arrived at by males or by females—should not be equally compelling for people of the opposite sex. Nor should it mean that the others are precluded from investigating such topics cogently. One need no more be a male to study male anatomy or male behaviors than one need be a chimpanzee to study chimpanzees. The provenience of an investigator (be it as male/female or as young/old or as caucasian/non-caucasian) places no inherent limits on domains of investigation. And it is not—and should not be—an obstacle to objectivity.

To be sure, science covers a lot of ground. Where is a particular scien-tist to settle? Is a physicist to work on quarks or quasars? Will a zoologist study mice or elephants? Provided the talent is there at all, the rest is, clearly, a subjective issue—a matter of individual inclinations and prefer-ences. Such *thematic* subjectivity is there, all right, but *doctrinal* subjectivity is something else again. Once a substantive question is decided on—Do elephants live longer than mice? Do they weigh more? or the like—we would expect all complex investigations to come to the same result. With the selection of problem areas we would accept—nay expect—a gender-specific or culture-specific sensibility. But with the selection of answers to definite questions, sensible people would *not* be prepared to take gender boundedness in stride.

After all, it is important in this context to distinguish between: (1) *Sociological* questions regarding the recruitment of women into scientific work, their career paths, etc.; (2) *Psychological* questions about the sorts of issues that interest women, the kinds of problems and methodologies that appeal to them, etc.; and (3) *Substantive* questions of the extent to which women bring special sensitivities and values to bear in the solution of scientific problems. The salient issue here is the extent to which, once a particular issue is concretely defined (e.g., "How do Polynesians conduct burial rituals?"), it would be expectable—and indeed even acceptable—that men and women should arrive at discrepant answers.

The flaw in the reasoning of the epistemic feminists lies in their insistence that one's emotional attitudes do or should somehow determine one's cognitive findings. As already indicated, it is unquestionably true that personal attitudes will influence which problems one addresses—what one finds interesting or not, and what engages one's attention. But once a particular problem is chosen for investigation and the questions to be addressed decided, then the idea that emotions and attitudes appropriately can—let alone *should*—exert a further influence to determine the result of a well-conducted inquiry is something that is doubtful on the very face of it. Men and women certainly can and probably often do find different issues interesting and engaging. But that on a given question their differential sensitivities could or should lead them to different and discordant answers is an idea doubtful in the extreme.[12] There is no more reason why a female and a male cosmologist should come up with different interpretations of the same data than why a female and a male physician should come up with different diagnoses for the same patient. There can be no feminist electrodynamics that differs from a masculinist version.

Nor does it make sense to see the traditional "objective" standards of rational cogency in science and inquiry as somehow reflecting peculiarly male values. Cogent reasoning, conscientious care for evidence, testing conjectures against observations, and all such trademarks of cognitive rationality hold just as much for females as for males.

Some feminist theoreticians tell us that the seventeenth century saw a crucial turning to the "masculinization of scientific thought," which crowded out an earlier more feminine "symbolic, intuitive, empathic associational" version of science in favor of a model in which detachment, clarity, and impersonality became the dominant factors.[13] But to regret this shift is to ignore the fact that this turning was a forced one. It was forced because scientists then as now wanted to obtain cogent answers to their questions, and the questions changed at that time. Technology came to the foreground and with it the demand for predictive and operative control. The shift from Renaissance to modern science was not driven by a preju-dicial masculinization of the enterprise; it occurred because the impact of new and increasingly powerful observational technologies led people to ask new questions. The issues that came into the agenda were questions to whose resolution issues of control—both cognitive (predictive) and ma-nipulative (operative)—became crucial. The historical reality is that the old purportedly "feminist" parameters (symbolic, intuitive, empathetic, etc.) were driven out not by a change of ideology but by the crude and cruel fact that the science they engendered just didn't work. They were driven out not by prejudice or gender politics but by a cognitive Darwinism that operated on behalf of the survival of the fittest. The long and short of it is that subjectivity has given way to objectivity as a guide-post of rational inquiry in science (and elsewhere) not because brute male chauvinism pushed touchy-feely science aside but because in the natural sciences, at any rate, the prospect of gender gearing has not proven productive in ac-complishing the tasks at hand. The history of scientific rationality as we now understand it was not a victory of gender politics; it was a victory of pragmatism.

7. MARXISTS AND CLASS-INTEREST THEORISTS

Marxists maintain that science (and indeed all of human culture) is a social product whose nature is determined by the impetus of class inter-ests upon the processes of production. And sociologists analogously insist that social interests determine the acceptance of scientific hypotheses.[14] Accordingly, such class-interest theoreticians argue roughly as follows:

> All our knowledge—scientific knowledge included—is a human product, resulting from the labor of particular individuals working in particular circumstances and subject to the social pressures that characterize them. But human effort is always expended with a view to benefit and advantage. In consequence, our cognitive produc-

tions are bound to reflect the nature of human interests and pre-occupations.

Now this is certainly true as far as it goes. But these social determinism critics of traditional science also fail to heed with sufficient care the critical distinction between questions and answers. The questions we ask may well be socially determined by our personal interests and parochial concerns. But if we do our work competently then the answers that we obtain to a *given* question will have to be independent of this. Where we shine the light of scientific attention may well be—and largely is—determined by considerations of interest (in both senses of the term). But the resolutions at which we arrive will—if we are sensible—be determined by the (generally changeable and indeed changing) body of evidence at our disposal. Here interest and social allegiance do not—or certainly *should* not—come into it: there is no reason why capable and conscientious inquirers should reach different conclusions from the same evidence because they have different (noncognitive) preferences. And this is all the more decidedly true where issues of natural science rather than (say) political history are concerned.

One need not deny that interest is a prime motivation of scientific effort. But of course the whole ethos and modus operandi of the scientific enterprise is so designed as to provide advantages for those who do objectively cogent work. The scientific enterprise harnesses the pursuit of interest to the effective realization of its characteristic goals because the reward structure of science is designed to provide recognition to *competent* work.

To reemphasize: there can be no valid capitalist arithmetic that differs from a Marxist version. There is no upper-class cytology that differs from a proletarian variant. Different social groups may possibly have different scientific preoccupations. But as regards the concrete questions, those resolutions should reflect the facts investigated rather than the idiosyncratic predilections of investigators. The melting point of lead does not vary to accommodate the variable interests and predilections of different economic or social groups. Jewish physics, bourgeois biology, or feminist algebra are no more than mirages in the eyes of misguided ideologists. The subjectivity of scientific preoccupation is certainly a fact of life. But the objectivity of problem-solving cogency is so every bit as much. And it is to this fact of life that the reward and recognition structures of the scientific enterprise have become geared.

8. POST-MODERNISTS

While radical Marxists see objectivity as a deception that throws the sheepskin of respectability over the wolf of the class–interest of an elite, post-modernist theorists, by contrast, see it not as a covering but as the non-covering of the Emperor's New Clothes. They reason along the following lines:

> The objectivity of scientific knowledge is something about which (as with so much else) people are simply deluded. Truth and rational cogency are mere chimeras, comforting self-delusions like Santa Claus or the Tooth Fairy. We live in a biased and cruel world where all there is, is what people find it convenient to think. Nothing we ever have deserves the name of *knowledge:* all we ever have is mere *opinion.*

Accordingly, post-modernists maintain that there simply is no such thing as objectivity. The very idea at issue is, so they insist, a vestigial remnant of the obsolete epistemology of an outmoded era—of a time when people still deemed the pursuit of rational cognition to be a feasible project. But we sophisticates of the present, so they hold, have learned that truth, reason, rational cogency, objectivity, and the like are mere chimeras. There is only the fashion of the day—the ideas and beliefs that happen to find wide acceptance. The idea of impersonal cogency has no valid basis in the facts of scientific life.

With the Sophists of classical antiquity, the post-modernists maintain that all so-called human "knowledge" is simply a matter of so many transitory beliefs. The whole idea of normativity—of reason, evidences, cogency, appropriateness, etc.—has no proper place in this domain. There is simply what people believe, what they agree and disagree about. And any idea of an impartial rational inquiry into the justification of these beliefs—into their inherent cogency and appropriateness—is so much fraud and delusion. In the final analysis, everything we call "cognition" is a matter of opinion through and through.

Seeing, however, that these objections themselves are offered up not as mere take-them-or-leave-them opinions, but as correct assessments of the situation, the obvious flaw of such a position is its internal incoherence. It saws off the very limb which alone is able to sustain it.

The post-modernist himself may well be willing to accept this. His stance is likely to be: "We hold no position in doctrine at all. No such formula can ever be appropriate. Our doctrinal discourse is just a ladder that you must kick away once you have used it to climb to the vantage point of a higher insight." There is nothing to stop post-modernist epistemologists from taking up such a position and being prepared to see their own position prevail in the all-consuming deconstructive fire. But there is no earthly reason why we, who are not among the already persuaded, should join them there. Nor—on their own telling—will any such reason ever be forthcoming.

9. SOCIAL ACTIVISTS

It is a widespread—and often condemnatory—allegation among contemporary social scientists that objectivity implies detachment and disengagement from issues of practice and policy.[15] The general line of reasoning adduced here runs as follows:

> Being objective calls for being detached and nonjudgmental—for putting one's own convictions aside. In consequence, objectivity requires passivity and disengagement from the problems of personal and social life. Objective people are mere bystanders who will not take a stand against the world's evils.

This view of the matter involves a grave misconception. Being objective about determining the facts does not demand being prepared to welcome them as is and refusing to try to change the condition of things that they represent. It is clear on the very face of it that using conscientious care to recognize a situation for what it indeed is in no way involves approving of it.

The idea that objectivity implies passivity fails to reckon properly with certain essential distinctions, in particular those between: (1) objectivity as contrasted with subjectivity/parochialism in matters of cognition, and (2) detachment as contrasted with engagement in matters of policy and praxis. The crucial point is that these two distinctions are independent of one another. They relate to totally separate issues: taking a particular stance in the one domain does not settle what sort of stance one is to take in another.

The "fixation of belief" about the facts of the matter as inquiry reveals them is one sort of thing: the goals and objectives one wants to pursue in one's actions are something quite different. To be objective is to settle one's beliefs on the basis of rational standards and cogent evidence rather than to form them in line with one's wishes, preferences, or the like. It is a matter of having the results of conscientiously conducted inquiry rather than the dictates of attitudes play the determinative role. And, so understood, there is nothing about objectivity that somehow constrains or encourages passivity and disengagement. But, of course, understanding the facts as the evidence indicates them to be does not require *approving* them in a way that inhibits or discourages change. A commitment to conducting inquiry on the basis of the principles of rationality (of objectivity and disinterestedness of inquiry) does not carry in its wake a disengagement and detachment from practical endeavors to change the course of things so as to bring one's values to fuller realization and to implement one's vision of "the good life." The idea that the disinterestedness of objective inquiring enjoins a passive disengagement from action is simply wrongheaded.

Given this state of affairs, it follows that objectivity is emphatically *not* the enemy of evaluation and action. It does not require one to be nonjudgmental and passive. "Objective appraisal" is not a contradiction in terms, nor is "appropriate action." To be sure, objectivity calls for evaluating things and situations and eventuations by those standards that reasonable people in general assert to. And it accordingly requires laying aside one's personal preferences and prejudices and trying not to accommodate the parochial predilections of one's group at face value. This does not mean objectivity is at odds with evaluative judgment as such. What is required is that such evaluations should be supported by good reasons rather than by appeal to the mere customs of the group—let alone individual likes and dislikes. And there is nothing about a commitment to objectivity that discourages actions that implement such rational and reasonable assessments. Quite to the contrary! It would surely be totally unreasonable to disconnect one's actions from one's conscientiously made evaluations.

• • •

All in all, then, it must be acknowledged that objectivity has been under attack from many sides. But the substance of the charges at issue is almost invariably misguided. Like old, toothless lions, these currently fashionable critiques of objectivity have much roar but little bite. For all of the objections rest on some sort of misunderstanding or misappreciation of what objectivity is really about. The reason why this is so calls for detailed scrutiny.

— three —

OBJECTIVITY AND CONSENSUS

Synopsis

(1) Objectivity calls for putting one's idiosyncratic inclinations and biases aside. But this does not necessarily require joining in a communal consensus. (2) After all, agreement among people offers no sure route to the rational appropriateness at which objectivity aims. (3) Only in ideal circumstances is consensus probatively decisive, and not amidst the messy complexities of the real world. (4) To be sure, there are many limited cognitive contexts in which consensus can play a positive and supportive epistemic role. (5) Science, in particular, is one of these. (6) All that can be said at the level of general principles is that, while the quest for consensus provides a potentially useful resource, it is no royal road to adequacy where matters of objectivity and rationality are concerned.

1. COGNITIVE OBJECTIVITY DOES NOT DEMAND CONSENSUS

Objectivity calls for putting aside one's idiosyncratically personal and affective predilections and inclinations, by doing what *any* reasonable person would do in one's place. It requires that we do what sensible people at large would agree to as being appropriate in the circumstances. Does this mean that the objectivity-concerned rational person would aim at consensus with others, come what may?

Some theorists equate objectivity with consensuality, deeming the attainment of a consensus to be an indispensable requisite of reason. But there are deep problems here—not least in the cognitive case, where the idea that the lack of consensus undermines our own claims is particularly questionable. In characterizing a belief as objectively rational we are certainly not claiming that there is a universal consensus about it. No matter how sensible a contention on any significant issue may be, there is an ever-present prospect that some people—perhaps even many—will nevertheless quite defensibly and appropriately dissent from it. The validity of our judgments is emphatically *not* destroyed by finding that there are people who reject them.

Failure of consensus is often used as a basis for questioning objective factuality. A dismissive relativism takes the line: *no consensus → no objectivity*. It insists that objectivity requires a rationally enforceable consensus and is predicated on the principle that "if different people can (justifiably) think differently about some issue, then there just is no objective fact with regard to it." Accordingly, it is maintained that when consensus is lacking, the issue is not an objective one: there is no "fact of the matter," it is entirely a matter of mere opinion, of arbitrary decision, of a-rational (if not outright irrational) allegiance, or some such.

This attribution of dire implications to unavailable consensus dates back to the teachings of the skeptics of classical antiquity—to the last of the ten *tropes*, the arguments for skepticism inventoried in classical antiquity by Sextus Empiricus.[1] This argument pivots on the variety encountered across the range of man's culturally diverse views in matters of opinions and custom, manners, laws, and above all beliefs. Throughout the skeptical tradition, this variation of customs has been invoked to mean that a lack of consensus betokens an absence of the objective factuality needed for meaningful deliberation. The prospect of different constructions, different interpretations or opinions, is taken to annihilate the matter in view as an objective issue admitting of some sort of rational resolution.

This sort of position suffers from a vitiating flaw, however. For to validate an inferential move from "People do not agree about Z" to the conclusion "Z does not represent a genuine issue of objective fact," what is required is clearly a premise to the effect that : "If Z is an authentic factual issue, then rational people must come to agree about it." But the closer one looks at this salient mediating premise, the less plausible it appears. Where is the Moses who has come down from the mountain with a stone-graven guarantee that, whenever there indeed are facts, we imperfect mortals can come to discern them with an accuracy that precludes disagreement?

A view of this sort fails to reckon satisfactorily with the reality of an *evidential* diversity that obtains (and must obtain) because different people are differently situated and accordingly have different bodies of evidence at their disposal. And this circumstance makes for a perfectly warranted—

indeed rationally mandated—differentiation of belief. In the cognitive case, for example, there are clearly different defensible answers to such factual questions as: "What sort of person was Napoleon?" or "What motivated Caesar's decision to cross the Rubicon?" But de-objectification certainly does not follow; our inability to reach consensus in factual inquiry on the basis of the available information certainly does not entail that there is no sort of objective "fact of the matter" at issue. Nor does it mean that any set of opinions is as good as any other. Then too, in the case of evaluation, the circumstance of experiential diversity (the fact that different people have different bodies of experience at their disposal) makes for a perfectly warranted, indeed rationally mandated, differentiation of appraisal. (And the same holds for judgments about the appropriateness of actions.)

This situation is vividly illustrated with reference to the natural sciences. The history of science is a story of changes of mind. Where are those generally accepted "scientific truths" of yesteryear—the absolute space of the Newtonian era, the luminiferous aether of turn-of-the-century physics? And there is no good reason to think this process will come to a stop. The scientist of the year 3000 will think our theories to be every bit as inadequate as we deem those of our predecessors of 300 years ago. There is no reason to believe that progress will ever come to a stop in a final consensus enduring across the generations. Different eras possessing different bodies of information do—and must—reach discordant views of things. But such diversity is no ground for seeing science as a failed effort at objective inquiry, as a misconceived activity dealing with nonfactual matters.

The fact is that the partisans of relativism misconstrue the significance of unavailable consensus. After all, consensus as such need be neither a means to nor a consequence of people's commitment to rational cogency and objectivity. We have to come to terms with the epistemic realities, which include:

- the diversity in people's experiences and cognitive situations
- the variation of "available data"
- the underdetermination of facts by data (all too frequently insufficient)
- the variability of people's cognitive values (evidential security, simplicity, etc.)
- the variation of cognitive methodology and the epistemic "state of the art"

Such factors—and others like them—make for an unavoidable difference in the beliefs, judgments, and evaluations even of otherwise "perfectly rational" people. Rationality can be counted upon to lead to *consensus* only in situations of uniform experience—which are, of course, not generally realized. Short of a biological and situational cloning that equips every inquirer with exactly the same cognitive basis for the formation of opinion, it is clear that consensus is unrealizable. In the circumstances in which we labor in this world, consensuality is neither a requisite for nor a consequence of rationality in the conduct of inquiry.

No doubt, disagreement will (and should) engender caution by undermining any facile confidence that we have actually got it right. But there are no adequate grounds for construing disagreement—even stubbornly enduring disagreement—to mean that there just is not objective fact there to disagree about.

The truth as such hinges on what the facts of the case are. Consensus in the community of inquirers, on the other hand, is a matter of human doings and dealings—a question of how people think about things on the basis of the evidence at their disposal. It is clearly problematic to contend that whenever there is a fact of the matter we are bound to acquire enough of the right sort of evidence of find it out. The argument "No consensus, therefore no factual objectivity" is thus deeply flawed. After all, the absence of consensus is not all that serious, nor is its presence all that significant. Consensus—real-world consensual agreement, that is—is a matter of what people happen to concur on. The basis here can be what it will—mere chance, group pressure, fashion, or whatever. But the only rationally meaningful consensus is one that pivots not on what people do happen to agree on, but on what they *should* agree on. It is a consensus that has to emerge in a particular sort of way, namely, on the basis of the weight that good reasons carry with rational people. Consensus does not determine rationality; rationality determines *meaningful* consensus.

These considerations support an important conclusion. Objectivity is essential to rationality but consensuality is not. Consensus is a matter of the development of people's views and hinges on such variable matters as evidence, education, and "climate of opinion." Consensus turns on what people *do* think: objectivity on what they *ought* to think, on what it is reasonable for them to think in the circumstances at issue. And the two converge only in the ideal limit, only where people do as they ought. Only "ideal" consensus—consensus in an idealized community of perfectly rational agents with shared evidence and experience—has a substantial bearing on rationality as such. The crucial point for present purposes is that objectivity—which indeed *is* linked to rationality—does *not* stand coordinate with consensuality.

2. THE CRITICS OF COGNITIVE CONSENSUS

Given that consensus is neither a guarantor for nor a precondition of rationality, it is perhaps unsurprising that, despite the many and eminent partisans of consensus, theorists who reject any and all probative appeal to consensus have never been lacking. In this regard, several major groups of consensus dismissers stand out.

One group of theorists who have rejected the quest for consensus are those who might be called *cognitive elitists*. Their first spokesman was the pre-Socratic philosopher, Heraclitus of Ephesus. Heraclitus distinguished humanity's common *capacity* for reason from the imperfect *exercise* of this capacity, which can produce bizarre misunderstandings even in entire communities. He taught that: "It is necessary to follow 'the common'; but although reason (the *Logos*) is common, the many live as though they had a private understanding" (Frag. 195).[2] Whether individually or collectively, people just are not all that rational: "For although all things happen according to reason (the *Logos*), men act like people of no experience . . . [and] fail to notice what they do after they wake up just as they forget what they do when asleep" (Frag. 194). The great majority have a befuddled understanding; they fail to realize the truth and do not recognize that "the real constitution of things is accustomed to hide itself" from the careless observation of "the many" (Frag. 208). Heraclitus accordingly saw no need to give credence to the views of the herd, and viewed consensus as devoid of probative value.

The most prominent disciple of Heraclitus in this matter of disdaining the general consensus was Plato, who also emphatically rejected the idea that credence should be given to the views of "the many." He insisted in the *Republic* that only a small, select, and trained elite can be expected to achieve insight into the truth of things. Most people are content simply to amuse themselves with shadows whose underlying basis in reality is beyond their grasp.

Plato and Heraclitus thus inaugurated a tradition of cognitive elitism that has found its adherents in every place and era. On a such a view of the matter, what the consensual opinion of people-in-general ("the common herd") deserves is not respect but scornful rejection. From the cognitive point of view, consensus is counterproductive: insight belongs to the few, not the many.

Consensuality also has its *social science critics* who emphasize that, in point of empirical fact, people's dedication to consensus has its limits. For even when inquirers speak a shared opinion or form an attachment to a favored "school of thought" they seldom stick by it through thick and thin. And if people fail to reach agreement relatively quickly in deliberating about matters of fact, then the chances of their not doing so at all increase dramatically with time (see table 3.1). Additional interaction becomes increasingly unlikely to produce agreement; at some point, further discussion becomes unprofitable. The social dynamic of discussion does not automatically promote consensus.

TABLE 3.1

Statistics on Hung Juries in a Study of 2,001 Trials of 1-10 Days in Length

Total hours of deliberation	% of total deliberations	% of these deliberations failing to reach a unanimous verdict
0–1	55	1
1–2	19	8
2–3	10	10
3–4	6	11
4–5	4	24
5+	6	30

Source: Harry Kalven, Jr., and Hans Zeisel, *The American Jury* (Chicago: University of Chicago Press, 1966), p. 459.

Considerations of this sort indicate that an insistence on actually achieving consensus is not really very practical. But with the rise of the "social sciences," worries about the quest for consensus have come to be equipped with a more formal theoretical basis. Consideration of deep-rooted general principles were now invoked to reveal grave problems about using majority opinion as a touchstone of adequacy or correctness. An early example of this approach is Condorcet's argument against the internal consistency of majority opinion. He observed that it is perfectly feasible that a majority should endorse each one of a group of mutually incompatible beliefs, such as the following:

(1) Plato is wiser than Aristotle

(2) Aristotle is wiser than Socrates

(3) Socrates is wiser than Plato

Concretely, in a hypothetical group of three individuals, A-B-C, just two of whom accept each of those several incompatible propositions (P_1, P_2, P_3), let the acceptance situation with respect to those contentions stand as in table 3.2. This majoritarian consensus here endorses *all* of the propositions at issue. But these contentions, being inconsistent overall, cannot possibly all represent truth. The inconsistent "consensus" yielded by majority opinion is not a rational one.[3] It is perfectly clear that consensus offers us no universally safe route to truth.

TABLE 3.2

A Register of Acceptances

	P_1	P_2	P_3
A	–	+	+
B	+	–	+
C	+	+	–

A comparable situation obtains when matters of probability are at issue. Consider, for example, a lottery with 100,000 tickets. Vast majorities will agree that 537 will not come up. And exactly the same will hold for any other *particular* number. But if we proceed to settle questions of truth on this (probabilistically guided) majoritarian basis, then the resultant body of "truth" will be collectively inconsistent.[4] Again, "consensus" procedures cannot yield a rationally satisfactory result.

Nor need an evaluative consensus be all that meaningful. The "Arrow Paradox" encapsulated in the economist Kenneth J. Arrow's well-known Impossibility Theorem is a case in point.[5] The argumentation at issue demonstrates that when, in situations of choice, several inherently plausible requirements are set for forming a collective group consensus from the distributive preferences of individuals, then no rationally viable process of consensus formation will be available at all. Theoretical obstacles to forming a "social aggregate" from an amalgamation of individual opinions thus

indicate the infeasibility—as a matter of fundamental principle—of forming an appropriate preference-consensus mechanism. (And it does not
matter whether the preferences at issue are preferences for action or preferences for thesis-acceptance; since the move from individual to collective
preference is generally problematic, what holds for the goose of action
holds for the gander of belief as well.)

For considerations drawn from various areas of cognitive concern all
combine to indicate that the link of consensuality with rationality—and
thus with objectivity—is by no means as tight as the partisans of consensus epistemology have been inclined to suppose.

3. SCIENTIFIC CONSENSUALISM

Perhaps the most eloquent and committed exponent of scientific relativism is Ludvik Fleck.[6] His basic thesis is that "scientific facts" are always
so in virtue of what the relevant scientific community accepts as such. And
this, of course, is a changeable aspect of the "state of the art" of scientific
thought. But what is often overlooked in such discussion is that the role
of Fleck's "thought style" and its reference to the *Zeitgeist* and the state of
opinion of the scientific community of the day do little if anything to
countervail objectivity. For one thing, the "state of the opinion of the
day" is itself something objective and matter-of-factual and not something
dependent on the variant perspective of particular individuals. And for another, what is at issue in these potentially variable belief systems is a matter
of belief regarding the objective reality of things—about how things actually stand in the world. After all, scientific investigation addresses our
questions about the world's processes and not questions about what people
think about them. Nonscientists standing outside the subject may investigate the acceptability of scientific theories by examining the state of
opinion of the community and looking for consensus, but natural scientists cannot proceed in this way without ceasing to qualify as such.

Consensus accordingly fails us as an all-purpose instrument for the determination of objective appropriateness. But it does, nevertheless, play an
important *limited* role in the conduct of our cognitive affairs in more narrowly defined, special-purpose contexts. Let us pursue this line of thought
with respect to scientific inquiry.

In science—and, above all, in the natural sciences—the pursuit of objectivity via a quest for consensus is a well-established phenomenon,

manifested in the scientific community's insistence on two interrelated consensus-geared desiderata. The first is the *reproducibility of experiments,* subject to the stipulation that only those observations are qualified to furnish scientifically acceptable data which can be repeated and reconfirmed by other investigators; only those experiments merit endorsement as providing scientifically usable results which reproducibly and uniformly yield one and the same generally obtainable outcome. The second desideratum is the *verifiability of claims,* subject to the requirement that scientifically appropriate reasonings (inferences and calculations) must be described in sufficient detail that any qualified investigator can retrace and recheck independently the argumentation on whose basis a given conclusion is advanced. Both of these factors of observational and discursive robustness provide strong impetus toward seeing consensus in a favorable light in such contexts of inquiry. To be sure, this does not mean that consensus is a necessary condition for, or an indispensable requisite of, objective factuality.[7] After all, scientists are also impelled toward consensus by a conformism imposed by promotion committees, funding agency appraisers, and peer review boards.

Moreover, an emphasis on communal consensus in science needs to be qualified. For one thing, a scientific consensus is certainly not stable over time—and is not expected to be. Scientists in different periods will differ not only as regards beliefs but even as regards basic values. (Take chance and chaos, for example; against the young quantum theorists, Einstein insisted on envisioning a God who does not play dice with the universe.) And so in science even the contemporaneous situation of the day will constantly manifest diversity and controversy about fundamentals. (One need look no further than current debates over cosmology or evolutionary theory for examples of this phenomenon.)

And so, despite all its striving for agreement, science is not an inherently consensual affair. Controversy is all too common in this domain. At and near the creative edge of science there are always disagreements. Throughout the areas near a research frontier there are always controversial issues that divide the community into conflicting and discordant schools of thought. Putting astronauts on the moon did not end controversies over the moon's origin; it shifted the areas of dispute, but did not diminish them. The progress of science sees the unfolding of an ever-widening area of agreement as regards specifics. But with the development of the field as a whole, the area of *disagreement* also increases. In science as in other areas of inquiry or of evaluation we cannot and do not simply let the community speak for us. We do—and should—do the best we can to achieve an *appropriate* answer, and consensuality is not determinative here because the community is not always right. (*Vox populi* is certainly not *vox dei.*)

The bottom line of these deliberations is that consensus—actual real-world agreement among people—affords no failproof guarantee of rational appropriateness and is not an indispensable component of the demand for objectivity. But what cultivating consensus can actually accomplish is to provide us with a useful instrument in this regard—a device for factoring our own idiosyncratic biases and predilections out of the modus operandi in question. The quest for consensus is not a royal road to adequacy but, more mundanely, a facilitator of its realization—a means of overcoming at least some of the obstacles to an objectivity that seeks to avoid the potentially misleading impetus of individual idiosyncrasies.[8]

— four —

AGAINST COGNITIVE RELATIVISM

Synopsis

(1) Cognitive relativism rejects objectivity on grounds of an egalitarianism that sees every group's standards for the acceptability of claims as equally valid and legitimate. (2) But such a basis-egalitarianism fails to recognize that the very idea of equivalent "alternative standards of rationality" is inappropriate. In our discussion of rationality it must be our standard—our own basis-framework—that is decisive. (3) To be sure, this invariance with respect to what rationality is does not impede a contextualistic pluralism that reflects different bodies of experience. To reject relativism is not to abandon the inherent contextualism of rational proceedings. (4) The untenability of relativism validates a—perfectly appropriate—commitment to the idea of "the pursuit of truth." (5) The Achilles' heel of a relativistic basis-egalitarianism in the cognitive sphere lies in the fact that inquiry is a purposive enterprise and that some modes of procedure serve our purposes better than others. The purposiveness of human enterprises affords a standard that enforces a rationalistic monism's insistence on objective adequacy.

1. COGNITIVE RELATIVISM

Does the rejection of consensual agreement as a decisive test of adequacy leave us bereft of viable standards? Does not abandoning consensus as an unrealistic demand lead straightaway to an objectivity-destroying relativism of "to each his own"?

Relativism is the doctrine that people make their judgments by standards and criteria that have no inherent validity or cogency because their standing and status lie solely and wholly in their acceptance by the group. It dismisses objectivity by insisting that judgments of any orientation—be it regarding the true, the good, the right, etc.—are always made relative to

a potentially variable basis: a norm, standard, criterion, or evaluative perspective regarding acceptability that differs from one group to another in
a more or less arbitrary way, with those different norms entirely on a par
with one another. In particular, such cognitive relativism holds that there
is never any cogent reason for thinking some possibilities to be better can-
didates for claims to truth, or even as being more probable or plausible.
Different people (let alone different cultures!) occupy different "situations"
that make the things that are rational for some to believe or to do quite
different from those that are rational for others. To all appearances, rational
validation is something that is variable with individual and group circumstances, and thus ceases to have any claim to universality and objectivity.
And so, the problem of relativism arises—one person's or group's rationality may conceivably be another's foolishness.[1] There is simply no place
for an objectivity that transcends parochialism. Impersonal cogency is an
illusion.

Egalitarian relativism thus holds that it is no more rational to opt for one
alternative than for any of its rivals. It does not deny that those who have
a particular commitment (who belong to a particular school or tendency
of thought) do indeed have a standard of judgment of some sort. But it
insists that only custom speaks for that standard, that it is nothing more
than another contingent characteristic of the cognitive position of the particular group. The matter is simply one of the parochial allegiances of the
community—there is no larger, group-transcending "position of impersonal rationality" on whose basis one particular standard could reasonably
and appropriately be defended as inherently superior to any other. The
cognitive relativist, in particular, insists that no actual or possible group of
inquirers whatsoever is in a privileged epistemic position. Every group's
resolutions in this regard are final; each is its own definitive arbiter. There
is no higher court of appeal, no inherently cogent basis of cognitive acceptability that has any real claim to validity. Thus one opinion is every bit
as justified as any other. Objectivity is beyond our reach. It is all just a
matter of what people happen to think. To believe anything else is no
more than a recourse to the myth of the God's-eye point of view, a point
of view which, in the very nature of things cannot possibly be ours.

Over the last century, indifferentist relativism of this sort has gathered
strength from various modern intellectual projects. As the sciences of man
developed in the nineteenth century, especially in historical and sociological studies, the idea increasingly gained acceptance that every culture and
every era has its own characteristic fabric of thought and belief, each ap-

propriate to and cogent for its own particular context. Historicist thinkers from Wilhelm Dilthey onwards have lent the aid and comfort of their authority to cultural relativism. And the aftermath of Darwinian biology reinforced this doctrinal tendency in giving currency to the idea that our human view of reality is formatively dependent upon our characteristically human cognitive endowments—as opposed to those of other possible sorts of intelligent creatures. Not only do the data that we can acquire about the world come to us courtesy of the biological endowment of our senses, but the inferences we can draw from those data will be analogously dependent on the biological endowment of our minds. Various turn-of-the-century philosophers of otherwise very diverse theoretical orientations—ranging from Nietzche and Vaihinger to Henri Bergson and Samuel Alexander—all drew heavily on Darwinian inspiration to support a syncretist perspectivism of one sort or another. Under such inspiration, William James wrote:

> Were we lobsters, or bees, it might be that our organization would have led to our using quite different modes from these [actual ones] of apprehending our experiences. It *might* be too (we cannot dogmatically deny this) that such categories, unimaginable by us today, would have proved on the whole as serviceable for handling our experiences mentally as those we actually use.[2]

Different cultures and different intellectual traditions, to say nothing of organically different sorts of creatures, will, so it is contended, describe and explain their experience—their world as they conceive it—in terms of concepts and categories of understanding substantially different from ours but in principle every bit as good.

Such a view of the cognitive situation also diffuses across various other fields and disciplines. In the social sciences, for example, anthropological and sociological investigations militated towards relativism on similar grounds. Moreover, theorists relying on ideas drawn from psychology, F. S. C. Schiller and John Dewey, for example, were impelled in very much the same direction. And writers who addressed the "historicity" of science generally stressed the extent to which the scientists of one era have different (and yet to all appearances circumstantially plausible and appropriate) views of nature's modus operandi, and feel compelled on this basis to support a particular kind of (historical) relativism.[3]

In this way, as we have seen, investigations in various modern fields of inquiry have combined to provide aid and comfort for the partisans of cognitive relativism. The position thus came to have countless adherents. But is it correct?

2. THE PRIMACY OF OUR OWN STANDARDS OF RATIONALITY

Even a superficial scrutiny is enough to indicate that an egalitarian approach to standards of rationality faces serious difficulties. Any view that prevents us from differentiating between superstition and science, or between uninformed guesswork and expertise, is inherently problematic.

There is nothing particularly problematic about the question "Are there indeed different norms and standards of rationality?" The answer is clearly an immediate and emphatic "yes." Just as with *autres temps, autres moeurs*, so also other cultures, other standards. Rather, the salient question is: "Are we well advised—perhaps even rationally obligated—to see all those various alternative norms and standards as equally appropriate, equally correct?" Must we adopt that principle of basis-egalitarianism: "All of the various standards of judgment have equivalent justifications. *Ours* is on an equal footing with *theirs* in point of acceptability. It is a matter of indifference which basis we adopt—each one is every bit as good (or poor) as the next." And here the answer is an immediate and emphatic "no." There is no good and sufficient reason to see this principle as plausible. Basis indifferentism is daring and exciting—but also untenable. For, at this point we must turn relativism against itself by asking: "*Indifferent to whom?*" Certainly not to us! For, we have in place our own basis of rational judgment, and it speaks loud and clear on its own behalf. Nor yet by parity of reasoning is *ours* equally acceptable to *them*. From just what "angle of consideration" is that claim to merit equivalency going to be made? Not from *ours* surely— for this, after all, is ours precisely because we deem it superior. And by parity of reasoning not from *theirs* either. (From God's? Well . . . perhaps. But he, of course, is not a party to the discussion—and if he were, then what price indifferentism?)

Perhaps from the point of view of the universe all experiential perspectives are of equivalent merit; and perhaps they are equal in the sight of the Cosmos—and even of God. But we ourselves cannot assume the prerogative of these mighty potencies. We humans can no more contemplate information with our minds without having a perspectival stance than we can contemplate material objects with our bodily eyes without having a perspectival stance. We ourselves do and must occupy a particular position, with particular kinds of concerns and particular practical and intellectual tools for dealing with them. And for us, there indeed is one particular set of standards for making such appraisals and adjudications, namely, our own, the one we actually accept in the conditions and circumstances of our existence.

To be sure, people often say the following sort of thing:

> [All] those cognitive concepts that philosophers have taken to be the most fundamental—whether it be the concept of rationality, truth, reality, sight, the good, or norms—all such concepts must be understood as relative to a specific conceptual scheme, theoretical framework, paradigm, form of life, society, or culture, [since] there is no one single framework or single metalanguage by which we can rationally adjudicate or universally evaluate the competing claims of alternative paradigms.[4]

But this exciting contention is eminently questionable. For, there indeed is a single and unique thought-framework that *we* can use in making such appraisals and adjudications, namely, our own, the one we actually accept. (Were we to trade it in for another, then of course that other one would automatically become ours.) Only for someone who has no scheme or framework at all—who is located wholly outside the realm of linguistic and epistemic and cognitive commitments—is there an open and uncommitted choice among alternatives. But of course none of us do or can find ourselves in *that* position.

The normative perspectives at issue with our cognitive (or evaluative or normal, etc.) standards do not come to us *ex nihilo*. From the rational point of view such standards themselves require validation. And this process is itself something that is standard-presupposing. For, of course, we cannot assess the adequacy of a standard-perspective in a vacuum, it must itself be supported with reference to standards of some sort. But in this world we are never totally bereft of such a basis: in the order of thought as in the world's physical order we always have a position of some sort. By the time one gets to the point of being able to think at all, there is always a background of available experience against which to form one's ideas. And just there is where one has to start. It is precisely because a standard-deploying certain position is appropriate *from where we ourselves actually stand* that makes this particular position of ours appropriate *for us*.

In evaluating alternatives we in fact have no real choice except to do so from the perspective of our cognitive posture—our own cognitive position and point of view. (It wouldn't *be* our point of view if we didn't use it as such.) We cannot cogently maintain a posture of indifference. Assuming that we are rational about it, we are committed to the standard that (as best we can tell) rational people in general ought to use—that is, the one which represents our conception's best estimate of the rationally appropriate standard. So "appropriate for us" here comes down to "appropriate (as best we can tell) for rational people" and thus represents our best effort to speak for rational people in general.

If we are going to be rational we must take—and have no responsible choice but to take—the stance that our own standards (of truth, value, and choice) are the appropriate ones. Be it in employing or in evaluating them, we ourselves must see our own standards as authoritative because this, exactly, is what it is for them to *be* our own standards—their being our standards *consists in our seeing them in this light*. We have to see our standards in an absolutistic light—as the uniquely right appropriately valid ones—because exactly this is what is at issue in their being our standards of authentic truth, value, or whatever. To insist that we should view them with indifference is to deny us all prospects of having any standards at all. Commitment at this level is simply unavoidable. Our cognitive or evaluative perspective would not be our perspective did we not deem it rationally superior to others.

And so, in discussions about "alternative modes of rationality" we do indeed have a "higher standpoint" available to us—namely, our own. And this is rationally justified by the consideration that no real alternative is open to us—we have to go on from where we are. Accordingly, while one must recognize the reality of alternative cognitive methodologies, one certainly need not see them as equally valid with one's own. "You have your standards and I have mine. There are alternatives." True enough. But this fact is bound to leave me unaffected. I myself have no real choice about it: I *must* judge matters by my own lights. (Even if I turn to you as a consultant, I must ultimately appraise the acceptability of your recommendations on my own terms.)

The basis-egalitarian thunders: "You have no valid right to your own particular basis! How can you possibly justify taking it to be superior to others?" But of course we *can* justify it; many philosophical discussions endeavor to do so, and some do quite well. "This sort of justification is something you can accomplish only by reasoning, by reflective and judicious appraisal. And on what basis can this reasoning proceed?" Why . . . by our own, of course! (Who else's would we use?) "But surely this approach is circularity vitiating, self-undermining?" By no means! It is inevitable—and desirable. The unavoidable self-justification of rationality signalizes the fact that a rational basis which would not thus support itself would ipso facto stand condemned as inadequate. "But what makes you think your basis is any better than all those others?" That is a perfectly fair question. We had better have a good story to tell to justify our greater satisfaction with our own epistemic basis. (And of course we do—though this is hardly the place to unfold it.)[5] But this validation of cognitive rationality will clearly have to proceed in its own terms.

There is, of course, no denying that all human endeavors are conducted within the setting of place and time, of cultural and historical context. All our works—those of reason included—transpire within the framework of history and culture. We cannot extract ourselves from the setting of our history and society and technology to enter into a timeless and acircumstantial realm. But the fact that we work from within a historio-cultural context does not limit the validity of what we say to such a context. Our pyramids have a vertex or top just as much as do those of the Egyptians. That two shekels plus two shekels make four shekels is just as true for us as for the Babylonians; that the interior angles of a plane triangle sum to 180 degrees is just as true for us as it was for Euclid—simply because that "for X" is out of place. If others have indeed asserted those claims that our *form* of words *conveys,* then they have asserted what is true—and true unqualifiedly rather than "true for us" or "true for them." The fact that the affirmation of a fact must proceed from within a historio-cultural setting does not mean that the correctness and appropriateness of what is said will be restricted to such a setting. The fact that we make our assertions within time does not prevent us from asserting timeless truths.

One can in theory contemplate two very different lines of approach here: (1) We find that certain types of creatures have somehow been precertified as rational (by the World Spirit?), and we then inquire empirically into what it is that all of these predeterminedly rational beings have in common. Or again: (2) We make use of our conception of what rationality is to characterize certain types of creatures as rational, and *then* ask (analytically) what it is that all of them *must* have in common simply in virtue of qualifying under this conception of ours. Clearly, the second approach is the only practicable one; it makes no sense to try to implement the first (seeing that we simply have no way to get in touch with the

World Spirit). But when we proceed in this second way, the only commonalties we can get out are the ones that we put in. We must ask what
features beings must possess in virtue of qualifying as the sort of creature
that *we ourselves are prepared to accept as answering to our conception of "rationality."* Clearly, this approach puts that conception of ours at the forefront
as the determinative pivot-point.

In the final analysis, then, one can and should turn the weapons of
relativism against itself. If indeed each group has its own standards against
which there is no further, external, higher appeal, then we ourselves have
no viable alternative but to see our conception of rationality as decisive
for any judgments that we conscientiously make on these matters.

The salient point is that we are entitled—indeed, rationally constrained—to see our own criteriological basis of rational judgment as
rationally superior to the available alternatives. In the setting of *our* deliberations it is our standards that must be determinative. If we did not
take this stance—if we did not deem our cognitive posture effectively optimal—then we could not sensibly see ourselves as rationally justified
in adopting it. We cannot responsibly think that this variant scheme is co-
meritorious with our own, because (if rational) it is precisely because we
deem that scheme superior that we have made it ours. It would, ipso
facto, fail to be our real position—contrary to hypothesis.

For us, then, it is a fact of life that the primacy of our own position is
decisive. Recognizing that others see such matters differently from ourselves need not daunt us in attachment to our own views. It may give us
"second thoughts"—may invite us to rethink—but this is not to move us
to admit their standards but rather to make more careful and conscientious use of our own. In this regard, our commitment to our own
cognitive position is (or should be) unalloyed. We ourselves are bound to
see our own (rationally adopted) standards as superior to the available alternatives—and are, presumably, rationally entitled to do so on the basis
of the cognitive values we ourselves endorse.

Admittedly, there are cognitive postures different from ours—different
sorts of standards altogether. But what does that mean *for us*? What are *we*
to do about it? Several stances towards those various bases are in theory
open to us:

(1) accept none: reject ours
(2) accept one: retain ours
(3) accept several: conjoin others with ours

(4) "rise above the conflict": say "a plague on all your houses" and take
the path of idealization, invoking the "ideal observer," the "wise
man" of the Stoics, the "ideally rational agent" of the economists,
or the like

The first option is mere petulance—a matter of stalking off in "fox-and-
grapes" fashion because we cannot have it all our own preferred way. The
third option is infeasible: different bases do not combine, they make mutually incompatible demands, and set mutually inconsistent priorities; in
conjoining them we will not get something more comprehensive and complete—we will get a mess. The fourth option is utopian and unrealistic. We
have no way to get there from here. Only the second alternative makes
sense—having the courage of our convictions and standing by our own
guns (or, rather, our own *lights*) where cognitive matters are concerned. In
evaluating contentions and positions (of any sort) we just have no plausible
alternative to doing so from the perspective of our cognitive values, our
own conscientiously adopted cognitive point of view. But of course we
do have the option—and from the rational point of view even the obligation—to make sure that the standards we adopt as ours are, as best we can
manage to tell, those which are appropriate for rational people in general.

But how, short of megalomania, can one take the stance that one's own
view of what is rational is right, that it ought to be binding on everyone?
How can I appropriately claim an agreement between my position and
that of "all sensible people"? Not, surely, because I seek to impose *my*
standard on *them*, but rather, only because I have assessed their standards in
the course of shaping my own. Coordination is achieved not because
I insist on their conforming to me, but because I have made every *reasonable* effort to make my position that which (as best I can tell) ought to
be everyone's. The issue is one not of domineering but of submissive
conformity. In the end, I can thus insist that they should use the same
standards that I do because it is on this very basis of a commitment to
commonalty that I have made that standard my own in the first place. The
conformity of rational standards is, or ought to be, produced not by megalomania but by humility.

It is, accordingly, important to stress that the reflexive primacy of our
own standards is not in conflict with objectivity. To defend objectivity, it
is not necessary to maintain the (absurd) thesis that everyone, regardless of
time, place, and culture, holds to one and the same epistemic standard. All
that is necessary is that one should design one's own standard in a way that

everyone who is rational ought (by virtue of this rationality) to proceed on its basis. It is through a humble submission to the demands of reason—and *not* through a megalomania of insistence that everyone should conform to one's own standard—that the objectivity and universality of one's standard is to be assured.

"But is it not possible for someone to go out and get another normative standard?" It certainly is. But on what basis would one do this? You might *force* me to change standards. Or you can, perhaps, brainwash me. But you cannot *rationally persuade* me. For, rational persuasion at the normative level has to proceed in terms of norms that I accept and, by the norms I actually have, my present standards are bound to prevail, if I am rational in the first place.[6]

Gestalt switches are certainly possible, but they are just that: unpredictable leaps. We do not reason our way into them by the use of existing standards—if it were so it would be an implementation of the old standard that is at issue and not, as per hypothesis, a Gestalt switch. They are only seen as rational *ex post facto*, from the vantage point of the *then* prevailing "established" standard—i.e., the new one.

Thus, even while acknowledging that other judgments regarding matters of rationality may exist, we have no choice but to see our standards as appropriate for us. (In using someone else's with "no questions asked" we would, ipso facto, be making them ours!) To use another standard (categorically, not hypothetically, as an experiment) is to make it ours—to make it no longer *another* standard. Of course, to see our own standards as the appropriate ones for us to use here and now is not to deny the prospect of a change of standards. But when this actually occurs, our stance toward the new standards is identical to our present stance towards the presently adopted ones. Like "now" and "here," the "our" of *our standards* follows us about no matter where we go. A commitment to the generic appropriateness of his present standards follows the rational man about like his own shadow. Objectivity cannot be detached from its claims to universality.

To acknowledge that other people hold views different from ours, and to concede the prospect that we may, even in the end, simply be unable to win them over by rational suasion, is emphatically not to accept an indifferentism to the effect that their views are just as valid or correct as ours are. To acquiesce in a situation where others think differently from oneself is neither to endorse their views nor to abandon one's own. In many departments of life—in matters of politics, philosophy, art, morality, and so on—we certainly do not take the position that the correctness of our own views is somehow undermined and their tenability compromised by the circumstance that others do not share them. And there is no good reason why we should see matters all that differently in matters of inquiry—or even evaluation.

But are we really entitled—rationally authorized—to place such reliance on our own standards without worrying about others? Assuming that we indeed have done what reason, as best we can understand it, demands for their substantiation (and this is a long story best reserved for another occasion), the answer is and has to be an emphatic *yes*. Rational people should not and need not be intimidated by the fact of disagreement; it makes perfectly good sense for a person to do the best possible towards securing evidentiated beliefs and justifiable choices without undue worry about whether or not others disagree.

In his important and influential book on epistemic standards,[7] Alasdair MacIntyre seeks to navigate the narrow passage between a relativism that acknowledges rival epistemic traditions and an absolutism that sees these as subject to rational appraisal by impartial quality-control standards. Traditions, as he sees it, can be developmentally self-critical. They can encounter checks and crises in their *internal* development, so as to become transformed under such internal pressures into something different from an earlier, less tenable version. Accordingly, one need not be relativistic about it and see every alternative tradition as being on all fours with every other. However, traditions cannot be assaulted successfully from without. Progress can be assessed tradition-internally but not as between different traditions. To stand outside a tradition is not to play the part of a cogent critic at all: "To be outside all traditions is to be a stranger to inquiry; it is to be in a state of intellectual and moral destitution, a condition from which it is impossible to issue . . . [any meaningful] challenge" (p. 367). Much of this seems plausible and cogent. But just where does it lead?

It leads MacIntyre to the idea of rival traditions of inquiry in whose presence "there are no tradition-independent standards of argument by appeal to which they can be shown to be in error" (p. 403). But just here there beckons the primrose path towards relativism, a road along which MacIntyre's traditionalistic pluralism is inexorably impelled.

To be sure, he is carried along reluctantly, kicking and screaming. His concluding pronouncement is emphatic here: "The several claims to truth of contending traditions of inquiry depend for their validation upon the adequacy and the explaining power of the histories which the resources

of each of these traditions in conflict enable their adherents to write"
(p. 403). And at this point MacIntyre's discussion stops—to its decisive
detriment. For exactly here it needs to take a deep breath and go forward. If "validation" makes sense in that "adequacy" can be appraised and
explanatory power determined by some meaningful standard for assessing
the "rival claims to truth" of those contending traditions, then what price
autonomy and self-contained finality for traditions? What then becomes
of that vaunted impossibility of impartial criticism? If MacIntyre's general analysis is carried to its logical conclusion with rigorous consistency,
then the evaluational process has to be seen as tradition-based all the way
through, and we had best forget about asking for the cogent validation of
a tradition vis-à-vis contending rivals.

But the proper and ultimately only defensible course is to see the issue
of impartial adequacy validation for what it is—a red herring. There is no
point in entering on an inquiry into the merits of "rival claims to truth."
For us, our own standards, our own values, our own traditions are and
must be the only real prospect. We have no choice but to go on from
where we are—and no choice but to see this as the only viable alternative
for any sensible person. Our position on matters of reason and rationality
would not be what it is if we deem it to be the only ultimately correct and
viable option. The issue of a correct standard is and must be "merely academic" for us because the very nature of the issue is such that we must see
its resolution as a foregone conclusion. The only standard it makes any
sense for us to use is the one we *endorse*. There is no point in my applying
someone else's standard of value or worth or interest or appropriateness or
whatever. God's standard I cannot apply, since I do not have it. Your standard I will not apply, if I do not share it. The standard we have got to use
is just exactly the standard that we have got. And we have no way to evaluate standards save in our terms. After all, if we do not subscribe to that
rival standard, then how can we rationally use it; and if *we do*, then we
have thereby already made it ours!

Relativism accordingly ends where charity begins—at home. The implications of our own conception of rationality are absolutely decisive for
our deliberations. We ourselves must be the arbiters of tenability when
the discussion at issue is one that we are conducting. And so, we cannot
at once maintain our own rational commitments as such while yet ceasing to regard them as results at which all rational inquirers who proceed
appropriately ought also arrive if their conditions and circumstances were

the same as ours. In this sort of way, the claims of rationality are inherently universal.

3. THE EXPERIENTIAL CONTEXTUALISM OF RATIONALITY

To be sure, this invariance with respect to what rationality is does not impede a contextualistic pluralism that reflects different bodies of experience. To reject relativism is not to abandon the inherent *contextualism* of rational proceedings.

In matters of cognition, as elsewhere, our normative orientations do not come to us ex nihilo but emerge from experience. And in this world we are never totally bereft of an experiential basis: in the order of thought as in the world's physical order we always have a position of some sort. By the time one gets to the point of being able to think at all, there is always a background of available experience against which to form one's ideas. And just there is where one has to start. It is precisely because a certain position is appropriate *from where we stand* (i.e., in our context) that this particular position of ours is appropriate for us. The posture that emerges from this way of approaching the issue is thus that of a contextualistic rationalism:

> Confronted with a pluralistic proliferation of alternative positions you have your acceptance-determination methodology, and I have mine. Yours leads you to endorse *P;* mine leads me to endorse not-*P.* Yours is just as valid for you (via your methodology of validating principles) as mine is for me. The situational differences of our contexts simply lead to different rational resolutions. And that's the end of the matter.

The fact that the cognitive venture viewed as a whole incorporates other positions does nothing to render a firm and fervent commitment to one's own position somehow infeasible, let alone improper.

For me, my own experience (vicariously obtained experience included) is something unique—and uniquely compelling. You, to be sure, are in the same position—your experience is compelling, *for you*—but that's immaterial *to me.* "But isn't such an experiential absolutism just relativism by another name—is it not itself just a relativism of a particular sort—an experiential relativism?" Whatever relativity there may be is a relativization to evidence, so that relativism's characteristic element of indifference is lacking. It is just this, after all, that distinguishes indifferentist *relativism* from a rationalistic *contextualism*. And there is nothing *corrosive* about such a contextualization: it does not dissolve any of our commitments. Its absolutism lies in the fact that, for us, our own experience—taken in broadest extent—is bound to be altogether compelling for us.

The case of perceptual objectivity poses special problems. For it is often said that perceptual objectivity—in the case of vision in particular—is something unachievable. After all any scene must be apprehended from some *point of view*, with some particular visual apparatus, and by an individual who brings on the scene various personal endowments and characteristics. Myopia, color blindness, personal association ("the old homestead"), or symbolic significance ("our flag") will all influence how we see things and will make for a large range of variation. Yet despite this vast range of possible phenomenal variation there will be many facts regarding what we perceive that are actually objective and transcend what lies "in the eye of the beholder." For one thing, there is the matter of *classification*: is it a cat that we see or a dog? For another thing, there is the matter of (at least approximate) *measurement:* is the object a foot long for us or 100 feet? is the sound high-pitched or low? Some features of things are such that different observers will adjudge them differently (quite reasonably so, in ways that third parties can explain perfectly well). But other features are such that we would expect any and every reasonable individual to come to essentially the same conclusion in sufficiently similar circumstances. Such perception-mediated features will ipso facto qualify as objective. And of course where *conception* rather than *perception* is concerned the case is even more straightforward.

Its commitment to universality notwithstanding, the cultivation of objectivity thus need not issue in homogeneous uniformity. For in seeking to do what any reasonable person would do in my circumstances I will have to reckon with the fact that others will be operating in circumstances that differ very substantially from mine. Differences in time and place loom large. The cognitive state of the art is one thing in the twentieth century and another in the Greece of Aristotle's day; it is one thing in an Oxford college and another in the Brazilian rain forest. The uniformity of rational process need not constrain a substantive uniformity of belief. It would be utterly contrary to reason for differently situated thinkers confronted with different bodies of evidence to think exactly alike.

4. ON PURSUING "THE TRUTH"

Regrettably, many people have—under the influence of relativism—simply given up on the idea of a real and objective truth. The very idea of "the truth" is of small interest to various theorists nowadays. Heidegger, for one, regarded those so-called absolute truths as no more than "remnants of Christian theology in the problem-field of philosophy."[8] Of themselves, truth and falsity, correctness and incorrectness, adequacy and inadequacy, reason and unreason, sense and nonsense—approached as issues of logic, semantic theory, or epistemological explication—simply do not interest the hermeneuticist. He wants to know what role the *ideas* about these issues have in the sphere of authentic human experience; he does not ask about what these ideas *mean* but about what people *do* with them. Truth as such is something he is eager to abandon.

And he is not alone. In stressing the pluralism of philosophizing, William James wrote:

> *The* Truth: what a perfect idol of the rationalistic mind! I read in an old letter—from a gifted friend who died too young—these words: "In everything, in science, art, morals, and religion, there *must* be one system that is right and *every* other wrong." How characteristic of the enthusiasm of a certain stage of young! At twenty-one we rise to such a challenge and expect to find the system. It never occurs to most of us even later that the question "What is *the* Truth?" is no real question (being irrelative to all conditions) and that the whole notion of *the* truth is an abstraction from the fact of truths in the plural.[9]

Inspired by James, various contemporary pragmatists are quite prepared to abandon concern for truth.

But any such reaction is gravely misguided. Epistemological pluralism has no substantive consequences for the nature of truth as such. The fact that "our truth," the truth as we see it, is not necessarily that of others, that it is no more than the best *estimate* of the real truth that we ourselves are able to make, should not disillusion us in our inquiries and should not discourage us in "the pursuit of truth." In inquiry as in other departments of human endeavor we are well advised simply to do the best we can. Realizing that there are no guarantees we have little sensible choice—*pro tem* at least—but to deem the best we can do as good enough.

What people *think* to be true is clearly something that is person-variable and thus relative. We can take the line that "What is *true*?" is a question that different people can quite appropriately answer differently because of the interpersonal variability of available information. But what *truth* is all about is something that is, on the approach proposed here, altogether definite and fixed. The *evidentiation* at issue in the epistemic sector is doubtless interpersonally and intercommunally variable. But variability on the side of information does not make for variation on the side of concepts.

In this context one must also take care to distinguish the internal assertoric substance of a claim. ("The cat is on the mat") from the claim-external epistemic qualification made by the claimant to reflect its evidentiary state ("*It is probable that* the cat is on the mat"). Clearly, "probably on the mat" is simply no place for the cat to be. Two separable and indeed separate items are at issue and two different questions are being answered:

Q. Where is the cat?
A. On the mat.
Q. How sure are you of this?
A. Reasonably sure.

One question relates to the location of the cat; the other to the status of the grounding or evidentiation of our claims about this. And only the latter has a status that is subject to relativistically degree-like qualification. After all, degrees of confidence may be—indeed are—person-relative and variable, but truth status is not. Even mere opinions are still opinions about facts. And even merely to conjecture that *p* is to conjecture that *p is true;* is not to think that *p is conjecturally-true.* The dimension of epistemic qualification enters into the *external semantical status* of claims, not into their *internal assertoric constitution.* And differences in evidentiation do not make for differences in truth-value. The truth-status of claims is not pluralized by the fact that different people can have different views about it. Small-ish evidence that *p* is true is not firm evidence that *p* is smallishly true. Admittedly many of our truth claims are no more than that—mere claims or estimates. But there are contentions for which, given the operative ground rules, we can stake greater claims, particularly insofar as we render them vague. With G. E. Moore's "this is a human hand," with the classical "The cat is on the mat" in its experiential immediacy, and with "yon tree is higher than an inch and less high than a mile," one need not be all that diffident. Such claims are themselves sufficiently modest that there is room for not more than a neurotic doubt as to how "the structure of reality" is fixed in regard to the matter.

Moreover, even if we are relativists regarding *evidence* we need not be so regarding *evidentiation*. Once I learn what evidentiation is about, I can no longer reasonably believe that *q* constitutes evidence for *p* for Jones but not for Smith. They may or may not *realize* this. But evidentiation works in such a way that what is evidence for the goose is evidence for the gander. To be sure, people's *views* of evidentiation may vary. But if they have a concept of evidence at all, it is one that they will deem "objective" in the sense of rejecting the idea that evidentiation is person-variable. Of course *information* does vary from person to person. So I may lack evidence that you have. But if it is *evidence* that is at issue, that is something we have to see as person-indifferent in just the way that our standard conception of evidentiation has it.

Recognizing that others see matters differently in contexts of inquiry need not daunt us in attachment to our own views of the matter. There is clearly no conflict between our commitment to the truth as we see it and a recognition that the adoption of a variant probative perspective leads others to see the truth differently. Given that we ourselves occupy our perspective, we are bound to see *our* truth as *the* truth. But we nevertheless can and do recognize that others who operate in different times and conditions see matters in a different light. The circumstance that different people see something differently does not destroy or degrade the thing as such.

After all, our factual claims must one and all be made in a setting of place and time, in the context of a cultural and technological state of the art. But their being provisional and contextual claims to truth does not metamorphose them into claims to conditional and contextual truth. The flaw of relativism is that it conflates the *status* of our truth-claims with their *substance*.

We have no choice but to pursue *the* truth by way of cultivating *our* truth; we have no direct access to truth unmediated by the epistemological resources of rational inquiry. And, given the ground rules of rational inquiry, this means that one's view of the truth is bound to be linked to one's cognitive situation. To say that this is not good enough and to give up on our truth—to declare petulantly that if we cannot have *the* absolute, capital-T Truth that of its very nature constrains everyone's allegiance, then we will not accept anything at all—is automatically to get nothing and to abandon the pursuit of truth as such. It is foolishness to reject an orientation-bound position as not worth having in a domain where a position is only to be had on this basis. The only truth-claims worth staking are those which can be seen as rational on the standards that we ourselves endorse.

An experiential pluralism of cognitive positions is thus no impediment to a commitment to the pursuit of truth. There is no reason that the mere existence of different views and positions should leave us immobilized like the ass of Buridan between the alternatives. Nor are we left with the gray emptiness of equalitarianism that looks to all sides with neutrality and un-committed indifference. In important matters like inquiry (or evaluation, etc.) we cannot—and in good conscience should not—bring ourselves to view disagreement in the light of a "mere divergence of opinion."

It is, in the eyes of some, a disadvantage of pluralism that it supposedly undermines one's commitment to one's own position. But this is simply fallacious. There is no good reason why a recognition that others, circum-stanced as they are, are inclined—and indeed rationally entitled *in their circumstances*—to hold a position of variance with ours should be construed to mean that we, circumstanced as we are, need feel any rational obligation to abandon our position. Once we have done our rational best to substan-tiate our position, the mere existence of alternatives need give us no pause.

A sensible cognitive pluralism, which is to say a contextual evidential-ism, accordingly does not imply that one must:

- abandon the truth (skepticism);
- fragment truth by adopting a doctrine of truth pluralism (Averroism);
- remain indifferent as between different truth criteria (indifferentism);
- abandon rationality altogether (irrationalism).

Rather, it means that we can (quite appropriately) disagree about what it is that is true and what good reasons are at hand, while yet maintaining an (appropriately) absolutistic view of what truth and good reasons are. The ideal nature of *actual* truth and of *actual* good reasons that inhere in our (defining) conception of inquiry establishes a clear limit to the implica-tions of cognitive relativism.[10] To reemphasize: A pluralistic contextualism of potential basis-diversity is altogether compatible with an absolutistic commitment to our own basis. One can accept the prospect of alternatives as available to the community at large without seeing more than one of them appropriate for oneself. One can combine a pluralism of possible al-ternatives with an absolutistic position regarding ideal rationality and a firm and reasoned commitment to the standards intrinsic to one's own position. We ourselves are bound to see our own (rationally adopted) stan-dards as superior to the available alternatives—and are, presumably, rationally entitled to do so in the light of the cognitive values we in actual fact endorse. The crux of the pluralism issue lies in the question of just what it is that one is being pluralistic about.

5. THE ACHILLES' HEEL OF RELATIVISM

The decisive weakness of relativism's commitment to an indifferentist basis-egalitarianism in matters of cognition lies deep in the nature of the human condition. It emerges as follows: Be it contentions, beliefs, doctrines, practices, customs, or whatever that may be at issue, relativists insist that rationality does not come into it. As they see it, people are led to adopt one alternative over another by *extra-rational* considerations (custom, habituation, fashion, or whatever); from the rational point of view there is nothing to choose—all the alternatives stand on the same footing. But the fatal flaw of this position roots in the fact that our claims, beliefs, doctrines, practices, customs, and so on, all belong to sectors of purposive human endeavor. And all (or virtually all) human enterprises are at bottom teleological—conducted with some sort of end or objective in view. And what chastens the impetus to relativism is the existence of absolutistic constraints within the purposive teleology of the cognitive enterprise with respect to explanation, prediction, and control. The Achilles' heel of relativism lies in the fact that inquiry is a purposive enterprise and that some modes of procedure among the available possibilities will serve our purposes better than others.

In particular, rational inquiry aims at providing implementable information about our natural and artificial environments—information that we can use to orient ourselves cognitively and practically in the world. After all, explanation, prediction, and effective intervention constitute definitive enterprise-characterizing goals for the cognitive project. (And the moral enterprise is also purposive, its mission being to define, teach, and encourage modes of action that bring the behavior of individuals into alignment with the best overall interests of the group.) Human endeavors in general have an inherent teleology, seeing that *Homo sapiens* is a goal-pursuing creature. Now in this context the crucial fact is that some claims, beliefs, doctrines, practices, customs, etc. are bound to serve the characteristic purposes of their functional domain better than others. For it is pretty much inevitable that in any goal-oriented enterprise, some alternative ways of proceeding serve better than others with respect to the relevant range of purpose, proving themselves more efficient and effective in point of goal-realization. And in the teleological contexts at issue these ways *thereby* establish themselves as rationally appropriate with respect to those goals. It lies in the nature of the thing that the quintessentially rational thing to do is to give precedence and priority to those alternatives that are more effective with respect to the range of relevant purposes.

There is no doubt that such a position qualifies as a version of "prag-matism." But it is crucially important to note that it is *not* a version of practicalism. It stands committed to the primacy of purpose, but it cer-tainly does not endorse the idea that the only possible (or only valid) sort of human purpose is that of the type traditionally characterized as "prac-tical"—one that is geared to the physical and "material" well-being of people. Purposive enterprises are as diverse and varied as the whole spec-trum of legitimate human purpose, and such purposes can relate not only to the "material" but also to the "spiritual" side of people—their knowl-edge, artistic sensibility, social dispositions, etc. (To differentiate this broader position from the classical range of specifically *practical* purposes, such a pragmatism might perhaps better be characterized as *functionalism*.)

Such a functionalist perspective is decisive in its impetus against a rela-tivism that insists that at bottom it just does not matter, at any rate as far as the rationality of the issue is concerned. For once we see the issues in a purposive perspective, this line just doesn't work. Where specific pur-poses are at issue—and, in particular, cognition-coordinate purposes like effective communication, prediction, and control—alternatives are not in general portrayable as rationally indifferent. Rationality not only permits but demands giving preference to purposively effectual alternatives over the rest, at any rate as long as other things are anything like equal. It is quintessentially rational to prefer what works. The teleological aspect pro-vides a basis for rationality in a way that puts relativism into a thoroughly problematic and dubious light.[11]

five

OBJECTIVITY AND QUANTIFICATION

Synopsis

(1) Measurement is more than a matter of mere quantification; only in special cases do quantities actually measure *something. (2) Quantification in and of itself is no guarantor of objectivity. And actual measurement, though indeed sufficient for objectivity, is certainly not necessary to it. Objectivity, after all, does not require quantification.*

1. DOES QUANTIFICATION ASSURE OBJECTIVITY?

A fetish for measurement is astir among our contemporaries. We worship at the altar of statistics: the penchant for quantities is a salient characteristic of contemporary Western culture. Everything we touch turns to numbers: intelligence quotients, quality of life indices, feminine beauty (ranked on a scale from zero up to a "perfect 10"), and so on. It is often said that quantification provides a high-road to objectivity in science and rational inquiry in general. And this seems plausible because of the dramatically prominent role of measurement in these domains. All the same, there are problems here. For quantification is no guarantor of objectivity, simply because numbers, even robustly determined ones, may in fact fail to be effectively meaningful.

Notwithstanding an extensive literature on the subject, the existing state of the art is such that our understanding of exactly what measurement is all about still leaves much to be desired.[1] Many treatises on the subject routinely assume that each and every observationally based quantification represents a measurement.[2] But this is nonsense. Quantification as such does not automatically constitute measurement. To see this, consider some examples of effectively meaningless quantities, such as "the number of 3's in the distance (in kilometers) between two cities" or again, "the number of times (on average) that the sentences of a given English text end with a proper name." It is very doubtful that such numbers do any measuring.

There are quantities and quantities. Some actually effect specifications (in at least estimates) of the measurable features of things. But others are simply meaningless numbers. For there is nothing about qualification as such that guarantees objectivity. People's subjective reactions are just as quantifiable as their physical dimensions—that, after all, is what public opinion polling is largely about.

Certainly not every quantity represents an actual measurement of some sort. "How many of those girls remind you of your mother?" you ask me. "Two," I respond. A lovely quantity, that! But what in heaven's name am I *measuring?* It is thus all too clear that we must reject the claim of S. S. Stevens that "measurement [is] the assignment of numerals to objects or events according to a rule—any rule."[3] But this is very questionable. "Tell me the first number that comes to your mind" is a rule—but what does it signify? A measurement, after all, has to be a quantitative characterization of some meaningfully descriptive facet of reality, as opposed to one that is arbitrary and uninformative.

But exactly what is at issue here? A well-known pair of philosophical authors has told us that measurement consists in "indicating the quantitative relations between [intensive] qualities."[4] But this idea that quantitative measurements must represent actually qualitative features of things is deeply problematic. Presumably the rate of exchange between dollars and yen constitutes some sort of measurement. But it is far from clear that the qualities or attributes of something are at issue. Again, birth rates or inflation rates do not discernibly reflect qualities of anything—unless we blatantly *invent* something (a social or economic or political *system*) for them to be qualities of.[5] We can measure the annual snowfall of a place, but it is far from evident that one of its *qualities* is at stake.

Perhaps, then, one should simply abandon any reference to qualities in this context. Perhaps getting numbers is all that counts for measurement. Following in the footsteps of the operationalist school of P. W. Bridgman, the British philosopher of science Herbert Dingle has insisted that "instead of supposing a pre-existing 'property' which our operation measures, we should begin with our operation and its result, and then if we wish to speak of a property (which I do not think that we should do) define it in terms of that."[6] But here we are caught in a dilemma. If we tie measurement to specifically physical processes of quantity determination—linking it to apparatus manipulation and instrument pointer readings as with the measurement of length or mass—then we proceed in so restrictive a way that we have difficulties accommodating the sorts of quantities at issue with social affairs. Interest rates or the velocity of money circulation are some examples. In macroeconomics, after all, we get our quantities not by reading off the position of a pointer from a scale but by copying suitably related numbers from pieces of paper. And yet the claims of these quantities to count as measurements seem to be conceded on all sides. It is thus very problematic to insist that measurements have to result from a *physical* measuring process of some sort. If, on the other hand, we loosen up the linkage of *measuring* to *measurement* too much, then how far are we to go?

Actually to *measure* something is to affix a numerical yardstick to some quantitative *parameter* that has its operative foothold in the world's scheme of things—length, temperature, mass, electric charge, money-circulation, or the like. A measurement, after all, is a number assignment made under a particular description such as:

- is x inches long
- measures x units on the Richter scale
- rates x units of acquisitiveness on the Spencer phrenology scale

And when numerical assignments fail to capture any lawfully descriptive features of things, then they just do not *measure* anything. Measurements must, ideally, represent an objective, well-defined quantitative aspect of the qualitative makeup of things in the real world.

With a genuine measurement two questions arise:

(1) *What* is it that one is measuring? (the *object* question)
(2) *How* is it that one is measuring what is at issue? (the *process* question)

And, moreover, the issues involved in (1) and (2) must be separable and distinct, that is, one must in principle be able to provide an answer to the *what* question independently of one's answer to the *how* question. Thus a person's weight and age represent cogent measurements, but not:

- age in years divided by waistline in inches
- height in feet plus years resided at present address

It is clear in this context that a wide roadway leading from meaningful to meaningless numbers is provided by mathematical compounding. This is indicated by such examples as:

- the product of the longest and shortest sides of a polygon
- weight of a person in kg minus months resided at present address
- volume of an object (in cc^3) divided by its age (in years)

Such amalgamations are problematic precisely because there is no non-circular reply to the question: Just what is it that is being purportedly measured in this way? That is, we have no workable way of distinguishing the *what* of the putative measurement from its *how*. And so, such "oddball" quantities, albeit defined in a perfectly "objective" way in the epistemic mode that renders them in principle accessible to everyone, do not thereby acquire the sort of ontological objectivity that makes information about them capable of contributing significantly to the description of things.

The issue of dimensionality is clearly serviceable in providing a cogent factor that disqualifies such Rube Goldberg quantities from counting as genuine measurements. Regrettably, however, it is not easy to say just what is at issue here (which may explain why recent treatments of measurement in general simply bypass this issue of descriptive dimensionality). Philosophers of science have in recent years deliberated a good deal about what is or is not a *natural kind* when it comes to *classification*, but they have largely ignored the closely parallel and inherently no less important issue of what constitutes a *natural dimension* in point of *mensuration*.[7] However difficult this issue may be to resolve, it is clear that such descriptive dimensionality—or something very like it—must be insisted upon for genuine measurement.

Yet is even this sufficient? There is good reason to think that it is not. For one thing even perfectly meaningful quantities can be contextually problematic. It makes sense to ask for the market price of gold or of lead specifically but not of metal in general. We can make good sense of the idea of the average birth-weight of human females in specific, but can make little of that of the average death-weight of fish in general. And even graver difficulties lurk around the corner. Consider, for the sake of an example, the person-correlative quantity:

$$\text{fage} = \text{age} \times \frac{\text{\# of fingers}}{\text{\# of toes}}$$

This clearly quantifies an aspect of a person's individual makeup in a way that (1) has a meaningful dimension (chronological age, seeing that the fractional multiplier is dimensionless), and (2) behaves lawfully since for the vast majority of humans *fage* = *age* and a person's age factors lawfully in many contexts and as biological development and life expectancy. Despite all this, however, the Rube Goldberg nature of the conception would leave one disinclined to consider "fage"-determination as a meaningful measurement process. What we want and need is a more cogent and discriminating account. But it is one thing to ask for such an account and another to know where it can be found.

And so, in the end, it appears that we are confronted with a distinctly discomfiting situation. It is clear *that* we need a cogent way of distinguishing between meaningless quantities and genuine measurements. But it is far from clear *how* we are to draw this distinction.

Some numbers can be acknowledged as measurements because, like weight and distance, they are paradigmatic of the very concept. Others are clearly not measurements because they violate one or another of the necessary conditions of the conception. But there is a considerable gray area where we do not see the way clear, and where we have good reason for caution and unease.

2. LARGER VISTAS

In the aggregate, then, these deliberations indicate the need for recognizing that, even when we are dealing with a perfectly fine *quantity*, the conditions needed for this to qualify as an authentic *measurement* may nevertheless not be satisfied. The importance of science in modern life has engendered a quantitative prejudice. People incline to think that if something significant is to be said, then you can say it with numbers and thereby transmute it into a meaningful measurement. They endorse Lord Kelvin's dictum that "When you cannot express it in numbers, your knowledge is of a meager and unsatisfactory kind."[8] But when one looks at the issue more clearly and critically, one finds that there is no convincing reason to think this is so on any universal and pervasive basis.

Science has succeeded in mathematicizing the realm of our *knowledge* to such an extent that we tend to lose sight of the fact that the realm of our *experience* is not all that congenial to measurement. Learning to talk or

to read are life-determining projects, but little about them is all that quantitative. We readily forget how very special a situation actual *measurability*
is—even in contexts of seeming precision.

Moreover, reliance on numbers brings in its wake a host of problems
of its own. For one dangerous thing about numbers is that small errors in
their use can produce large—and very unfortunate—consequences. A
minor mistake in the number encoding of a prescription medication can
prove lethal. Again, for many years, spinach has enjoyed great prestige as
a valuable source of iron because a misplaced decimal point credited this
vegetable with an iron content ten times its actual value.[9]

It is thus easy to see why the prospect of meaningless quantities should
cause unease. For in this measurement-enchanted time of ours we constantly depend on quantitative information as a basis for decision-making
and policy guidance. But garbage in, garbage out. If those quantities that
people throw about so readily are in fact meaningless, then the decisions
we so enthusiastically base upon them are built on sand.

Numbers do not always tell the story. The wise strategist realizes that
God is not always on the side of the big battalions. "How many divisions
has the Pope?" Stalin asked. It was not a question that bemused General
Jaruzelski in Poland. By all quantitative yardsticks—body counts and all
that—the U.S. was ahead throughout the Vietnam conflict and duly won
all the battles; but it lost the war. One does not need to enroll oneself, with
Goethe, as an opponent of measurement's entry into the domain of
human doings and dealings to feel a deep disquiet regarding the particular
ways in which people have sought to introduce measurement into the
social sphere. The fact is that in everyday life, professional practice, and
public affairs alike, stubborn reliance on numbers can sometimes prove
more of an obstacle than an aid to critical and reflective thought.[10]

The immense success of quantitative techniques in the mathematicizing sciences has misled people into thinking that quantification is the only
viable road to objectively cogent information. But think—is it really so?
Where is it written that numbers alone yield genuine understanding—that
judgment based on structural analysis or qualitative harmonization is
unhelpful and uninformative, so that where numbers cannot enter, intel-
ligibility flies away? (Modern mathematics itself is not all that quantitative,
since it is deeply concerned with issues such as those of topology and
group theory that deal with structures in a way that puts quantitative issues
aside.) The difference between *killing* in general and *murder* as specifically
unjustified killing is mirrored in the difference between *quantification* in

general and *measurement* as specifically appropriate quantification. The latter—measurement—can prove to be an aid towards objectivity if only because where we do not achieve robust and interpersonally determinable quantifiers we do not speak of measurement at all. But in the end we must come to terms with the fact that quantification as such is no guarantor of objectivity.

To be sure, to acknowledge the limits of measurability is not to downgrade the whole process, let alone to propose its total abandonment. It is precisely because we are well advised to push the cause of measurement as far as we legitimately can that we need to be mindful of the line between meaningful measurements and meaningless quantifications. That we cannot draw this line better than seems to be the case at present is—or should be—a proper cause for justified chagrin.

But for present purposes the salient point is that quantification does not carry measurability in its wake nor necessarily indicate objectivity. Polls quantify public opinion, but need they indicate anything objective? The sales prices of entries in an art auction are perfectly good quantities, but they reflect no more than the elusive fashion and passion of the moment. There is nothing about quantities as such to indicate that they measure anything objective.

Three lessons emerge:

- While measurement requires quantification, quantification is not sufficient for measurement.
- Quantification is neither necessary to nor sufficient for objectivity.
- Actual measurement, while indeed sufficient for objectivity, is not necessary for it.

The long and short of it is that the linkage between objectivity and quantification is more distant and more complex than is commonly envisioned.[11]

— six —

OBJECTIVITY AND COMMUNICATION

Synopsis

(1) Ordinary language as we usually employ it in everyday discourse is committed to the existence of objective standards. (2) The cultivation of objectivity is substantially advantaged through establishing an intercommunicating community. (3) Our conceptions of things are always provisional. To have a correct conception of a thing we must have all of its important properties right. And this is something we generally cannot ascertain, if only because we cannot say what is really important before the end of the proverbial day. (4) Human cognition pivots on the prospect of communal inquiry into and interpersonal communication about an objective order of reality. Without a presupposition of ontological objectivity, the project of communication about a shared world would become inoperable. Ontological and epistemic objectivity are thus linked together in that the latter has the former as a functional (or "regulative") presupposition. (5) Ontological objectivity is not something we discover but something we postulate. For if our "subjective" conceptions were determinative, the very idea of communication would become impracticable.

1. HOW ORDINARY DISCOURSE IS COMMITTED TO OBJECTIVITY

Ordinary discourse—language as we usually employ it in everyday discourse—is inherently committed to the existence of objective standards. The very way in which we use language takes objectivity for granted. In particular, personal attributions of competence are inextricably geared to the idea of impersonal appropriateness.

Let us begin with specifically *cognitive* competence. Consider the contrast between the A-column and the B-column.

A	B
accepts that p	realizes that p
believes that p	knows that p
thinks p's reason to be q	understands p's reason to be q

The A-locutions describe the agent's cognitive posture without any commitment on our part. They characterize the situation in terms of what the individual in view deems acceptable by his lights. Mere reporting is at issue here. No position-taking on *our* part as assertors is involved: we make no endorsement and do not editorialize on the agent's position.

But with B-locutions the situation is very different. It would be a contradiction in terms to say:

- "X realizes that p, but is mistaken"
- "X knows that p, but p is false"
- "X understands that p's reason is q, but it isn't"

Assertoric endorsement is inherent in such competence-imputing A-locutions. To eliminate this factor of concurrence, reformulations will be necessary that explicitly detach the assertor from what is going on with respect to the agent:

- "X thinks he realizes that p, but . . ."
- "X thinks he knows that p, but . . ."
- "X thinks he understands . . . , but . . ."

Those initial attributions of intellectual competence (realizes, knows, understands) involve an inherent commitment to objective appropriateness. They do not simply report the agent's posture but characterize it as appropriate by objective standards. To say that someone realizes (knows, understands) something is *not* just to say that he thinks certain things and not even just to add that I as reporter agree with him. The way the language works, "X realizes that p" is not just to say that he believes p and I do so as well. That initial claim involves the contention that this belief is appropriate and warranted as correct by impersonally objective standards. Our declarations here function in such a way as to immerse those attributions of cognitive competence in a commitment to objective standards.

This is why anthropologists who ascribe to other cultures or peoples a knowledge different from and discordant with ours speak sloppily and inappropriately (though not unintelligibly) when they say things like "The

Wazonga know that the swamp spirits cause fever," the ground rules of proper usage are cast to the winds. To be sure, there is no difficulty of understanding. We grasp easily enough what corrections are in order: we know full well what is going on, namely, that the Wazonga *think* (or *believe* or *accept*) that they know that those swamp spirits are at work. But we cannot conscientiously speak of knowledge where we have reservations about endorsement. To reemphasize: Strictly construed, "X knows that p but I incline to doubt it" is a contradiction in terms, given the language as it stands.

This situation obtains not just in the cognitive case but is replicated across the board. Take the setting of *evaluation*. Consider here the difference between

A	B
values	appreciates
does justice as he sees it	acts justly
does what he sees as right	acts morally

In each instance we have an analogous situation. The *A*-locutions characterize a state of affairs in terms of the agent's situation: they are shortly reportorial. The *B*-locutions incorporate an imputation of appropriateness by putatively objective standards. Thus saying "X appreciates p" is not just a claim that he values it, but rather asserts that he values it rightly, prizing it out of a recognition that it *ought* to be prized—that is, deserves to be prized by standards that are objectively appropriate. One can unproblematically say "X values (or prizes) z even though it is utterly worthless" but it would be paradoxical to say "X appreciates z even though it is utterly worthless." In such axiological matters of assessing value or justice or morality—in matters of evaluation even as in cognitive matters—we distinguish between how things appear subjectively in the eyes of the agent and additionally the larger issue of whether this stance merits endorsement on the basis of objective standards. And it is exactly this matter of objectivity that is built into the *B*-assessments.

Again, in *practical* contexts we have the same situation. Thus an agent acts *successfully* if he does what yields his desired result—if he does what proves to be goal-attaining. But he only acts *sagaciously* if he does what proves to be successful in the appropriate (objectively warranted) belief that it would (most probably) succeed in realizing a worthy aim. And at this last stage—the stage of competence assessment—a commitment to objective standards is once again at work.

The critical difference is exhibited by the contrast between:

- *X* does *A* because he *believes* that it is the correct thing to do (be it morally or practically, or whatever).

and

- *X* does *A* because he *realizes* (i.e., *appropriately* believes) that it is the (morally, practically, etc.) correct thing to do.

The former is a mere report of the agent's position. But in the second case, where we attribute competence, we not only impute to the agent a certain belief (that *A* is the correct thing to do) but we go on to endorse this belief on our own account as being objectively correct and to claim (implicitly) that the agent also appreciates (understands) this to be so. The commitment to objective standards is imprescindable here: all such attributions of competence carry an implicit commitment of this nature. They go beyond the issue of seeming (subjective) appropriateness as the issue stands in the agent's sight (according to *his* lights) to involve a commitment to what is objectively warranted and in order.

In all of the attribution of competence at issue with B-style locutions, the matter is not one of someone's merely *thinking* that a certain answer is going to be correct—and not even so if one lucks out and matters by chance so eventuate that this answer proves to be correct. The crux here is that the agent so thinks on the basis of appropriate grounds—grounds which deserve to be seen by anyone as compelling on the basis of objectively valid standards.

The fact is that the very language we use in these matters—and the conceptual scheme that it embodies—stands committed to the idea of impersonally correct standards. Be it in cognitive or evaluative of practical contexts, the terminology we employ making attributions of competence involves us in an implicit subscription to the idea of objectively cogent standards.

To be sure, the mere fact that our language involves a commitment of some sort does not establish that commitment as correct. But it does indicate a strong presumption in its favor, a presumption that only a cogent and convincing case to the contrary could manage to defeat.

That such a case is unlikely to be forthcoming is shown by a rather more fundamental analysis of language use, namely its service as an instrumentality of interpersonal communication.

2. COGNITIVE OBJECTIVITY AND COMMUNICATION

William James somewhere says that "Each of us literally chooses, by his ways of attending to things, what sort of a universe he shall appear to himself to inhabit."[1] This is in its own way perfectly true, being saved from disaster by that qualifying "appear to himself." But the fact remains that all of us need to some extent and most of us need to a great extent to live in a world we share with others. And in such a common shared world we need to proceed objectively—to be efficient and effective in the crucial business of coordinating beliefs and actions with those of people with whom we need to interact.

One of the main merits of cognitive objectivity thus arises in the context of communication—in its role in rendering people's thoughts and actions mutually accessible and making one person's information and ideas available to others. In doing what *any* reasonable person would do in the existing circumstances, we enter upon a universalization that renders one's own proceedings generally intelligible to the rest. Cognitive objectivity clearly supports communication. And the reverse is true as well. The cultivation of objectivity is greatly facilitated by an interpersonal communication that enables one to test one's view of things against the views of other people. For one thing, objectivity is powerfully fostered through the creation of an intercommunicating community, seeing that effective intercommunication provides a crucial objectivity check. But even more importantly, objectivity is a pivotal function in the context of the community that we require for well-being and survival. We need not only to answer questions and make statements in such a way that they can be *understood* by others but also in such a way that they will be *accepted* by them.

The relation between objectivity and communication is thus a two-way street. Objectivity facilitates communication because by proceeding objectively, by doing as others would do, we render ourselves intelligible to them. Conversely, communication aids the pursuit of objectivity because information about what others are doing—and how and why they do it—enables us to benefit from their efforts at understanding a common, shared world. Since objectivity encompasses interpersonal coordination (doing what others would in my place), communication with others is clearly both a facilitation of and an incentive to the impetus to objectivity.[2]

To pursue objectivity in practice means doing the best we can to assure the rationality of our own proceedings, to seek to do what other reasonable people would do in our situation. And there is no more effectively practicable way to achieve this than by entering into a communicative commerce with them that enables us to learn by study—and even interrogation—how other sensible people manage those affairs. We are well advised to do so not because we should wish to pursue consensus as such and desire to be conformist, but because we do (or should!) want to do what is the rational and appropriate thing. Interpersonal communication, and impersonal objectivity with it, are part and parcel of rationality's concern for cost-effective means to sensible ends.

Why, after all, do we credit people with communicative potential—with the capacity to provide us with information? Note that the purported fact, *In uttering "the cat is on the mat" he is engaged in asserting that the cat is on the mat*, represents a belief of ours, or at any rate a supposition on our part. We make such communicative suppositions initially in desperation, as it were, because this provides the only feasible way for us to derive any benefit from the content of someone's assertions, but ultimately because we eventually accumulate evidence that indicates (with the wisdom of hindsight) that this supposition was well advised (warranted), if not invariably then at least by and large. On this basis, we are rationally well advised (for example) to treat their declarations as epistemically innocent until proven otherwise, exactly because this is the most cost-effective thing to do. Our communicative procedures are motivated—and justified—by the essentially economic objective of extracting the maximum benefit from our information-oriented interactions.

The policy of believing what we are told in the absence of case-specific counterindications represents the course of wisdom because it is always in our interest to proceed in ways that are efficient and effective in meeting our informational requirements. If playing safe were all that mattered, we would, of course, suspend judgment indefinitely. But it is simply not in our interest to do so, since safety is not all. In rational inquiry we seek not only to avert error but to achieve knowledge. We adopt an epistemic policy of credence in the first instance because it is the most promising avenue toward our goals, and then persist in it because we subsequently find, not that it is unfailingly successful, but that it is highly cost-effective.[3]

The guiding principle here is that of cost-benefit calculation. The standard presumptions that underlie our communicative practices are emphatically *not* validatable as established facts. (For example, it is certainly *not* true that people say what they mean, save at some level of statistical generality.) But their justification becomes straightforward on economic grounds, as practices that represent the most efficient and economical way to get the job done. For if we do not concede *some* credit to the declarations of others, then we lose any and all chance to derive informative profit from them, thus denying ourselves the benefit of a potentially useful resource. For the course of experience would soon teach us that, even where strangers outside the family circle are concerned, the benefits of trust, of credibility concession, generally overbalance the risks involved.

Communication is accordingly predicated on conceding and maintaining credibility. Communication too is a commercial system of sorts. Credit is extended, drawn upon, and enlarged. And with communicative and financial credit alike, one could not build up credit (prove oneself credit-worthy) unless given *some* credit by somebody in the first place. For credit to be obtainable at all, there has to be an initial presumption that one is credit-worthy. Clearly, such a presumption of innocent until proven guilty (i.e., fault-free until shown to be otherwise) can be defeated; one can of course prove oneself to be unworthy of credit or credence. But initially the presumption must be made.

And the issue has another important aspect. The circumstances of human life are such that, like it or not, we are enmeshed in a variety of needs which must be satisfied in the interests of a viable and satisfactory existence. The need for knowledge to guide our actions and satisfy our curiosity is paramount among these. Without knowledge-productive inquiry we cannot resolve the cognitive and practical problems that confront a rational creature in making its way in this world. But in matters of knowledge-production life is too short for us to proceed on our own. We simply cannot start at square one and do everything needful by ourselves. We must—and do—proceed in the setting of a larger community that extends across the reaches of time (through its cultural traditions) and space (through its social organization). This requires communication, coordination, collaboration. And so even as the pursuit of objectivity is aided by an agent's recourse to the resources of the envisioning community, so, conversely, is objectivity an indispensable instrumentality for the creation and maintenance of intercommunicative community. For there can be no community where people do not understand one another, and it is the fact that I endeavor to proceed as any rational person would in my place that renders my proceedings efficiently intelligible to others. The objectivity of rational procedure is a crucial coordination mechanism that renders people mutually understandable by one another. It positions each of us to benefit by a mutually advantageous commerce that is indispensable for the cooperation and collaboration without which the cognitive enterprise—and other social enterprises in general—would become infeasible. In communicative situations everyone profits from objective ways of proceeding. The whole process is one of reaching out to establish and maintain commonalties with others. Objectivity is an integral and indispensable component of this enterprise.

3. THE PROVISIONALITY OF CONCEPTIONS

Clear thinking about interpersonal communication requires recognizing that there is a significant and substantial difference between a true or correct statement or contention on the one hand, and a true or correct conception on the other. To make a true contention about a thing we merely need to get *one particular fact* about it right. To have a true conception of the thing, on the other hand, we must get *all of the important facts* about it right. And it is clear that this involves a certain specifically normative element, namely, what the "important" or "essential" facts of something are.

Anaximander of Miletus presumably made many correct contentions about the sun in the fifth century B.C.—for example, that its light is brighter than that of the moon. But Anaximander's *conception* of the sun (as the flaming spoke of a great wheel of fire encircling the earth) was totally wrong.

To assure the actual correctness of our conception of a thing we would have to be sure—as we very seldom are—that nothing further can possibly come along to upset our view of just what its important features are and just what their character is. Thus, the qualifying conditions for true conceptions are far more demanding than those for true claims. With a correct contention about a thing, all is well if we get the single relevant aspect of it right, but with a correct conception of it *we must get the essentials right*—we must have an overall picture that is basically correct. And this is something we generally cannot ascertain, if only because we cannot say with confidence what is really important or essential before the end of the proverbial day.

With *conceptions*—unlike propositions or *contentions*—incompleteness means incorrectness, or at any rate *presumptive* incorrectness. Having a correct or adequate conception of something as the object it is requires that we have all the *important* facts about it right. But since the prospect of discovering further important facts can never be eliminated, the possibility can never be eliminated that matters may so eventuate that we may ultimately (with the wisdom of hindsight) acknowledge the insufficiency or even inappropriateness of our earlier conceptions. When our information about something is incomplete, obtaining an overall picture of the thing at issue becomes a matter of theorizing , or guesswork, however sophisticatedly executed. A conception of its overall content must be largely conjectural, and thus must be *presumed* to contain an admixture of error. And then we have no alternative but to suppose that this overall picture fall short of being wholly correct in various (unspecifiable) ways. With conceptions, falsity can thus emerge from errors of omission as well as those of commission, resulting from the circumstance that the information at our disposal is merely incomplete rather than actually false (as would have to be the case with contentions).

To be sure, an inadequate or incomplete *description* of something is not thereby false—the statements we make about it may be perfectly true as far as they go. But an inadequate or incomplete *conception* of a thing is by virtue of this very fact something that we have no choice but to presume to be *incorrect* as well,[4] seeing that where there is incompleteness we cannot justifiably take the stance that it relates only to inconsequential matters and touches nothing important. Accordingly, our conceptions of particular things are always to be viewed not just as cognitively *open-ended* but as *corrigible* as well.

We are led back to the thesis of the great idealist philosophers (Spinoza, Hegel, Bradley, Royce) that human knowledge inevitably falls short of "perfected science" (the Idea, the Absolute). Our knowledge of the world's objects must be presumed deficient both in its completeness and its correctness. And this epistemic modesty—this preparedness to entertain contrast between our own potentially imperfect conception of a thing and its real nature—is something crucial. For if we took our conception as definitive, if we *identified* "the thing itself" with "the thing exactly as we ourselves conceive of it," then we would be unable to communicate with others about a common world. The achievement of ontological objectivity requires self-abnegation; we cannot claim definitive authority for our own conception of things.

4. OBJECTIVITY AND COMMUNICATION

Human cognition as we understand it would be impossible without communal inquiry into and interpersonal communication about an objective order of reality. And without a presupposition of ontological objectivity the very idea of investigating a shared world would become inoperable.

To communicate about real-world issues we must avoid claiming finality for our conception of things. To communicate about common, shared objects we need not claim to have it right—and we need not even agree on the *descriptions* of things. But it is crucial that we come together with respect to their identity. (That is why a consensus in matters of description is ultimately dispensable.)

Our concept of a *real thing* is such that it provides a fixed point, a stable center around which communication revolves, an invariant focus of potentially diverse conceptions. What is to be determinative, decisive, definitive, etc., of the things at issue in my discourse is not my conception, or yours, or indeed anyone's conception at all. The conventionalized intention discussed means that a coordination of conceptions is not decisive for the possibility of communication. Your statements about a thing may well convey something to me even if my conception of it is altogether different from yours. To communicate we need not take ourselves to share views of the world, but only take the stance that we share the world being discussed.

Our commitment to an objective reality that lies behind the data that people secure is indispensably demanded by any step into that domain of the publicly accessible objects which is essential to communal inquiry and interpersonal communication about a shared world. We could not establish communicative contact about a common object of discussion if our discourse were geared to the substance of our own idiosyncratic ideas and conceptions. But the objectivity at issue in our communicative discourse is a matter of its *status* rather than one of its *content*. For the substantive content of a claim about the world in no way tells us whether it is factual or fictional. This is something we have to determine from its *context*: it is a matter of the frame, not the canvas. The fact-oriented basis of our information-transmitting exchanges is provided a priori by a conventionalized intention to talk about "the real world." This intention to take real objects to be at issue—objects having a nature that reaches well above and beyond our knowledge of them and far transcending our potentially idiosyncratic conceptions—is fundamental because it is overriding; that is, it overrides all of our other intentions when we enter upon the communicative venture. Without this conventionalized intention we should not be able to convey information—or misinformation—to one another about a shared "objective" world.

We are able to say something about the (real) moon or the (real) Sphinx because of our submission to a fundamental communicative convention of "social contract" to the effect that we *intend* ("mean") to talk about it— that very thing itself as it "really" is—our own private conception of it notwithstanding. We arrive at the standard policy that prevails with respect to all communicative discourse of letting "the language we use," rather than whatever specific informative aims we may actually "have in mind" on particular occasions, be the decisive factor with regard to the things at issue in our discourse. When I speak about the Sphinx (even though I do so on the basis of my own conceivably strange conception of what is involved here), I will be discussing "the *real* Sphinx" in virtue of the basic conventionalized intention governing our use of referring terms.

This fundamental intention of objectification, the intention to discuss "the moon itself" regardless of how untenable one's own *ideas* about it may eventually prove to be, is a basic precondition of the very possibility of communication. It is crucial to the communicative enterprise to take the egocentrism-avoiding stance that rejects all claims to a privileged status for *our own* conception of things. In the interests of this stance we are prepared to "discount any misconceptions" (our own included) about things over a very wide range indeed; we are committed to the stance that factual disagreements as to the character of things are communicatively irrelevant within very broad limits. The incorrectness of conceptions is venial.

If we were to set up our own conception of things as somehow definitive and decisive, we would at once erect a barrier not only to further inquiry but—no less importantly—to the prospect of successful communication with one another. Communication could then only proceed with the wisdom of hindsight, at the end of a long process of tentative checks. Communicative contact would be realized only in the implausible case where extensive exchange indicated retrospectively that there had been an *identity* of conceptions all along. And we would always stand on very shaky ground. For no matter how far we push our investigation into the issue of an identity of conceptions, the prospect of a divergence lying just around the corner—waiting to be discovered if only we pursued the matter just a bit further—can never be precluded. One could never advance the issue of the identity of focus past the status of a more or less well-grounded *assumption*. And then any so-called communication would no longer be an exchange of information but a tissue of frail conjectures. The communicative enterprise would become a vast inductive project, a complex exercise in theory-building, leading tentatively and provisionally toward something which, in fact, the imputational groundwork of our language enables us to presuppose from the very outset.[5]

Communication requires not only common *concepts* but common *topics*, interpersonally shared items of discussion, a common world constituted by the self-subsistently real objects basic to shared experience. The factor of objectivity reflects our basic commitment to a communally available world as the common property of communicators. Such a commitment involves more than merely de facto intersubjective agreement. For such agreement is a matter of a posteriori discovery, while our view of the nature of things puts "the real world" on a necessary and a priori basis. This stance roots in the fundamental convention of a shared social instance on communication. What links my discourse with that of my interlocutor is our common subscription to the governing presumption (a defensible presumption, to be sure) that we are both talking about the shared thing, our own possible misconceptions of it notwithstanding. This means that no matter how extensively we may change our minds about the *nature* of a thing or type of thing, we are still dealing with exactly the same thing or sort of thing. It assures reidentification across discordant theories and belief-systems.

5. THE ROLE OF POSTULATION

The commitment to objectivity is basic to any prospect of communicative discourse with one another about a shared world of "real things" to which none of us is in a position to claim privileged access. This commitment establishes a need to "distance" ourselves from things by way of recognizing the prospect of a discrepancy between our (potentially idiosyncratic) conceptions of things and the true character of these things as they exist objectively in "the real world." The ever-present contrast between "the thing as we view it" and "the thing as it is" is the mechanism by which this crucially important distancing is accomplished. And maintaining this stance means that we are never entitled to claim to have exhausted a thing *au fond* in cognitive regards, to have managed to bring it wholly within our epistemic grasp. For to make this claim would, in effect, be to *identify* "the thing at issue" purely in terms of "our own conception of it," an identification which would effectively abolish the former item (the thing itself as an independent entity in its own right) by endowing our idiosyncratic conception with decisively determinative force. And this would lead straightaway to the unacceptable result of a cognitive solipsism that would preclude reference to intersubjectively identifiable particulars, thereby blocking the possibility of interpersonal communication and communal inquiry.

Any pretensions to the authoritative predominance, let alone the definitive correctness, of our own conceptions regarding the realm of the real must be set aside in the context of communication. In communication regarding things we must be able to exchange information about them with our contemporaries and to transmit information about them to our successors. And we must be in a position to do this on the presumption that *their* conceptions of things are not only radically different from *ours*, but conceivably also rightly different. Thus, it is a crucial precondition of the possibility of successful communication about things that we must avoid laying any claim either to the completeness or even to the ultimate correctness of our own conceptions of any of the things at issue. This renders it critically important *that* (and understandable *why*) conceptions are not pivotal for communicative purposes. Our discourse *reflects* our conceptions and perhaps *conveys* them, but it is not substantively *about* them.

What is crucial for communication, however, is the fundamental intention to deal with the objective order of this "real world." If our assertoric commitments did not transcend the information we have on hand, we would never be able to "get in touch" with others about a shared objective world. In actual communication no claim can be made for the *primacy* of our conceptions, or for the *correctness* of our conceptions, or even for the mere *agreement* of our conceptions with those of others. The fundamental intention to discuss "the thing itself" predominates and overrides any mere dealing with the thing as we conceive it to be. Certainly, that reference to "objectively real things" at work in our discourse does not contemplate a peculiar sort of *thing*—a new *ontological* category of "things-in-themselves." It is simply a shorthand formula for a certain communicative presumption or imputation rooted in an a priori commitment to the idea of a commonality of objective focus that is allowed to stand unless and until circumstances arise to render this untenable.

How do we really know that Anaximander of Miletus was talking about *our* earth when projecting his (to us fanciful) cosmological scheme in the sixth century B.C.? He is not here to reassure us. He did not leave elaborate discussions about his aims and purposes. How can we be so confident about what he meant in that strange talk about a slab-like object suspended in equilibrium in the center of the cosmos? The answer is straightforward. That he is *to be taken* to mean that *our* earth is such an object as something that turns, in the final analysis, on two very general issues in which Anaximander himself plays little if any role: (1) our subscription to certain generalized principles of interpretation with respect to the Greek language; and (2) the conventionalized subscription by us and ascription to other language-users in general of certain fundamental communicative policies and intentions. In the face of appropriate functional equivalences we allow neither a difference in language nor a difference of "thought-world" or worldview to block an identity of reference.

Seen in this light, the key point may be put as follows: it is indeed a presupposition of effective communicative discourse about something that we purport (claim and intend) to make true statements about it. But for such discourse it is *not* required that we purport to have a true or even adequate conception of the item at issue. On the contrary, we must deliberately abstain from any claim that our own conception is definitive if we are to engage successfully in discourse. We deliberately put the whole matter of conception aside—abstracting from the question of the agreement of my conception with yours, and all the more from the issue of which one of us has the right conception.[6] This sort of epistemic humility is the price we pay for keeping the channels of communication open.

A commitment to the ontological objectivity of an objective, impersonally defined order of things is accordingly absolutely crucial to the epistemic project as we standardly conceive of it. For the very idea of acquiring and transmitting knowledge of a real order of things is predicated in the supposition—the postulation, if you will—that there indeed are real objects in the world regarding whose nature our own information is not only incomplete but also possibly incorrect. Without a commitment to ontological objectivity the very idea of cognitive objectivity would be lost. Ontological and epistemic objectivity are thus indissolubly linked because the latter has the former as a functional (or "regulative") presupposition.

And so an important lesson emerges. The rationale of a commitment to ontological objectivity is in the final analysis cognitively driven. For without a presuppositional commitment to objectivity with its acceptance of a real world independent of ourselves that we share in common, inter-personal communication would become impracticable. Objectivity is an integral part of the sine qua non presuppositional basis of the project of meaningful communication. For, to reemphasize, if our own subjective conceptions of things were to be determinative, informative communication about a world of shared objects and processes would be rendered unachievable.[7]

seven

ONTOLOGICAL OBJECTIVITY GROUNDS COGNITIVE OBJECTIVITY

Synopsis

(1) Real-world objects outdistance the range of human cognition. Real things—actually existing physical objects—have a cognitive depth whose bottom we cannot possibly plumb. (2) This circumstance has a strongly realistic tendency. It means that the limits of our world—the world of our belief and of our information—cannot be claimed to be the limits of the world. It is the very limitation of our knowledge of things—our recognition that reality extends beyond the horizons of what we can possibly know or even conjecture about—that betokens the mind-independence of the real. (3) The ontological component of metaphysical realism—the idea that there indeed is an objective sphere of mind-independent reality which exists independently in its own right, without reference to anyone's ideas and conceptions about it—is not something that we learn from experience. It is a presupposition for our experience-exploiting inquiries, rather than a product thereof. (4) We have to do here with a postulation made on functional rather than evidential ground, which we endorse in order to be in a position to learn by experience at all. And its ultimate justification lies in the pragmatic consideration of its being an essential component of what is for us a useful and indeed necessary project.

1. THE COGNITIVE OPACITY OF REAL THINGS

Ontological objectivity has to do with the things that exist; cognitive objectivity with the nature of our knowledge or, at any rate, belief about things. The one deals with what exists, the other with our views about it. How are the two related?

The issue posed here is unquestionably complex. But the ultimate answer is that a particular sort of cognitive stance towards *ontological* objectivity lies at the base of our commitment to *cognitive* objectivity. The pursuit of cognitive objectivity—with its injunction to align our own thought with our best judgment of the demands of reason—calls for a commitment to ontological objectivity, requiring the supposition of real-world objects whose true character is independent of what any of us happen to think. The task of the present chapter is to unfold the rather intricate tale of how this is so.

The quest for objective knowledge will, in theory, beckon us onwards to the infinite. From finitely many axioms, reason can generate a potential infinity of theorems; from finitely many words, thought can exfoliate a potential infinity of sentences; from finitely many data, reflection can extract a potential infinity of items of information. Even with respect to a world of finitely many objects, the process of reflecting upon these objects can, in principle, go on unendingly. One can inquire about their features, the features of these features, and so on. Or again, one can consider their relations, the relations among those relations, and so on. Thought—abstraction, reflection, analysis—is an inherently ampliative process. As in physical reflection mirror-images can reflect one another indefinitely, so mental reflection can go on and on. Given a start, however modest, thought can advance *ad indefinitum* into new conceptual domains. The circumstance of its starting out from a finite basis does *not* mean that it need ever run out of impetus (as the example of Shakespearean scholarship seems to illustrate).

Any adequate theory of inquiry must recognize that the ongoing process of information acquisition at issue in science is a process of *conceptual* innovation, which always leaves certain facts about things wholly outside the cognitive range of the inquirers of any particular period. Caesar did not know—and in the then extant state of the cognitive arts could not have known—that his sword contained tungsten and carbon. There will always be facts (or plausible candidate facts) about a thing that we do not *know* because we cannot even *conceive* of them in a prevailing order of things. To grasp such a fact means adopting a perspective of consideration which holds that we do not have a definitive and complete view of the item at hand because the state of knowledge is not yet advanced to a point at which finality and definitiveness can reasonably be claimed. Any adequate worldview must recognize that the ongoing progress of scientific inquiry is a process of *conceptual* innovation that always leaves various facts about the things of this world wholly outside the cognitive range of the inquirers of any particular period.

The prospect of change can never be eliminated in the cognitive domain. The properties of a thing are literally open-ended: we can always discover more of them. Even if we were (surely mistakenly) to view the world as inherently finitistic—espousing a Keynesian principle of "limited variety" to the effect that nature can be portrayed descriptively with the materials of a finite taxonomic scheme—there will still be no a priori guarantee that the progress of science will not lead *ad indefinitum* to changes of mind regarding this finite register of descriptive materials. And this conforms exactly to our expectation in these matters. For where the real things of the world are concerned, we not only expect to learn more about them in the course of further scientific inquiry, *we expect to have to change our minds about their nature and modes of comportment.* Be the object at issue elm trees, or volcanoes, or quarks, we have every expectation that in the course of future scientific progress people will come to think about the origin and properties of the item differently from the way we do at this juncture. In sum, real things—actually existing physical objects—have a cognitive depth whose bottom we cannot possibly plumb. And cognitive changes or innovations are to be conceptualized as something that occurs on *our* side of the cognitive transaction, not on the side of the *objects* with which we deal.[1]

It is worthwhile to examine more closely the considerations that indicate the inherent imperfection of our knowledge of things.

To begin with, it is clear that, as we standardly think about things within the conceptual framework of our fact-oriented thought and discourse, *any* real physical object has more facets than it will ever actually manifest in experience. For every objective property of a real thing has consequences of a dispositional character and these are never surveyable in toto because the dispositions which particular concrete things inevitably have endow them with an infinitistic aspect that cannot be comprehended within experience.[2] This desk, for example, has a limitless manifold of phenomenal features of the type: "having a certain appearance from a particular point of view." It is perfectly clear that most of these will never be actualized in experience. Moreover, a thing *is* what it *does:* entity and lawfulness are coordinated correlates—a good Kantian point. And this fact that real things involve lawful comportment means that the finitude of experience precludes any prospect of the *exhaustive* manifestation of the descriptive facets of any real things.[3]

Physical things not only have more properties than they ever will overtly manifest, but they have more than they possibly *can* ever manifest.

This is so because the dispositional properties of things always involve what might be characterized as *mutually preemptive* conditions of realization. This cube of sugar, for example, has the dispositional property of reacting in a particular way if subjected to a temperature of 10,000°C and of reacting in a certain way if emplaced for one hundred hours in a large, turbulent body of water. But if either of these conditions is ever realized, it will destroy the lump of sugar as a lump of sugar, and thus block the prospect of its ever bringing the other property to manifestation. The perfectly possible realization of various dispositions may fail to be mutually *compossible*, and so the dispositional properties of a thing cannot ever be manifested completely—not just in practice, but in principle. Our objective claims about real things always commit us to more than we can actually ever determine about them.

The existence of this latent (hidden, occult) sector is a crucial feature of our conception of a real thing. Neither in fact nor in thought can we ever simply put it away. To say of the apple that its only features are those it actually manifests is to run afoul of our conception of an apple. To deny—or even merely to refuse to be committed to the claim—that it *would* manifest particular features *if* certain conditions came about (for example, that it would have such-and-such a taste if eaten) is to be driven to withdrawing the claim that it is an apple. The process of corroborating the implicit contents of our objective factual claims about something real is potentially endless, and such judgments are thus "non-terminating" in C. I. Lewis's sense.[4] This cognitive depth of our objective factual claims is inherent in the fact that their *content* will always outrun the evidence for making them and means that the endorsement of any such claim always involves some element of evidence-transcending conjecture.

The very concepts at issue—namely "experience" and "manifestation"—are such that we can only ever *experience* those features of a real thing that it actually *manifests*. But the preceding considerations show that real things always have more experientially manifestable properties than they can ever actually manifest in experience. The experienced portion of a thing is like the part of the iceberg that shows above water. All real things are necessarily thought of as having hidden depths that extend beyond the limits, not only of experience, but also of experientiability. To say of something that it is an apple or a stone or a tree is to become committed to claims about it that go beyond the data we have—and even beyond those which we can, in the nature of things, ever actually acquire. The "meaning" inherent in the assertoric commitments of our factual statements is never exhausted by its verification. Real things are cognitively opaque—we cannot see to the bottom of them. Our knowledge of such things can thus become more *extensive* without thereby becoming more *complete.*

This cognitive opacity of real things means that we are not—and will never be—in a position to evade or abolish the contrast between "things as we think them to be" and "things as they actually and truly are." Their susceptibility to further elaborative detail—and to changes of mind regarding this further elaborative detail—is built into our very conception of a "real thing." To be a real thing is to be something regarding which we can always, in principle, acquire more and possibly discordant information. This view of the situation is supported rather than impeded once we abandon the naive cumulativist/preservationist view of knowledge acquisition in recognizing that new discoveries need not *supplement* but can *displace* the old. We realize that people will come to think differently about things from the way we do—even when thoroughly familiar things are at issue—since scientific progress generally entails fundamental changes of mind about how things work in the world.

In view of the cognitive opacity of real things, we must never pretend to a cognitive monopoly or cognitive finality. This emphasis on the *tentative* (rather than definitive) nature of our information about things—its provisional rather than definitive nature which makes our knowledge of things into merely purported knowledge—led Kant to contrast the empirical/experiential objects that feature in our knowledge with "something = X, of which we *know*, and with the present constitution of our understanding can *know*, nothing whatsoever."[5] This recognition of incomplete information is inherent in the very nature of our conception of a "real thing." It is a crucial facet of our epistemic stance towards the real world to recognize that every part and parcel of it has features lying beyond our present cognitive reach—at *any* "present" whatsoever.

Much the same story holds when our concern is not with physical things but with *types* of such things. To say that something is copper or magnetic is to say more than that it has the properties we think copper or magnetic things have, and to say more than that it meets our test conditions for being copper (or being magnetic). It is to say that this thing *is* copper or magnetic. And this is an issue regarding which we are prepared at least to contemplate the prospect that we have got it wrong.

It is, of course, imaginable that natural science will come to a stop, not in the trivial sense of a cessation of intelligent life, but rather in Charles Sanders Peirce's more interesting sense of eventually reaching a condition after which even indefinitely ongoing effort at inquiry will not—and indeed actually *cannot*—produce any significant change. Such a position is, in theory, possible. But we can never *know*—be it in practice or in principle—that it is actually realized. We can never establish that science has attained such an omega-condition of final completion: the possibility of further change lying "just around the corner" can never be ruled out finally and decisively. We thus have no alternative but to *presume* that our science is still imperfect and incomplete, that no matter how far we have pushed our inquiries in any direction, regions of terra incognita yet lie beyond. And this means that we must, to be realistic, take the stance that our conceptions of real things, no matter how elaborately developed, are nevertheless provisional and corrigible. Reality always has hidden reserves; it is always "deeper" than our knowledge of it.

It is instructive in this context to contemplate some of the great discoveries of twentieth-century formal and empirical science:

- Gödel's incompleteness theorem and such of its cousins as Turing's halting problem and various noncomputability results
- the proliferation of logical, geometric, and mathematical systems
- the development of quantum physics with its statisticization of all nature (the cognitive domain included)
- the rise of scientific epistemology with its idea that theories are everywhere underdetermined by evidence

These developments combine to indicate and substantiate an important lesson. They go beyond the general-principle argumentation of traditional skepticism to provide detailed substantive grounds for acknowledging that our knowledge of things is incomplete and incompletable, imperfect and imperfectible. All we can do at this—or any—stage of inquiry is to project the most plausible overall account relative to the information at hand so as to achieve the best estimates for resolving our questions about the world that are realized in the existing state of the art.[6] Our science represents not the definitive truth of things but only our best currently attainable effort in this direction. The fact of the matter is that reality everywhere outruns our knowledge of it.

2. PERSPECTIVES ON REALISM

Physical realism claims the objective reality of physical existents. But what is involved with this ontological mode of being "objective"? What are we committing ourselves to in saying of something that it is "a real thing," an object existing as part of the world's furniture? Clearly, as regards objectivity we stand committed to several (obviously interrelated) points.

- *Substantiality of entity*. Being a "something" (entity) with its own unity of being. Having an enduring identity of its own.
- *Physicality or reality*. Existing in space and time. Having a place as a real item in the world's physical scheme.
- *Publicity or accessibility*. Admitting universality of access. Being something that different investigators proceeding from different points of departure can get hold of.
- *Autonomy or independence*. Being independent of mind. Being something that observers find rather than create.

The first two of these interrelated factors are ontological; the second two epistemological. And the latter hook on to the former. In rational inquiry—in science in particular—we try to get the objective matters of fact regarding physical reality in ways that are accessible to all observers alike. (The "repeatability of experiments" is crucial.) And another salient factor enters in with that fourth and final issue—autonomy. The very idea of a real thing so functions in our conceptual scheme that actually existing things are thought of as having an identity, a nature, and a mode of comportment wholly indifferent to the cognitive state-of-the-art regarding them—and potentially even very different from our own current conceptions of the matter.

The conception of a *thing* that underlies our discourse about the things of this world reflects a certain sort of tentativeness and fallibility—the implicit recognition that our own personal or even communal conception of particular things may, in general, be wrong, and is in any case inadequate. At the back of our thought about things there is always a certain wary skepticism that recognizes the possibility of error. The objectivity of real existents projects beyond the reaches of our subjectively conditioned information.

There is wisdom in Hamlet's dictum: "There are more things in heaven and on earth, Horatio. . . ." The limits of our knowledge may be the limits of *our* world, but they are not the limits of *the* world. We do and must recognize the limitations of our cognition. We cannot justifiably equate reality with what can, in principle, be known by us, nor equate reality with what can, in principle, be expressed by our language. And what is true here for our sort of mind is true for any other sort of finite mind as well. Any physically realizable sort of cognizing being can know only a part or aspect of the real.

The issue of "objectivity" in the sense of mind-independence is pivotal for realism. A fact is *objective* in this mode if it obtains thought-independently—if any change merely in what is thought by the world's intelligences would leave it unaffected. With objective facts (unlike those which are merely a matter of intersubjective agreement) what thinkers think just does not enter in—what is at issue is thought-invariant or thought-indifferent. What realism maintains from the outset—and traditional idealism often struggles valiantly to retain (with mixed success)—is just this idea that there are certain objective facts that obtain regardless of what we, or anybody else, think of them.

At this point we reach an important conjuncture of ideas. The ontological independence of things—their objectivity and autonomy from the machinations of mind—is a crucial aspect of realism. And the fact that it lies at the very core of our conception of a real thing that such items project beyond the cognitive reach of mind betokens a concept-scheme fundamentally committed to objectivity. The only plausible sort of ontology is one that contemplates a realm of reality that outruns the range of knowledge (and indeed even of language), adopting the stance that character goes beyond the limits of characterization. It is a salient aspect of the mind-independent status of the objectively real that the features of something real always transcend what we know about it. Indeed, yet further or different facts concerning a real thing can always come to light, and all that we *do* say about it does not exhaust all that *can and should* be said about it. In this light, objectivity is crucial to realism and the cognitive inexhaustibility of things is a certain token of their objectivity.

Authentic realism can exist only in a state of tension. The only reality worth having is one that is in some degree knowable. But it is the very limitation of our knowledge—our recognition that there is more to reality than what we do and can know or ever conjuncture about it—that speaks for the mind-independence of the real. It is important to stress against the skeptic that the human mind is sufficiently well attuned to reality that *some* knowledge of it is possible. But it is no less important to join with realists in stressing the independent character of reality, acknowledging that reality has a depth and complexity of makeup that outruns the reach of mind.

Peirce and others have located the impetus to realism in the limitations of man's will, in the fact that we can exert no control over our experience and, try as we will, cannot affect what we see and sense. Peirce's celebrated "Harvard Experiment" of the Lowell Lectures of 1903 makes the point forcibly:

> I know that this stone will fall if it is let go, because experience has convinced me that objects of this kind always do fall; and if anyone present has any doubt on the subject, I should be happy to try the experiment, and I will bet him a hundred to one on the result. . . . [I know this because of an unshakable conviction that] the uniformity with which stones have fallen has been due to some *active general principle* [of nature]. . . . Of course, every sane man will adopt the latter hypothesis. If he could doubt it in the case of the stone— which he can't—and I may as well drop the stone once and for all—I told you so!—if anybody doubt this still, a thousand other such inductive predictions are getting verified every day, and he will have to suppose every one of them to be merely fortuitous in order reasonably to escape the conclusion that *general principles are really operative in nature*. That is the doctorate of scholastic realism.[7]

No doubt, the ordinary man, and usually the philosopher, also stands committed to the conviction that whatever happens in the world of observations occurs in line with the causally lawful machinations of an underlying mind-independent physical reality.

In this context it is, however, important to distinguish between mental *dependency* and mental *control*. Peirce is clearly right in saying that we cannot *control* our conviction that the stone will fall: do what we will, it will remain. Nevertheless, this circumstance could conceivably still be something that *depends on us*—exactly as with the fearsomeness of heights for the man with vertigo. If the unconscious sphere of mind actually dictates how I *must* "see" something (as, for example, in an optical illusion of the Mueller-Lyer variety), then I evidently have no control. But that does not in itself refute mind-dependency—even of a very strong sort. There is always the prospect that we are deluding ourselves in these matters— that the limitations at issue appertain only to our conscious powers, and not to our power as such.

This prospect blocks Peirce's argument in the way already foreseen by Descartes in the *Meditations*:

> I found by experience that these [sensory] ideas presented themselves to me without my consent being requisite, so that I could not per-

ceive any object, however desirous I might be, unless it were present. . . . But although the ideas which I receive by senses do not depend on my will I do not think that one should for that reason conclude that they proceed from things different from myself, since possibly some facility might be discovered in me—though different from those yet known to me—which produced them.[8]

This line of reflection rightly suggests that we may simply be deluding ourselves about the range of the mind's powers: lack of control notwithstanding, dependency may yet lie with the "unconscious" sector of mind. The traditional case for realism based on the deficiencies of causal control—the limits of the human *will*—thus fails to provide a telling argument for mind-independence.

However, a yet more potent impetus to realism lies in the limitations of man's *intellect*, pivoting on the circumstance that the features of real things inevitably outrun our cognitive reach. In placing some crucial aspects of the real altogether outside the effective range of the mind's capacity to understand, it speaks for a position that sees mind-independence as a salient feature of the real. We cannot write stories in a language we do not know; we cannot solve problems in a domain we do not understand. The very fact of fallibility and limitedness—of our absolute confidence that our putative knowledge does *not* do justice to the real truth of the matter of what reality is actually like—is surely one of the best arguments for a realism that pivots on the basic idea that there is more to reality than we humans do or can know about. Traditional scientific realism sees the basis for realism in the extent and nature of our scientific knowledge; the present realism, by contrast, sees its basis in our realization of the inevitable *shortcomings* of our scientific knowledge.

This line of thought preempts the preceding sort of objection. If we are compelled to be modest about the reach of our cognitive powers, acknowledging they do not adequately grasp "the way things really are," then this very circumstance clearly *bolsters* the case for ontological objectivity. The cognitive intractability of things is something about which, in principle, we cannot delude ourselves, since such delusion would illustrate rather than abrogate the fact of a reality independent of ourselves. The very inadequacy of our knowledge is one of the most salient tokens there is of a reality out there that lies beyond the inadequate grasp of mind. It is the very limitation of our knowledge of things—our recognition that reality extends beyond the horizons of what we ourselves can possibly know or even conjecture about it—that betokens the mind–independence of the real.

Let us consider ontological objectivity's basic reality postulate somewhat more closely. Our standard conception of inquiry involves recognition of the following facts: (1) The world (the realm of physical existence) has a nature whose characterization in point of description, explanation, and prediction is the object of empirical inquiry. (2) The real nature of the world is in the main independent of the process of inquiry which the real world canalizes or conditions. Dependency is a one-way street here: reality shapes or influences inquiry, but not conversely. Our opinions do not affect the real truth but, rather, our strivings after the real truth engender changes in our opinions. (3) In virtue of these considerations, we can stake neither total nor final claims for our purported knowledge of reality. Our knowledge of the world must be presumed incomplete, incorrect, and imperfect, with the consequence that "our reality"—reality as we deem it to be—must be considered as an inadequate characterization of "reality itself." The strongest support for realism does not lie in the convictions of our knowledge but in the acknowledgment of our ignorance.

3. THE EXISTENTIAL COMPONENT OF REALISM

Realism has two indispensable and inseparable components—the one existential and ontological, the other procedural and epistemic. The former maintains that there indeed is a real world—a realm of mind-independent, objective physical reality. The latter maintains that we can to some extent secure adequate information about this mind-independent realm. This second contention obviously presupposes the first: objective, impersonally cogent knowledge requires objective facts about the actual world: we cannot achieve person-irrelevant adequation to facts without a realm of reality for these facts to be facts about. C. I. Lewis in his more Kantian moments envisioned a cognitive imperative of reason and characterized it as "the law of objectivity."[9] This imperative enjoins one to acknowledge that experience signifies an objective reality beyond what is presented in the experience itself. And this position is perfectly sensible as far as it goes. But we are left with the question: what can the justificating rationale of such an imperative be?

A metaphysical realism of thought-independent existence is clearly not an inductive inference secured through the scientific systematization of our observations, but rather a regulative presupposition that makes science possible in the first place. Our observations could not be informative if we did not *presuppose* an objective order of reality for them to be informative about. The realm of mind-independent reality is something we cannot *discover*—we do not learn that it exists as a fruit of inquiry and investigation. How could we ever learn by inference from observations that our observations are objectively valid, that our mental experience is itself largely the causal product of the machinations of a mind-independent matrix, that all those phenomenal appearances are causally rooted in a physical reality? All this is clearly something we do not *learn* from inquiry. For what is at issue is, after all, a *precondition* for empirical inquiry—a presupposition for the usability of observational data as sources of objective information. That experience is indeed objective, that what we take to be evidence *is* evidence, that our sensations yield information about an order of existence outside the experiential realm itself, and that this experience constitutes not just a mere phenomenon but an appearance of something extra-mental belonging to an objectively self-subsisting order: all this is something that we must always *presuppose* in using experiential data as "evidence" for how things stand in the world. Objectivity represents a postulation made on *functional* rather than *evidential* ground: we endorse it in order to be in a position to learn by experience at all. We do not learn or discover that there is a mind-independent physical reality, we *presume or postulate* it. As Kant clearly saw, objective experience is possible only if the existence of such a real, objective world is *presupposed* from the outset rather than seen as something that must be a matter of ex post facto discovery about the nature of things.[10]

The information that we may have about a thing, be it real or presumptive information, is always just that—information *we* lay claim to. We recognize that it varies from person to person. But our view of the world's things goes far beyond this. Our attempts at communication and inquiry are undergirded by an information-transcending stance—the stance that we communally inhabit a shared world of independently existing items, a world of "real things" amongst which we live and into which we inquire (but about which we do and must presume ourselves to have only imperfect information at any and every particular stage of the cognitive venture). This is clearly not something that we learn from the course of experience. The "facts of experience" can never reveal it to us. It is—to reemphasize—something that we postulate or presuppose. Its epistemic status is not that of an empirical discovery, but that of a postulate or presupposition whose ultimate justification is its role in possibilizing the (themselves pragmatically justified) projects of communication and inquiry as we standardly conduct them. (A Kantian concern for "condition under which alone" is at issue, so that we have a transcendental argument of sorts.) In this way, the crucial existential (ontological) component of realism is not a matter of discovery, a part of the findings of empirical research but rather a facilitating and formative assumption for inquiry and communication. Without subscribing to this idea, we could not think of our knowledge as we actually do. Our commitment to the existence of a mind-independent reality is thus a postulate whose justification pivots on its functional utility.

To be sure, that second, descriptive (epistemic) component of realism stands on a very different footing. Reality's *nature* is something about which we can only make warranted claims through examining it. Substantive information must come through inquiry—through evidential validation. Once we are willing to credit our observational data with objectivity, and thus with evidential bearing, we can, of course, proceed to make use of them to inform ourselves as to the nature of the real. After we postulate an objective reality and its concomitant causal aspect, then principles of inductive systematization, of explanatory economy, and of common-cause consilience can work wonders towards furnishing us with plausible claims about the nature of the real. But we indispensably need that initial existential presupposition to make a start. Without commitment to a reality to serve as ground and object of our experience, its cognitive import would be lost. Only on this basis can we proceed evidentially with the exploration of the interpersonally public and objective domain of a physical world-order that we share in common. In the end, our conception of objective reality is the focus of a family of convenient regulative principles—a functionally useful instrumentality that enables us to transact our cognitive business in the most satisfactory and effective way.

Such an endorsement of mind-independently real unobserved causes in nature is not based on science but on metaphysics. Science does not (cannot) teach us that the observable order is explicable in terms of underlying causes and that the phenomena of observation are signs or symptoms of this extra- and sub-phenomenal order of existence; we know this a priori of any world in which observation as we understand it can transpire. It is a presupposition for evidentiation and not a result of it. What science does teach us (and metaphysics cannot) is the objectively descriptive character of this extraphenomenal order.

As C. S. Peirce insisted, the epistemologically crucial question is this: Assuming by way of supposition that there indeed *are* objective facts, how can we possibly come to acquire knowledge of them? What sort of pre-suppositions must we make if our subjective experience—which is limited and episodic—is to provide a basis of legitimacy for maintaining objective and general claims?

Two gulfs must be transcended:

- From experiential appearances to objective facts—from "That looks like a red apple to me" to "That is a red apple"; from phenomena to real things.
- From particular cases to universals—from "These apples contain seeds" to "All apples contain seeds."

To effect these transitions, we must simply *presuppose* (for how could we possibly *preestablish* this?) that such moves can be made on a basis of available evidence: that subjective phenomena can be indicators of objective realities and that particular cases can be exemplifications of universal arrangements.

The foundations of objectivity do not rest on the findings of science. They precede and underlie science, which would itself not be possible without a precommitment to the capacity of our senses to warrant claims about an objective world order. Objectivity is not a *product* of inquiry; we must precommit ourselves to it to make inquiry possible. It is a necessary input into the cognitive project and not a contingent output thereof. The objective bearing of experience is not something we can preestablish; it is something we must presuppose in the interest of honoring Peirce's cogent injunction never to bar the path of inquiry.

It is important to recognize how different the present position is from the usually accepted view, which holds that the success of epistemic objectivity grounds the acceptance of ontological objectivity by way of an inductive inference to the best explanation. On this basis, ontological objectivity has the status of a fact established ex post facto by observational means. By contrast, the present position takes the line that the success of the inquiry processes that we base on the supposition of epistemic objectivity retro-validates this initial postulation (presumption) of ontological objectivity by way of a pragmatic justification. On this basis, ontological objectivity has the status of a postulate validated by its functional efficacy. In the former (best explanation) case we are dealing with an inductively validated conclusion, in the latter (retro-validated presupposition) case with a functionally efficient postulate. The epistemic status of the thesis at issue with ontological objectivity is thus radically different in the two approaches.

4. REALISM IN ITS REGULATIVE / PRAGMATIC ASPECT

What legitimates metaphysical realism's postulation that experience affords information about an objective and mind-independent domain and thus provides for viable information about the real? Given that the existence of such a domain is not a product of empirical inquiry but a precondition for it, its acceptance has to be validated in the manner appropriate for postulates and prejudgments of any sort, namely, in terms of its prospective utility. Bearing this pragmatic perspective in mind, let us take a closer look at this issue of utility and ask: What can postulation of a mind-independent reality actually do for us?

The answer is straightforward. The assumption of a mind-independent reality is essential to the whole of our standard conceptual scheme relating to inquiry and communication. Without it, both the actual conduct and the rational legitimation of our communicative and investigative (evidential) practice would be destroyed. Nothing that we do in this cognitive domain would make sense if we did not subscribe to the conception of a mind-independent reality.

To begin with, we indispensably require the notion of reality to operate the classical concept of truth as "agreement with reality" (*adaequatio ad rem*). Once we abandon the concept of reality, the idea that in accepting a factual claim as true we become committed to how matters actually stand—"how it really is"—would also go by the board. Semantics constrain realism; we have no alternative but to regard as real those states of affairs claimed by the contentions we are prepared to accept. Once we put a contention forward by way of serious assertion, we must view as real the states of affairs it purports, and must see its claims as facts. We need the notion of reality to operate the conception of truth. A factual statement on the order of "There are pi mesons" is true if and only if the world is such that pi mesons exist within it. By virtue of their very nature as truths, true statements must state facts; they state what really is so, which is exactly what it is to "characterize reality." The conceptions of *truth* and of *reality* come together in the traditional notion of adequation, the venerable principle that to speak truly is to say how matters stand in reality, in that things actually are as we have said them to be.

In the second place, the nihilistic denial that there is such a thing as reality would destroy once and for all the crucial Parmenidean divide between appearance and reality. And this would exact a fearful price from us: we would be reduced to talking only of what we *think* to be so. The crucial contrast-concept of the *real* truth would now no longer be available: we would only be able to contrast our *putative* truths with those of others, but could no longer operate the classical distinction between the putative and the actual, between what we think to be so and what actually *is* so. We could not take the stance that, as the Aristotelian commentator Themistius put it, "that which exists does not conform to various opinions, but rather the correct opinions conform to that which exists."[11]

The third point is the issue of cognitive coordination. Communication and inquiry, as we actually carry them on, are predicated on the fundamental idea of a real world of objective things, existing and functioning "in themselves," without dependence on us and so equally accessible to others. Intersubjectively valid communication can be based only on common access to an objective order of things. All our ventures at communication and communal inquiry are predicated on the stance that we communally inhabit a shared world of objectively existing things. There is a realm of "real objects" among which we live and into which we inquire as a community, but about which we ourselves as individuals presumably have only imperfect information that can be criticized and augmented by the efforts of others.

This points to a fourth important consideration. Only through reference to the real world as a *common object* and shared focus of our diverse and imperfect epistemic strivings are we able to effect communicative contact with one another. Inquiry and communication alike are geared to the conception of an objective world: a communally shared realm of things that exist strictly "on their own," comprising an enduring and independent realm within which, and more importantly with reference to which, inquiry proceeds. We could not operate on the notion that inquiry estimates the character of the real if we were not prepared to presume or postulate a reality for these estimates to be estimates of. It would clearly be pointless to devise our characterizations of reality if we did not stand committed to the proposition that there is a reality to be characterized.

The fifth advantage of a recourse to mind-independent reality is that it makes possible a "realistic" view of our knowledge as potentially flawed and thereby corrigible. A rejection of this commitment to reality *an sich* (or to the actual truth about it) exacts an unacceptable price. For in abandoning this commitment we also lose those regulative contrasts that canalize and condition our view of the nature of inquiry (and indeed shape our conception of this process as it stands within the framework of our conceptual scheme). We could no longer assert:"What we have there is good enough as far as it goes, but it is presumably not 'the whole real truth' of the matter." The very conception of inquiry as we conceive it would have to be abandoned if the contrast-conceptions of "actual reality" and "the real truth" were no longer available. Without the conception of reality we could not think of our knowledge in the fallibilistic mode we actually use—as having provisional, tentative, improvable features that constitute a crucial part of the conceptual scheme within whose orbit we operate our concept of inquiry.

Objective reality (on the traditional metaphysicians' construction of the concept) is the condition of things answering to "the real truth"; it is the realm of what really is as it really is. The pivotal contrast is between "mere appearance" and "reality as such," between "our picture of reality" and "reality itself," between what actually is and what we merely think (believe, suppose, etc.) it to be. And our allegiance to the conception of reality, and to this contrast that pivots upon it, roots in the fallibilistic recognition that, at the level of the detailed specifics of scientific theory, anything we presently hold to be the case may well turn out otherwise—indeed, certainly will do so if past experience gives any auguries for the future.

Our commitment to the mind-independent reality of "the real world" stands together with our pervasive acknowledgment that, in principle, any or all of our *present* scientific ideas as to how things work in the world, at *any* present, may well prove to be untenable. Our confidence in a reality that lies beyond our imperfect understanding of it (in all the various senses of "lying beyond") roots in our sense of the imperfections of our scientific commitment to a mind-independent reality. In the absence of this view of the matter we would lose any and all impetus to inquiry.

Sixth and finally, we need the conception of reality in order to operate the causal model of inquiry about the real world. Our standard picture of man's place in the scheme of things is predicated on the fundamental idea that there is a real world (however imperfectly our inquiry may characterize it to be) whose causal operations produce inter alia causal impacts upon us, providing the basis of our world-picture. Reality is viewed as the causal source and basis of the appearances, the originator and determiner of the phenomena of our cognitively relevant experience. "The real world" is seen as causally operative both in serving as the external molder of thought and as constituting the ultimate arbiter of the adequacy of our theorizing. (Think here again of C. S. Peirce's "Harvard experiment.")

In summary, then, we need that postulate of an ontologically objective order of mind-independent reality for at least six important reasons.

- To preserve the distinction between true and false with respect to factual matters and to operate with the idea of truth as agreement with reality.
- To preserve the distinction between appearance and reality, between our *picture* of reality and reality itself.
- To serve as a basis for intersubjective communication.
- To furnish the basis for a shared project of communal inquiry.
- To provide for the fallibilistic view of human knowledge.
- To sustain the causal mode of learning and inquiry and to serve as basis for the objectivity of experience.

The conception of a mind-independent reality accordingly plays a central and indispensable role in our thinking with respect to matters of language and cognition. In communication and inquiry alike we seek to offer answers to our questions about how matters stand in this "objective realm." It is seen as the epistemological *object* of veridical cognition, in the context of the contrast between "the real" and its "merely phenomenal" appearances. Again, it is seen as the target or *telos* of the truth-estimation process at issue in inquiry, providing for a common focus in communication and communal inquiry. (The "real world" thus constitutes the "object" of our cognitive endeavors in both senses of this term—the *objective* at which they are directed and the *purpose* for which they are exerted.) And further, reality is seen as the ontological *source* of cognitive endeavors, affording the existential matrix in which we move and have our being, and whose impact upon us is the prime mover for our cognitive efforts. All of these facets of the concept of objective reality are integrated and unified in the classical doctrine of truth as it corresponds to fact (*adaequatio ad rem*), a doctrine that makes sense only in the setting of a commitment to mind-independent reality.

Accordingly, the justification for this fundamental presupposition of objectivity is not based on some sort of inference from the observational data. The rationale of an objectivistic realism is not *evidential* at all; rather, it is *functional*. We need this postulate to operate our conceptual scheme. The justification of this postulate thus lies in its utility. We could not form our existing conceptions of truth, fact, inquiry, and communication without presupposing the independent reality of an external world. We simply could not think of experience and inquiry as we do. (What we have here is a "transcendental argument" from the character of our conceptual scheme to its inherent presuppositions.) The primary validation of that crucial objectivity postulate lies in its basic functional utility in the pursuit of our cognitive aims.

We return, then, to this chapter's initial question: How are ontological and epistemic objectivity connected? What linkage is there between the ontological dimension of how people think of things and the epistemic dimension of the way things actually are, independently of how people happen to think of them? We have contended here that this linkage is effected by a dual idealization. For the step from the former to the latter makes (1) the shift from real to *truly rational* people and (2) the shift from actually prevailing to *ideal* cognitive circumstances (that is from the presently available data base to a completed or ideally perfected data base).[12]

Such an idealization-mediated linkage between the epistemology of truth determination and the ontology of actual fact is inescapable. For the concept of truth is inseparably bound to the ideal of *adaequatio ad rem*: effectively by definition true claims are those which characterize things as they actually are. And it lies in the nature of the thing that in ideal cognitive circumstances ideally rational people will (ex hypothesi) arrive at the truth. The two modes of objectivity are thus coordinated and conjoined—albeit only as the result of an extrapolation into the order of idealization.

The extrapolation involved in this leap into idealization is not fanciful but pragmatic. For what we have here is a postulation made on *functional* rather than *evidential* ground, a precommitment that we endorse in order to be in a position to learn by experience at all. This postulation is justified in the first analysis on the grounds of a functional requirement, because it is an indispensable requisite for our standard conceptual scheme with respect to inquiry, cognition, and discourse. In the end, our commitment to ontological objectivity rests on the idealistic foundation of a mind-projected postulation whose validation is, in the end, functional and pragmatic, validated in the first instance not by evidence but by considerations of utility. It is a presumption to which we subscribe in order to make a go of the epistemic project as we practice it. And it is justified in the end by the pragmatic validation inherent in the success of this project as a whole. This pragmatic dimension of objectivity deserves closer consideration.[13]

eight

THE PRAGMATIC RATIONALE OF COGNITIVE OBJECTIVITY

Synopsis

(1) Why follow reason's injunction to the cultivation of cognitive objectivity? After all, even the most objectively rational of arrangements can go awry: there is no way to establish with categorical certainty that objectivity will pay off in particular cases. Here we can only achieve the essentially pragmatic *justification of showing that, as best we can judge the matter, the counsels of reason afford the most promising systematic prospect of realizing our objectives. And the primacy of rationality automatically carries it its wake the appropriateness of cultivating objectivity in matters outside the realm of personal indulgence. (2) Why, then, heed rationality's call to being objective? Because it is the reasonable and rationally appropriate thing to do. In providing a* rational *justification of objectivity—and what other kind would we want?—the most and the best that one can do is to follow the essentially circular (but nonviciously circular!) line of establishing that reason herself endorses taking this course.*

1. THE PROBLEM OF VALIDATING OBJECTIVITY

What validates acting under the aegis of rationality and the objectivity that goes with it? Doing so is certainly not a guarantor of adequacy: for example, there is no way to establish on general principles that rationally conducted inquiries will (let alone *must*) achieve the actual truth. What we *can* say with confidence is that proceeding rationally and objectively enables us to avert a variety of recognizable sources of error, so that in conducting our inquiries on objective principles it becomes less likely that we will commit mistakes.

Rationality foregoes guarantees because it recognizes their unavailability. It is content to play the odds. And specifically as regards objectivity it does so with caution. The considerations at issue here can be posed at a very general level.

The rational person is, by definition, someone who uses intelligence to maximize the probability—that is, *the responsibly formed subjective probability*—that matters will eventuate favorably for the promotion of his real interests. Rationality calls for adopting the overall best (visible) alternative—the best that is, in practice, available to us in the circumstances. It is thus *actually* rational to do the *apparently* rational thing, provided that those appearances reflect the exercise of due care. And it is here that the impetus to objectivity lies.

Objectivity eliminates sources of error. But supposing that p is true, does decreasing the probability of believing not-p mean increasing the probability of believing p? Do we in general have the relationship that would have to be at hand here:

$$\text{pr (Bel (not-}p\text{))} = 1 - \text{pr (Bel } p) \text{ ?}$$

Now we certainly do have the unrestricted truth of the equation:

$$\text{pr (not-}p) = 1 - \text{pr } (p)$$

And by substituting "Bel p" for p, we shall also have:

$$\text{pr (not Bel } p) = 1 - \text{pr (Bel } p)$$

Now in the presence of *this* equation, we see that the equality at issue in our initially contemplated question would obtain only if we had:

$$\text{pr (Bel (not-}p\text{))} = \text{pr (not Bel } p)$$

This equality relationship calls for the unrestricted equivalency of "Bel (not-p)" with "not (Bel p)." But this equivalency holds only to the extent that we are dealing with cognitively competent agents who are not in a condition of ignorance imposing a suspension of judgment in the face of insufficient information. And this obviously fails to obtain in general. Accordingly, *decrease* in the probability that we accept something false does not make for an automatic *increase* in the probability that we accept something true.

Paradoxical though it may seem, to eliminate error is *not* necessarily to get closer to the truth (save in the case of omniscient knowers). Where the answer to a numerical problem has to be an odd number, one can eliminate as erroneous 2, and 4, and 6, and so on ad infinitum through the entire series of even numbers, without drawing any nearer to getting the correct result. And that, in fact, is all that cognitive objectivity ever does for us—it eliminates various common avenues to error. Being objective—avoiding bias, prejudice, and the like—is thus no guarantor of appropriate results in the absence of cognitive competence. It helps us only to the extent that our methodology of inquiry is otherwise effective. It is an aid to rational inquiry but no magic wand.

But we live in a world without guarantees. After all, why do we endorse the world-descriptions of the science of the day? Why do we follow the medical recommendations of the physicians of the day, or the policy recommendations of the economists of the day? Because we know them to be correct, or at any rate highly likely to be true? Not at all! We know or believe no such thing—historical experience is too strongly counterindicative. Rather, we accept them as guides only because we see them as more promising than any of the *identifiable* alternatives that we are in a position to envision. We accept them because they afford us the greatest available subjective probability of success—discernibly the best bet. We do not proceed with unalloyed confidence but with the resigned recognition that we can do no better at the moment. Similarly, the recommendations of reason afford not *assurance* of success but merely what is, to all achievable appearances, the *best overall chance* of averting failure with respect to our goals. We act, in short, on the basis of *faute de mieux* considerations: in real-world situations reason trades in courses of action whose efficacy is a matter of hope and whose rationalization is a matter of this-or-nothing-better argumentation.

In pursuing our goals, we do well to emulate the drowning man in clutching at the best available prospect, recognizing that even the most rationally laid scheme can misfire. In this world of imperfect inquirers reality is not always and inevitably on the side of the strongest arguments. Heeding the call of reason, constructive though it is, affords no categorical guarantees of success, only the reassurance of having made the best rational bet—of having done as well as one could in the circumstances of the case. In this world we are at risk: no means are at our disposal for preestablishing that following rationality's counsel actually pays. We have to be content to settle for the most promising pathway towards realizing our goals. The situation is such that even cognitive rationality must ultimately be validated in the prudential order of reason.

Why be objective? Because it is the sensible, the rationally appropriate thing to do. And why is this so? Because it is quintessentially rational to pursue one's best or real interests in the way that looks to be the most promising, and the use of reason—which carries objectivity in its wake—is part and parcel of this endeavor.

We do not (or need not) pursue objectivity for its own sake;[1] its value emerges in the context of ulterior purpose within the methodology of inquiry. The merit of a commitment to objectivity is utilitarian and lies in the positive things that it can do for us in the pursuit of normative adequacy in matters of belief, evaluation, and practical action.

In the specifically cognitive domain, the assets of objectivity preeminently include:

- *Robustness.* Objectivity provides us with checks and balances. It facilitates the aims of inquiry by providing a safeguard against biases and misimpressions. It is an instrument of verification.
- *Communication.* Objectivity open up avenues of exchange that serve productive ends. In proceeding objectively (as others would) we make ourselves intelligible to them and lay the basis for mutual understanding. And not just understanding but also—
- *Community and collaboration.* Objectivity facilitates an eminently useful sharing of concerns. Life is too short and the self too limited; to get pretty much anything done in this world we must proceed communally.

This last item is particularly important. No man is an island: only by getting onto a ground where others too are at work can one find possibilities of communication, cooperation, and (above all) collaboration. Only by joining with others—by shifting from I to we (and indeed even a cross-generational we!) can I manage to accept the tasks that life in this world sets before us.

The issue of caring about the views of others is thus rather different with respect to an epistemic virtue such as objectivity from what it is with respect to a moral virtue such as courtesy. For the prudential rationale of objectivity means that there is a matter of due care for *our* interests while the moral aspect of courtesy means that it is a matter of due care for *their* interests. With objectivity, I seek to align my proceedings with theirs in order to realize *my* interests; with courtesy I do so to cater to *their* sensibilities—at any rate in the first analysis. All the same, both modalities alike avoid self-aggrandizement. Neither is a matter of insisting that others shall do as I do, but rather one of conforming my own proceedings to theirs.

To be sure, being objective in matters relating to the public domain is no guarantee of success. Throughout our cognitive and practical affairs we have to conduct our operations under conditions of risk. We have to do the plausible thing—to "play the odds." And so, when we do the rational thing but it does not pan out, we simply have to "grin and bear it." The matter is one of calculated risks and plausibly expectable benefits. Rationality, to reemphasize, affords no guarantees. By the very nature of what is involved in rational procedure, the determinable odds are in its favor. But that may still be cold comfort when things go wrong. Then, all we have is the satisfaction of having done our best. The long and short of the matter is that nothing "obliges" us to be rational except our rationality itself. It lies in the nature of things that reason is on the side of rationality. Admittedly, reason offers us no categorical guarantees; yet, if we abandon reason there is no better place where we can (rationally) go.

The imperative "Act as a rational agent ought" does not come from without (from parents or from society or even from God). It roots in our own self-purported nature as rational beings—in the fact of its being an integral part of what our reason demands of us in the context of its own cultivation. (In Kant's words, it is a *dictamen rationis*, a part of the "internal legislation of reason.") And this obligation to rationality carries the obligation to objectivity in its wake, so that the validations of rationality and objectivity are of a piece.

2. THE SELF-RELIANCE OF RATIONALITY IS NOT VICIOUSLY CIRCULAR

This practicalistic line of argumentation adopted here may still seem to leave the situation in an unsatisfactory state. It says (roughly): "You should follow rationality's counsels towards objectivity because *it is rational to believe that* success in achieving your objectives will be optimally realized in this way." Now one would, no doubt, deem it preferable if that italicized clause were wholly suppressed. A skeptic is thus bound to press the following objection:

> The proposed practicalistic legitimation of following reason's counsels conforms to the pattern: "You should be rational about objec-

tivity just because that is the rational thing to do!" And this is clearly circular.

It might seem questionable to establish the jurisdiction of reason by appeal to the judgment of reason itself. But, in fact, of course, this circularity is not really vicious at all. Vicious circularity stultifies by "begging the question"; virtuous circularity merely coordinates related elements in their mutual interlinkage. The former presupposes what is to be proved, the latter simply shows how things are connected together in a well-coordinated and mutually symbiotic interrelationship. The self-reliance of rationality merely exemplifies this latter circumstance of an inherent coordination among its several components.

Admittedly, the reasoning at issue has an *appearance* of vitiating circularity because the force of the argument itself rests on an appeal to rationality:"If you are going to be rational in forming your beliefs, then you must also act rationally, because it is rational to believe that rational action is optimal in point of goal attainment." But this sort of question-begging is not only unavoidable in the circumstances, it is not a negativity. On the contrary, it is exactly what we want and need. Where else should we look for a *rational* validation of rationality but to reason itself? The only reasons for being rational that it makes sense to ask for are *rational* reasons. In this epistemic dispensation, we have no way of getting at the facts directly, without the epistemic detour of securing grounds and reasons for them. And it is, of course, rationally cogent grounds and reasons that we want and need. The overall justification of rationality *must* be reflective and self-referential. To provide a rationale of rationality is to show that rationality stands in appropriate alignment with the principles of rationality. From the angle of justification, rationality is a cyclic process that closes in on itself, not a linear process that ultimately rests on something outside itself.

There is accordingly no basis for any rational discontent here, no room for any dissatisfaction or complaint regarding a "viciously circular" justification of validation for heeding the counsels of reason. We would not (should not) want it otherwise. If we bother to seek for an answer to the question "Why be rational?" at all, it is clearly a *rational* answer that we require. The only sort of justification of anything—rationality included—that is worth having at all is a rational one. That presupposition of rationality is not vitiating, not viciously circular, but essential, an unavoidable consequence of the self-sufficiency of cognitive reason. There is simply no satisfactory alternative to using reason in its own defense. Already embarked on the sea of rationality, we want such assurance as can now be made available that we have done the right thing. And such reassurance can indeed be given, exactly along the lines just indicated. Given the very nature of the justificatory enterprise at issue, one just cannot avoid letting rationality sit in judgment on itself. (What is being asked for, after all, is a rational argument for rational action, a basis for rational conviction, and not persuasion by something probatively irrelevant like threats of *force majeure*.) One would expect, nay *demand*, that rationality be self-substantiating in this way, that it *must* emerge as the best policy on its own telling.

From the justificatory point of view, rationality is and must be autonomous. It can be subject to no external authority. Rationality in general is a matter of systematization, and the justification of rationality is correspondingly a matter of systemic self-sufficiency. Rather than indicating the defect of vicious circularity, the self-referential character of a justification of rationality is a precondition of its adequacy! The only validation of rationality and its involvements that is worth having is a rational one. It is clearly a rational legitimation that we want: any other sort would avail us nothing. And if such a rational validation were not forthcoming this would indicate a grave defect. A somewhat desperate objection yet remains. It runs as follows:"So rationality speaks on objectivity's behalf. Well and good. But why should I care for rationality? Why should I set myself to do the intelligent and appropriate thing?"

At this point there is little more to be said. As already remarked, if I want a reason at all, I must want a *rational* reason. But if I care about reasons at all, I am already within the project of rationality. And once I am *within* the project, there is nothing *further* external to reason that can *or need* be said to validate it. At *that* stage rationality is already at hand to provide its own support—it wears its justification on its sleeve. (The project of trying to reason with those who stand *outside* the range of rationality to coerce them into its fold is clearly an exercise in pointlessness and futility.) The point is that in the very act of posing these questions about validation and satisfactions I am asking for reasons, I am evincing my commitment to the project of rationality. And if I do not care for objectivity, truth, and good reasons, then there is really no point in raising these questions. For in this event I have *already* taken my place outside the precincts of rationality, beyond the reach of reason.

Failures of objectivity—wishful thinking, self-deception, bias-indul-
gence, and similar departures from the path of reason—may be convenient
and even, in some degree, psychologically comforting. But they are ultimately indefensible. For if it is a viable defense of a position that we want,
it is bound to be a rational one. In the final analysis, "Why be rational?"
must be answered with the only rationally appropriate response: "Because
rationality itself obliges us to be so." In providing a *rational* justification of
objectivity—and what other kind would we want?—the best we can do is
to follow the essentially circular (but *nonviciously* circular!) line of establishing that reason herself endorses taking this course. The only validation
of rationality's recommendations that can reasonably be asked for—and
the only one worth having—must lie in considerations of the systemic
self-sufficiency of reason. Reason's self-recommendation is an important
and necessary aspect of the legitimation of the rational enterprise. And in
those matters where rationality counts, objectivity is the best policy by
virtue of this very fact itself.[2]

—nine—

MORAL OBJECTIVITY: AGAINST MORAL RELATIVISM

Synopsis

(1) Morality by its very nature stakes categorical claims to objectivity. To see morality as subjective is actually to abandon it. (2) Morality is inherently something functional: the moral enterprise exists as what it is because it has a purpose of to serve. (3) Moral subjectivism is thus deeply flawed, because rational deliberation and controversy about morality become possible through morality's characteristic purposiveness. (4) While a sociological pluralism of behavioral codes is a fact of life, the basic principles of morality are uniform. But this uniformity exists only at the highest—or "most basic"—level of functional significance. (5) Here the hierarchical aspect of the situation becomes important. For a purposive hierarchy is at issue that involves ever greater diversity as we descend into particular social principles. This renders a universal relativism untenable. (6) Despite the pluralism of moral codes, the claims of our own community must be seen as being paramount for us.

1. IS MORALITY MERELY SUBJECTIVE?

The pervasive relativism of the age sees moral principles and standards as little more than a matter of custom based on practical convenience like the rules of the road for driving—useful devices to diminish conflict in contexts of human interaction, but lacking any deeper validation and legitimacy, and certainly without any claims to universality. Morality as regarded from this angle is predicated on local custom, as part of the mores of the group. And any such behavioral code is as good as any other: it is simply a matter of "When in Rome, do as the Romans do." All moralities are created equal. There is no place for moral objectivity.

This negativistic relativism is profoundly erroneous. And it will be the task of this chapter and its successor to set out in some detail how it is that a claim to moral objectivity and universality can be validated.

There are two distinct modes of moral egalitarianism. Both agree in holding that all moral codes are of equal validity-status—that each is as good as any other. But one mode sees all codes as being alike *valid*, while the other sees all as being alike *invalid*. The former, indifferentist approach takes the syncretistic line of an indiscriminate openness and acceptance; the latter, nihilistic approach takes the defeatist line of a total negativity and rejection. Either way, the prospect of a *reasoned* endorsement of one moral position over against others is excluded.

Both doctrines are deeply problematic, however. A syncretistic moral indifferentism is caught up in the evident implausibility of holding that any and every moral code, any set of moral rules whatsoever, is actually as good as any other for us here and now, in the circumstances in which we actually find ourselves emplaced in our interactions with others. Moral nihilism, on the other hand, is caught up in the no less striking implausibility of the contention that no moral code whatsoever is cogent—that none can make good a claim to effectiveness in safeguarding the best interests of people. Both forms of egalitarianism are deeply enmeshed in difficulties. Syncretism shatters on the fact that different codes issue conflicting, mutually incompatible injunctions. Nihilism comes to grief on our realization that it does really make a difference how people act and that some ways of acting are just plain wrong.

However, even greater obstacles than those posed by the moral egalitarianism of validity-equivalence arise with a subjectivism that maintains: "To each his own; such differences as there are between moral codes merely 'lie in the mind of the exponent'; while it is indeed the case that one moral code can be superior to others, this superiority is simply a matter of an inclination that varies with individuals and groups." As the subjectivist sees it, morality is a matter of societal convention along the lines of customs, attitudes, or tastes—we have our moral code and they have theirs, period. Accordingly, the moral subjectivist insists that there simply is no objective substance to a moral thesis such as "Cheating people is wrong." Insisting "That's just what people happen to accept in our set or our society," he takes the line that it is all a matter of local custom. The sole reason why moral judgments matter for us is one of conformity through "keeping in step" with the rest of our group, averting the disapproval of our fellows though conforming our behavior to socially accepted norms.

This sort of societally subjectivistic relativism has been popular among philosophers since classical antiquity.[1] And it is still going strong. In the present century, C. L. Stevenson's "attitudinal expression" theory is an influential instance of the general line of approach.[2] Stevenson holds that a moral evaluation merely characterizes the *subject* and not the *object* that is at issue. My contention that "You acted wrongly in stealing that money" has two components, one factual (you stole that money) and the other a personal avowal: "I disapprove of your doing this and urge you not to do similar things in the future." The former component stakes an objective, descriptive claim; the latter expresses the assertor's attitude towards it. The point of making moral contentions, Stevenson insists, "is not [simply] to indicate facts but to *create an influence*. Instead of merely describing people's interests they [seek to] *change or intensify* them. They recommend an interest in an object, rather than state that the interest already exists."[3] Moral claims are primarily designed to exhort people to approved lines of action. Morality is accordingly a matter of the variable inclinations of individuals and groups, a matter of "the custom of the country," of what people just happen to approve—of fashion, if you will.

This view of the matter denies that people's acts are ever actually wrong in themselves, but insists that people merely *think* they are. Moral language is only "used to express feeling about certain objects, but not to make any assertion about them."[4] Moral judgments are only prescriptions—oblique injunctions designed to incite others to action.[5] In any event, they do not really express authentic *evaluations* which, as such, are right or wrong, appropriate or inappropriate. Rather, they reflect the circumstance that individuals and groups only *attach* or *attribute* value to human actions, ascriptions which are always made on an entirely variable basis reflecting the makers' feelings or wishes, attitudes or customs—always without any real foundation of warrant in the nature of the object. There is nothing more to moral praise or condemnation than the attachments of particular individuals or groups. Rightness or wrongness simply lies in the view of the individual (or the group) as a mere expression of personal (or social) disapproval. Evaluation on the basis of valid principles is simply not at issue.

Such an interpretation of moral judgment is altogether untenable, however. Moral appraisal as we actually conduct it is something that cannot root in feelings or personal sentiments. For no adequate paraphrase of a moral thesis can ever eliminate the element of (moral) *evaluation*. The "emotive" disapproval/recommendation theory reinterprets "Pointless deception is wrong" somewhat along the lines of "I/we disapprove of point-less deception; do so as well!" And this equation is untenable because the two locutions simply do not have the same force. For "doing A is wrong" entails that "it is wicked (bad, reprehensible) to do A"; merely disapprov-ing of doing A does not. Contrariwise, a breach of the rules, even the moral rules, may on occasion plausibly gladden one's heart—I need not withdraw my judgment that someone who upset Hitler by cheating him at cards did something morally improper while averring that I am justifiably pleased by his having done so. After all, merely expressing an attitude or declaring a preference does not state or claim anything; only contentions (assertions) manage to state or claim. Expressing one's senti-ments just does not come to claiming something to be the case, be it factually or evaluatively. Our disapproving says something about us, while an evaluative appraisal says something about the item. The emotive theory runs very different things together in its identification of moral evaluation with a personal reaction. It lies in the very conception at issue that an act is immoral not because it is disapproved of but because it *deserves* disap-proval on the part of duly sensitive observers.

2. THE FUNCTIONAL/PURPOSIVE NATURE OF MORALITY

There nowadays prevails a widespread but nevertheless unfortunate tendency to deny the possibility of rational controversy about moral mat-ters—to relegate morality to the never-never land of matters of taste, feeling, or otherwise rationally insupportable opinion. Such a view is profoundly inappropriate. But once one recognizes the *functional* aspect of morality—as inculcating actions that safeguard the real interests of people—then moral issues become open to rational deliberation.[6] This functional aspect of morality as in its very nature representing an inher-ently appropriate end-oriented project blocks the prospect of indifferent-ism or of a relativistically detached view of morality as a mere matter of individual inclination or of "the customs of the tribe."

But such a radically subjective view along the lines that "With moral issues there is only what people think; there just are no objective facts of the matter" is ultimately untenable for anyone who, rejecting nihilism, gives credence to some sort of morality or other. For one cannot con-

sistently look on one's own moral convictions as "merely matters of opinion." In doing this one would thereby ipso facto fail to accept them as
such, that is, as *moral* convictions. In view of what can possibly qualify as
such, it lies in the very nature of our moral judgments that we regard
them as justified via a rationale regarding what is required by due heed of
the interests of people.

Morality, after all, is an end-governed purposive enterprise, one that is
structured by its having a characteristic functional mission of transparent
appropriateness. For it is morality's object to equip people with a body of
norms (rules and values) that make for peaceful and collectively satisfying
coexistence by facilitating their living together and interacting in a way
that is productive for the realization of the "general benefit" of the wider
community as a whole. The pursuit of righteousness that constitutes
morality is like the pursuit of health that constitutes medicine—both are
projects with an inherent teleology of their own—in morality's case one
geared to fostering patterns of action and interaction that promote the
best interests of people in general.

The functional nature of morality means that being *thought* to be
morally appropriate no more makes a certain action so than being *thought*
to be medically effective or transportationally efficient would render a
certain practice so. The claim that a rule or practice is morally appropriate—that in the conditions prevailing in a society it is effective in serving
and enhancing the real interests of people in general—is thoroughly objective and "factual." One is thus rationally constrained by considerations
of mere self-consistency to see one's own moral position as rationally superior to the available alternatives. If one did not take this stance—did not
deem one's moral position to be effectively optimal—then one could not
see oneself as rationally justified in adopting it, so that it would, in consequence, fail to be one's own real moral position, contrary to hypothesis.[7]
Because the claims of morality are categorical, to see morality as subjective is in fact to abandon it.

The validity of most moral appraisals is accordingly something that is
objectively determinable and nowise lies in the eye of the beholder. For
someone to say "You acted wrongly in stealing that money" is *not* simply
for them to assert that you stole the money and additionally to evince disapproval and urge a different sort of future conduct, but rather—and
most importantly—to *indicate a reason* for acting differently. For the claim
implies that your act instantiates a type of behavior (stealing) that does
injury to the legitimate interests of others. And this issue of human needs

and benefits, of people's real *interests*, such as their physical and psychological well-being, is not a matter of subjective reaction. What is in our interest—what is *advantageous* for our long-term, overall physical and psychological well-being, given the sorts of creatures we are—is in large measure a factual issue capable of empirical inquiry that lies open to general, public investigation.

Morality is by its very nature geared to safeguarding the interests of others as best we can manage it in prevailing circumstances. And people do not *choose* what it is that is in their interests.[8] Rather, this is something that is set for them by the physical, social, and situational circumstances of their lives. The issue of what advantages one (health, freedom of action, etc.) is something objective and not something that one makes up as one goes along. The fact that interests have a personal (individual and situation-variable) aspect does not make them subjective. (Even my mere preference of chocolate over vanilla ice cream is bound up with the impersonal benefit of "getting the flavor we prefer in an item of food that we like to eat." Even in matters of taste I do not *decide* that the one thing has a better flavor than the other, I *find* it to be so.)

Physicians, parents, public officials, and others constantly concern themselves with issues of what is good for people, what enables them to thrive and lead satisfying lives. People themselves are by no means themselves the definitive authorities regarding what is in their interests; their doctors, lawyers, or financial advisors can know a good deal more about these interests than the individuals themselves. In the final analysis, the objectivity of *moral* evaluations thus resides in the very nature of the issue. People are no doubt the definitive authorities regarding what *pleases* them, but certainly not regarding what *benefits* them. And this objectivity of people's interests carries in its wake also the objectivity of interest-promotion—and thus of morality. We cannot detach rational justification from objective validity in the moral sphere, because to say that a person is (rationally) justified in making a judgment is to say that he is (rationally) entitled to take it to be objectively true or correct. Nor can we detach objective validity from factuality, for where there is no appropriate claim to objective factuality (no "fact of the matter"), there can be no justification of endorsement either—though, to be sure, the facts of the matter may happen to be *evaluative* facts.

What renders morality objective is the fact that moral evaluations can—and should—be validated as cogent through considerations of purposive efficacy. To claim that someone ought (or ought not) to act in a certain way is thereby to commit oneself to the availability of a *good reason* why one should or should not do so, and a reason that is not only good but good in a certain mode, the moral mode, in showing that this sort of action is bound up with due care for the interests of others. And this matter of interest is something open to general view, something that can be investigated by other people as readily as by the agent himself. For since people's (real) interests root in their needs, the morally crucial circumstance that certain modes of action are conducive and others deleterious to the best interests of people is something that can be investigated, evidentiated, and sensibly assessed by the standards generally prevalent in rational discussion and controversy. The matters are not questions of feeling or taste, but represent something objective about which one can deliberate and argue in a sensible way on the basis of reasons whose cogency is, or should be, accessible to anyone. The modes of behavior of people that render life in their communities "nasty, brutish, and short" (or indeed even merely more difficult and less pleasant than need be) generally admit of straightforward and unproblematic discernment.

3. AGAINST MORAL SUBJECTIVISM

The salient point to emerge in the light of these considerations is that morality is not something merely subjective, not a matter of people's feelings or tastes or wants that "lies in the eyes of the beholder." It consists in the pursuit, through variable and context-relative means, of invariant and objectively implementable ends that root in a commitment to the best interests of people in general. In consequence, it inheres in the very meaning of moral "right" and "wrong" that issues of morality admit of appropriate and inappropriate resolutions, and can be deliberated about in sensible and foolish ways. A morality that is not objectively valid in this sense is no morality at all. And so, rational deliberation and controversy about moral judgments are possible precisely because claims about moral matters are, in their own way, preeminently objective and rational in nature.

To be sure, various theorists are eager to subjectivize the issue of what is in a person's interest. They propose to specify interests in terms of wants: in terms of people's wishes, preferences, and desires. But here they at once encounter the difficulty that people often want things (drink, drugs, revenge, etc.) that are patently self-destructive and run clean counter to anything that could *reasonably* be said to be in someone's interest. And to offset this unpalatable result, these subjective-interest theoreticians are led down the primrose path from actual to hypothetical desires and preferences, from what people *actually* want to what they *would-want-if.* They are, accordingly, led to the equation:

a person's real interests = what he/she would prefer (wish, choose, etc.) if only they were operating in circumstances X.

And here that parameter X opens up a considerable spectrum of possibilities:

- if the person were proceeding in a calm and unflustered state of mind, without any emotional stress.
- if the person were proceeding in conditions of full information and plausible foresight.
- if the person were proceeding with the benefit of ample hindsight.
- if the decision were being made under ideal (optimal, wholly unproblematic) conditions.

But of course as we move along such a list we are moving further and further away from the realistic situation of a person's own, actual, and idiosyncratic wishes and desires. We do well, therefore, to keep things in line from the very first by shifting from apparent interests (mere wants and desires) to real (true, "best," genuine) interests. That is, we arrive at something that is abstracted and idealized, namely: *what a disinterestedly benevolent, well-intentioned, well-informed, and ideally situated third-party chooser would select on behalf of the particular person at issue.*

On *such* an approach the person's own makeup (tastes, modulations, preferences) still figure critically in the choice. But they do so in a substantially objective way—in a way that other reasonable people would agree about. Impartial outsiders can be (and generally are) better judges of what is in someone's interests than the parties are themselves. That the interests of a creature constituted such as we humans are or claim to be are advantaged (or disadvantaged) by doing *A* rather than *B* follows straightforwardly from the reason-establishable fact that *A* is more (or less) consonant than *B* is with our nature as at once rational and embodied beings. Treating people's wounds serves their interests better than inflicting injuries. Only an over-narrow conception of reason that blocks it off from any appropriate concern with evaluative matters can open the way to moral subjectivism.

Morality, properly understood, is an inherently rational and objective enterprise. To gain moral credit for an action, the agent must have objective and impersonally cogent *reasons* for doing it, reasons that relate to the impact of the sort of action at issue on the valid interests of others. What makes such reasons into morally good reasons has nothing to do with what I (or anyone) want or what I (or anyone) feel, but lies in the nature of morality itself, hinging on the fundamental issue of what the moral enterprise as such is all about—to wit, protecting the real interests of rational agents. To reemphasize: morality is by definition geared to the interests of people even as refrigeration is by definition geared to cooling.

Of course, the circumstance that morality is objective does not mean that the subjective element has no place whatsoever in the moral domain. People's "feelings" unquestionably form an important part of what constitutes their interests, and thus deserve respect from the moral point of view. (It is clearly morally wrong to hurt someone's feelings unnecessarily.) And this consideration introduces a large element of personal variability into the moral domain. But there is nothing in *this* sort of variability that is at odds with the constancy of the fundamental principles at issue or with the objectivity of the factors invoked in them.

A crucial flaw of moral subjectivism is its failure to recognize that people—*reasonable* people at any rate—do not in general choose or endorse actions without having reasons which, to be sure, they need not necessarily articulate overtly. Sensible people incline to morally positive views towards actions when *and because* they recognize them to be beneficial—when they find something about them that conduces, on balance, to the advantage of people's interests. Underlying moral objectivism is the recognition, cogently formulated by W. D. Ross, that

> it is surely a strange reversal of the natural order of thought to say that our admiring an action either is, or is what necessitates, its being good. We think of its goodness as what we admire in it, and as something it would have even if no one admire it, something that it has in itself.[9]

The fact that there are good (and poor) reasons for action from the moral point of view means that morality is not simply a matter of subjective taste or feeling. That it is morally right to act in a certain sort of way (say, to keep one's promises) and not right to act in another (say, to steal) is capable of being established through perfectly objective considerations regarding subsumption under universal moral principles. Moral subjectivism is precluded by the reality of good reasons for action.[10] Objectivity has to come into play here.

Moral subjectivism takes roughly the following line:

> In moral judgments, as in judgments of taste, it is impossible to be mistaken. Whatever people think to be right is thereby rendered right. In matters of moral obligation and permission, thinking something to be so makes it so (even as in matters of taste, thinking something to be pleasing means that it *is* pleasing).

But this view of the matter is altogether wrong-headed. It is very much mistaken to think that a certain practice is rendered morally acceptable simply because people would like to have it so. For it lies in the very nature of the concept at issue that moral appropriateness has to hinge on how actions affect the real interests of people, and it is clear that the agent himself cannot be the decisive arbiter here. Morality turns on how actions affect people—on the negative side, for example, by doing them unwarranted harm, violating their rights, endangering their well-being, undermining their welfare, and the like. But that certain acts have such effects or tendencies is a perfectly objective matter—something that does not turn on the wishes, desires, tastes, or opinions of particular people. If causing someone needless suffering is morally wrong—which it indeed is—then this is so regardless of how people may think or feel about it. That you unwarrantedly did injury to another's interests is as objective a fact as that you absentmindedly forgot another's instructions. Accordingly, the moral quality of an act is emphatically not a matter of personal inclination, but one of rational evaluation.

Morality is thus a matter of reason and not of arbitrary, ungrounded choice. Moral values (honesty, kindness, and so on) rest on a ruling principle—the value of the person and the (moral) requirement to take due account of the interest of others in our own actions. That a purported moral evaluation actually qualifies as such is and must be capable of rational explanation and justification. We do not *choose* or *make* moral values, but *learn* about them by thinking through what it is that is required for safeguarding the best interests of people.[11] If morality were a mere matter of taste or of custom or of arbitrary choice, then harming helpless people needlessly, for example, might, in some society's scheme of things, be seen as *morally* preferable to helping them, and this perverted "morality" would have claims to appropriateness just as good as those of practices based on kindness and considerateness. And this is patently absurd. The capacity of certain modes of conduct to meet, or fail to meet, the requirements of morality—to safeguard the best (real) interests of people in general—is clearly not a matter of "decision" or "perspective," but one of impersonal fact, so that the appropriateness of moral judgments can be supported—or denied—in an intersubjectively cogent way.[12]

4. UNIFORMITY DESPITE DIVERSITY: THE ROLE OF BASIC PRINCIPLES AND IMPLEMENTATION HIERARCHIES

Yet there are complications here. For moral *pluralism* is unavoidable: moral codes can appropriately differ from one society to another. Does this fact not entail an indifferentist relativism to the effect that, in principle, "anything goes," by making morality into what is ultimately just a matter of local custom?

By no means! All modes of morality have important elements in common simply in view of the fact that *morality* is at issue. Since (by hypothesis) they all qualify as "modes of morality," they are bound to encompass such fundamental considerations as the following:

- What people do matters. Some actions are right, others wrong, some acceptable and some not. There is an important difference here.
- This is not just a matter of convention, custom, and the done thing. Violations of moral principles are not just offenses against sensibility but against people's just claims in matters where people's actual well-being is at stake.
- In violating the moral rules we inflict injury on the life, welfare, or otherwise legitimate interests of others—either actually or by way of putting them at unjustifiably at risk.

Attunement to consideration of this sort is *by definition* essential to any system of "morality," and serves to provide the basis for imperatives like: "Do not simply ignore other people's rights and claims in your own deliberations!" "Do not inflict needless pain on people." "Honor the legitimate interests of others." "Do not take what rightfully belongs to others without their appropriately secured consent." "Do not wantonly break promises." "Do not cause someone anguish simply for your own amusement." In the context of morality, principles and rules of this sort are universal and absolute. They are of the very essence of morality; in abandoning them we would withdraw from a discussion of *morality* and would in effect be changing the subject. What we say might be interesting—and even true—but it would deal with another topic.

"But moral objectivity is surely counterindicated by the circumstance that one cannot validly criticize the moral code of a society by any 'external' criteria." By no means! *Whether* a certain operational code is intended within the ambit of its social context to operate as a moral code may well be a proper subject of discussion and controversy. But once it is settled that it is indeed a *moral* code that is at issue, then in view of that very fact one can certainly bring principles of critical evaluation to bear. For at this point the question becomes paramount whether—and how effectively—this code accomplishes for its society those functions for which moral codes are instituted among people—to constrain their interactions into lines that safeguard their best interests.

When we are assessing a moral code in this way, we are *not* simply exercising a cultural imperialism by judging it against our own in asking how concordant or discordant it is with the prevailing moral standards of our environing group. We are judging it, rather, against those universal and "absolute" standards in terms of which the adequacy of any code, our own included, must be appraised. The evaluation of appropriateness is not one of ours against theirs, but one of judging *both* ours and theirs by a common, generic standard. What makes an action right or wrong (as the case may be) is exactly the issue of whether doing the sort of thing at issue injures or protects the interests of all the agents concerned. (To reemphasize: morality is by definition geared to the benefit of rational agents.)[13] This is part and parcel of the very meaning of "morally right" and "morally wrong." And it renders judgment in these matters factual, objective, and rationally disputable.

Even as there are many ways to build houses, fuel automobiles, or skin cats, so there are various ways of being moral. But that surely does not mean that there is no overarching unity of goals, functions, principles, and values to lend a definitional cohesion to the enterprise. Morality is a particular, well-defined sort of purposive project whose cohesive unity as such resides in its inherent function of molding the behavior of people in line with a care for one another's interests. Moral behavior can take many forms, but morality itself is a uniform project! Moreover, moral variability is more apparent than real—an absolute uniformity does, and must, prevail at the level of fundamentals. "Act with due heed of the interests of others" is a universal and absolute moral principle whose working out in different contexts will, to be sure, very much depend on just exactly how the interests of people happen to be reciprocally intertwined. But despite the diversity of the substantive moral codes of different societies, the basic overarching principles of morality are uniform and invariant, inherent in the very idea of what morality is all about.

Accordingly, different "moralities" are simply diverse implementations of certain uniform, overarching moral principles. There is ample room for situational variation and pluralism in response to the question: "What is the morally appropriate thing to do?" But there is no such room with respect to: "What is morality—and what are the principles at issue here?" The concept of morality and its contents are fixed by the "questioner's prerogative" inherent in the principle that it is the inquirer's own conception of the matter that is determinative for what is at issue in his inquiries. In *our deliberations* about moral rights and wrongs it is thus *our conception* of "morality" and its governing principles that is conclusive for what is at issue. When *we* engage in deliberations about morality—be it our own or that of others—it is "morality" *as we understand it* that figures in this discussion.[14] And this circumstance of theoretic fixity engenders a fixity of those project-definitive moral principles.

5. THE HIERARCHICAL DIMENSION

"But how could one plausibly pivot the issue of moral objectivity on 'the very idea of what "morality" is all about'? After all, different people have different ideas about this." Of course, different people do think differently about morality, even as they think differently about dogs or automobiles. But that's basically irrelevant. What is at issue with "morality" as such does not lie with you or with me but with all of us. What is relevantly at issue is how the word is actually used in the community—in the linguistic culture in which our discussion of the issue transpires. It is a matter not of what people think about the topic, but of how they use the terminology that defines it.

Yet how can this fixity of the conception of morality and of the basic principles that are at issue within it—inherent in the monolithic uniformity of "what *morality* is"—be reconciled with the plain fact of a pluralistic diversity of (presumably cogent) answers to the question: "What is it moral to do?" How can such an absolutism of morality's fundamentals coexist with the patent relativity of moral evaluations across different times and cultures?

At this point we have to return to the idea of a "cultivation hierarchy" already considered in sec. 4 of Chapter 1 (pp. 18–21). For in the case of morality, too, we have to deal with a descending hierarchy of characterizing aims, fundamental principles and values, governing rules, implementing directives, and (finally) particular rulings. (See table 9.1.) And the answer to our question lies in the fact that several intermediate levels or strata inevitably separate those overarching "basic principles of morality" from any concrete judgments about what it is moral to do.

TABLE 9.1

The Stratification Levels of the Implementation Hierarchy for
Moral Norms

Level 1	Characterizing Aims	"due care for the best interests of others"
Level 2	Governing Principles and Values	"honesty," "candor"
Level 3	Governing Rules	"Do not lie," "Speak truthfully"
Level 4	Operating Directives (Ground Rules of Procedure)	"When declaring what you believe, do not do so misleadingly"
Level 5	Particular Rulings	"Answer Jones truthfully (as best you can)"

At the topmost level we have the defining aims of morality, the objectives that identify the moral enterprise as such by determining its nature and specifying the aims and objectives that characterize what morality is all about. (Example: "Act with a view to safeguarding the valid interests of others.") These characterizing aims of morality represent the overarching "defining objectives" of the entire enterprise that characterize the project as such. They explicate what is at issue when it is with *morality* (rather than basket weaving) that we propose to concern ourselves. In spelling out the fundamental idea of what morality is all about, these top-level norms provide the ultimate reference points of moral deliberation. And they are unalterably fixed—inherent in the very nature of the subject.

And these fundamental "aims of the enterprise" also fix the basic principles and controlling values that delineate the moral virtues (honesty, trustworthiness, civility, probity, and the rest). Such values define the salient norms that link the abstract characterizing aims to an operational morality of specific governing rules. The norms embodied in these basic principles and values are "universal" and "absolute," serving as parts of what makes morality the thing it is. (Examples: "Do not violate the duly established rights and claims of others." "Do not unjustly deprive others of life, liberty, or opportunity for self-development." "Do not tell self-serving falsehoods." "Do not deliberately aid and abet others in wrongdoing.") Accordingly these high-level principles also lie fixedly in the very nature of the subject. At these two topmost levels, then, there is simply no room for any "disagreement about morality." Here disagreement betokens misunderstanding: if one does not recognize the fundamental aims, principles, and values that characterize the moral enterprise as such, then one is simply talking about something else altogether. In any discussion of *morality* these things are simply *givens*. But this situation changes as one moves further down the list and takes additional steps in the descent to concreteness.

At the next (third) level we encounter the governing rules and regulations that direct the specifically moral transaction of affairs. Here we have the generalities of the usual and accustomed sort: "Do not lie," "Do not cheat," "Do not steal," etc. At this level we come to the imperatives that guide our deliberations and decisions. Like the Ten Commandments, they set out the controlling dos and don'ts of the moral practice of a community, providing us with general guidance in moral conduct. Here variability begins to set in. For these rules implement morality's ruling principles at the concrete level of recommended practices in a way that admits of adjustment to the changeable circumstances of local conditions. A generalized moral rule on the order of the injunction "Do not steal" (= Do not take something that properly belongs to another) is in itself still something abstract and schematic. It still requires the concrete fleshing out of substantive implementing specifications to tell us what sorts of things make for "proper ownership." And so the next (fourth) level presents us with the ground rules of procedure or implementing directives that furnish our working guidelines and criteria for the moral resolution of various types of cases. (Example: "Killing is wrong except in cases of self-defense or under legal mandate as in war or executions.") At this level of implementing standards and criteria, the variability of local practice comes to the fore, so that there is further room for pluralistic diversification; we ourselves implement "Do not lie, avoid telling falsehoods," by way of "Say what you believe (to be the case)," but a society of convinced skeptics could not do so. The operating ground rules of Level 4 thus incorporate the situation-relative standards and criteria through which the more abstract, higher-level rules get their grip on concrete situations. Those general rules themselves are too abstract—too loose or general to be applicable without further directions to give them a purchase on concrete situations. They must be given concrete implementation with reference to local— and thus variable—arrangements.[15]

Finally, at the lowest (fifth) level we came to the particular moral rulings, individual resolutions with respect to the specific issues arising in concrete cases. (Example: "It was wicked of Lady Macbeth to incite her husband to kill the king.")

In such an "implementation hierarchy" we thus descend from what is abstractly and fixedly universal to what is concrete and potentially variable. Level 2 is contained in Level 1 simply by way of exfoliative "explication." But as we move downwards past Level 3 to the implementing specifications of Level 4, there is—increasingly—a looseness or "slack" that makes room for the specific and variable ways of different groups for implementing the particular higher-level objective at issue. (Further examples are given in table 9.2.)

TABLE 9.2

Illustrations from the Implementation Hierarchy of Morality

Level 1: *Characterizing Aims*
- To support the best interests of people and to avoid injuring them

Level 2: *Basic Principles (Controlling Values)*
- Do not cause people needless pain (GENTLENESS)
- Do not endanger people's lives or their well-being unnecessarily (CARE FOR SAFETY)
- Honor your genuine commitments to people; in dealing with people give them their just due (PROBITY)
- Help others when you reasonably can (GENEROSITY)
- Don't take improper advantage of others (FAIRNESS)

Level 3: *Operating Rules*
- Don't hurt people unnecessarily
- Don't lie; don't say what you believe not to be so
- Don't cheat

Level 4: *Operating Directives*
  • Be candid when replying to appropriate questions
  • Do not play with loaded dice
  • Where possible use anesthetics when operating on people

Level 5: *Concrete Rulings*
  • Return the money you borrowed from Smith
  • Don't pollute this river; dispose of your sewage elsewhere
  • Don't let these children play with those matches

The entire hierarchy contention culminates in a single, overreaching ruling imperative ("Support the interests of people!") that stands correlative with an enterprise-determinative value ("the best interests of people"). This overarching concern does not itself stand subordinate to further moral rules. After all, it is only possible up to a certain point that we can have rules for applying rules and principles for applying principles. The process of validating lower-level considerations in terms of higher-level ones must come to a stop somewhere. And with such implementation hierarchies it is the overreaching controlling teleology of "the aim of the entire enterprise" that gives at once unity and determinatives to the justificatory venture.

Note that the element of abstract generality at the top imposes the need for some suitable qualification lower down. Here some sort of qualification like "needless" or "unnecessary" or "inappropriate" (in their contraries) will become operative. The sorts of things that keep harms, etc., from being needless are clear enough. They include qualifications like "merely for personal convenience," "for one's own gain," "for one's own pleasure," "out of perversity or Schadenfreude," etc. To be sure, the list of inadequate reasons that render harms morally inappropriate is potentially endless, but the sort of thing at issue is clear enough to anyone but a moral imbecile.

The crucial fact is that one selfsame moral value—fairness, for example—can come into operation very differently in different contexts. In an economy of abundance it may militate for equality of shares, in an economy of scarcity for equality of opportunity. The particular circumstances that characterize a context of operation may importantly condition the way in which a moral value or principle can (appropriately) be applied. We cannot expect to encounter any universal consensus across cultural and temporal divides: physicians of different eras are (like moralists) bound to differ—and to some extent those of different cultures as well. There is—inevitably—substantial variability among particular groups, each with its own varying ideas conditioned by locally prevailing conditions and circumstances. But the impact of low-level variation is mitigated by the fact that justification at lower levels proceeds throughout with reference to superordinated standards in a way that makes for higher-level uniformity. Uniform high-level principles will have to be implemented differently in different circumstances. Medicine and morality alike are complex projects unified and integrated amidst the welter of changing conditions and circumstances by the determinative predominance of high-level principles.

Overall, then, we have to deal with a chain of subordination-linkages that connect a concrete moral judgment—a particular moral act-recommendation or command—with the ultimate defining aim of the moral enterprise. The long and short of it is that any appropriate moral injunction must derive its validity through being an appropriate instantiation or concretization of an overarching principle of universal (unrestricted) validity under which it is subsumed. It must, in short, represent a circumstantially appropriate implementation of the fixities of absolute morality. Thus even as in Roman Catholic theology there is a "hierarchy of truths" which places different teachings of the Church at different levels of doctrinal essentiality or fundamentality, so in the present context there is a comparable hierarchy of imperatival strata that place different injunctions at different levels of fundamentality in the moral enterprise, with some (the basic principles) as, in this setting, absolute, and others as variable and relative to context and circumstance. Fundamentals are fixed as essential to the moral domain as such, but agreement on concrete issues is itself something more marginal.

At the level of basic principles, then, morality is absolute; its strictures at this level hold good for everyone, for all rational agents. And lower-level rules and rulings must—if valid—preserve a "linkage of subsumption" to those highest-level abstractions, a linkage mediated by way of more restrictive modes of implementation. These implementing rules involve contextual relativity—coordination with contingently variable (setting-dependent and era- and culture-variable) circumstances and situations. Thus while moral objectives and basic principles—those top levels of the hierarchy of moral norms—are absolute and universal, "slack" arises as we move further down the ladder, leaving room for (quite appropriate) contextual variability and differentiation. "Do not unjustifiably take the property of another for your own use" is an unquestionably valid principle of absolute morality. But it avails nothing until such time as there are means for determining what is "the property of another" and what constitutes "unjustified taking." "Don't break promises merely for your own convenience" is a universal moral rule, and as such is global and absolute. But what sorts of practices constitute making a valid promise is something that is largely determined through localized social conventions and personal principles. Local context—variable history, tradition, expectation-defining legal systems, evaluative commitments, and the like—thus makes for substantial variability at the level of operational rules and codes for moral practices.

And so, the looseness of fit or "slack" that we encounter increasingly as we move down the hierarchy makes for considerable context-specific variability at that bottom level. Here underdetermination may come into play through the existence of plausible reasons for divergent positions without any prospect of categorical resolutions one way or the other. A situation of moral indeterminacy may arise where each one of several equally cogent positions can come into irreconcilable conflict. The same respect for life that leads one person to take up arms against a tyrant may lead another to walk in the path of pacifism and self-sacrifice. Either position is defensible and both deserve moral recognition and respect: in a dispute between these two variant appraisals there may well be no single unique right answer. In settings of scarcity (battlefield triage situations, for example) there may well be very real morally laden choices—relieve suffering vs. promote survival, for instance—where there is no definitive right or wrong.[16]

But a definite linkage of subordination and coordination is maintained throughout the implementation process. The validity of concrete rulings is always a matter of their attuning global (and abstract) prescriptions to local (and concrete) conditions. Without that linkage to the fixed highest-level absolutes, the linkage to morality is severed. For a particular ruling to be a proper moral ruling at all, there must be a suitable moral *rationale* for the action—a pathway of subordination linkages that connects it in a continuous manner all the way up to the characterizing aims of the moral enterprise. Varying practices and codes of procedure only possess moral validity insofar as they are implementations of a fixed and determinate set of moral principles. Moral validity must always root in a moral universality that is constrained by a *conceptual* fixity.

Morality's characteristic universality is thus inevitably mediated through factors that are variable, conventional, and culturally relative. That project-definitive general principle must be implemented in concrete circumstances and be adapted to them, even as the idea of hospitality towards strangers, for example, has to function differently in European and in Bedouin culture, since deserts and cities are very different human environments. Still, the deeper moral principles that underlie the moral rules and practices of a society ("Even strangers have their due—they too are entitled to respect, to courtesy, and to assistance in need") transcend the customs of any particular community. As concerns morality, culture is indeed a localizing and differentiating agent but one that merely conditions to local circumstances those fundamental invariants that are inherent in the very conception of morality as such.

To be sure, different societies operate with different moral ground rules at the concrete procedural level. Some societies deem it outrageous for women to expose their faces, their breasts, their knees; others view this as altogether acceptable and perhaps even mandatory. But behind this variation of mores stands a universal moral principle: "Respect people's sensibilities about the appropriate and acceptable appearance of fellow humans by conforming to established rules of proper modesty." This overarching principle is universal and absolute. Its implementation with respect to, say, elbows or belly buttons is of course something that varies with custom and the practices of the community. The rule itself is abstract and schematic, in need of implementing criteria as to what "proper modesty and due decorum" demand. The matter is one of a universal principle with variable implementations subject to "locally established standards and criteria" that are grounded in the particular customs of the community.

The local "moralities" of various communities merely canalize and implement such general principles in a way that attunes them to the character of local conditions and circumstances. For the universality of fundamental moral principles does *not* mean that all moral agents must proceed in exactly the same way at the level of concrete detail. (To revert to the preceding example: medical competence, too, is also based on uniform and universal principles—conscientious care to provide the best available treatment for one's patients; but that does not mean that competent doctors must in all times, places, and circumstances administer the same treatments.)

And so, while the concrete strictures of morality—its specific ordinances and procedural rules of thumb—will of course differ from age to age and culture to culture, nevertheless the ultimate principles that serve to define the project of "morality" as such are universal. The uniform governing conception of "what morality is" suffices to establish and stan-

dardize those ultimate and fixed principles that govern the moral enterprise as such. At the level of fundamentals the variability of moral codes is
underpinned by an absolute uniformity of moral principles and values.
At the highest levels alone is there absoluteness: here an impersonal cogency of acceptance prevails—the rejection of appropriate contentions at
this level involves a lapse of rational cogency. But at the lower levels there
is almost always some room for variation—and dispute as well. (How concern for the well-being of one's fellows can be brought to effective
expression, for example, will very much depend on the institutions of one's
society and also, to some extent, to one's place within it.)

It will not have escaped the reader that the case here developed against
moral relativism is substantially of the same structure as the case against *cognitive* relativism as set out in Chapter 4. And for good reason. Both simply
represent rationality's demand for an intelligent pursuit of appropriate objectives relating to our cognitive interests in the one case and our practical
interests in the other.

6. AGAINST MORAL RELATIVISM (ANTHROPOLOGICAL AND OTHER)

Moral relativism proclaims: "We have *our* moral convictions (rules, standards, values) and they have *theirs*. One is every bit as good as the other. To
each his own. Nobody is in a position to criticize or condemn the moral
views of others."[17] But to take this line at every point as regards moral matters is simply to abandon the very idea of morality. Such a position does
indeed hold good with respect to *mores*—we eat with cutlery, they with
chopsticks; we sleep on beds, they in hammocks; we speak one language,
they another, each with equal propriety. But this indifference does *not* hold
for matters of moral principle. "We treat strangers with respect; they (those
cannibals) eat them. We treat the handicapped kindly; they drown them
at sea. We treat darker-skinned humans as equals; they as inferiors. And
the one way of proceeding is just as appropriate as the other. It's all just a
matter of local custom." Rubbish! It is just not true from the moral standpoint. If crass selfishness, pointless maltreatment, wanton deceit, or the
infliction of needless pain is wrong for us, it is wrong for them too—and
conversely. At the level of fundamentals, matters of moral principle are
the same for everyone. What holds good for us holds good for them too.
A code that sees every mode of behavior as indifferent—every sort of

action as equally acceptable—is by its very nature not a moral code (whatever else it may be).

To be sure, even people who class themselves as flat-out relativists usually incline to regard *some* modes of behavior (political torture, random violence, senseless vandalism) as improper and undesirable. How, then, must they appraise their own position on such matters? They incline to say something like this: "Of course we ourselves (civilized sophisticates that we are) deem this sort of thing to be wicked. But others could, with equal validity, think it to be acceptable, nay even praiseworthy." The difficulty of course lies in that phrase, "with equal validity." From whose point of view does this equality obtain? Ours? Certainly not! On our standards, our own position clearly prevails. From God's? When did he become a party to the discussion? (And if he is a party to the discussion, then what price relativism?) In this matter as in any other, we must of course rely on *our own* basis of justificatory reflections to furnish a validation we can accept as satisfactory. We have no real choice but to proceed from where we are.

Relativists very mistakenly deem cultural variation to indicate that "it just doesn't make any real difference." But this slide from pluralistic variation to indifferentism roots in a grave error—a mistaken assimilation of morality to mere mores that are conventionally arbitrary and inherently indifferent. The fatal flaw of such radical relativism lies in its failure to distinguish sufficiently clearly between *matters of custom and social approval* on the one hand and *matters of principle and moral propriety* on the other.

From the Thrasymachus of Plato's *Republic* to Nietzsche, Marx, Freud, and the Existentialists, critics of "traditional morality" propose not to abolish morality as such, but to put *something different and better* in its place—to provide a new set of "superior" morality-improving values and principles. However, such revolutionism cannot be *altogether* revolutionary—at any rate, not as long as its advocacy rests on a rational basis. For insofar as its proponents set out to *convince* us, they must somehow argue that their variant moral code somehow affords a better way of life. They must hold that it better achieves the characterizing aims and purposes at issue in the moral enterprise—the safeguarding and enhancement of human well-being. And here, of course, "morality" is and must be "what people MEAN by 'morality'—i.e. 'morality' as standardly understood in relation to the interests of people-in-general." And that means that their arguments must ultimately pivot on the project of morality-as-we-understand-it, with those fundamental values that characterize the entire project's reason for being left wholly intact. (Clearly, if we are to accept those putatively superior moral values as indeed better than ones that we endorse, this evaluative conclusion can only be *argued* with reference to values we already hold.)

But what, then, of moral variability, of interpersonal and cross-cultural disagreement regarding moral matters? It is tempting to indulge in a convenient impoverishment of the range of alternatives: throughout morality we have *either* mere mores, mere customs of the tribe, *or* unvarying and all-pervasive absolutes. Given this choice, the reduction of morality to matters of mere convention seems relatively plausible. But of course this particular range of alternatives is too narrow; it overlooks another possibility far more promising than either of those considered, namely, that moral norms can operate at very different levels and that morality accordingly involves the implementation of fundamental and invariant principles within diversified and variable situations.

The uniformity of the higher-level norms determinative of morality means that different families of (appropriate) moral rules—different moral codes—simply represent diverse routes to the same ultimate destination. And, given the functional integrity of morality—as an endeavor aimed at safeguarding and promoting the best or real interests of rational agents as such—this is exactly how it should be. The mere fact that a single enterprise—morality—is at issue means that, despite the plurality of moral codes, we have to deal with a single uniform family of fundamentals, that the variability of moral rules is underpinned by an absolute uniformity of moral principles, the plurality of valid moral codes notwithstanding.

And the uniformity of these principles lies in the very nature of normality as the sort of project which, by definition, it actually is. From the moral point of view, the *empirical* search for "cultural invariants" as pursued by some ethnologists is thus entirely beside the point.[18] When such investigators embark on a cross-cultural quest for "moral universals" or "universal values" amidst the variation of social customs, they are engaged in a search which, however interesting and instructive in its own way, has nothing whatever to do with the sort of normative universality at issue with morality as such. Moral universality is not a matter of cross-cultural commonality but of a *conceptually* constrained uniformity. (It would be just as pointless to investigate whether another culture's forks have tines.)

A hermeneutical line of deliberation shows why the anthropological reduction of morality to mores just does not work. For it lies in the very nature of the issue that moral principles sometimes preclude flexibility. Certain things are wrong in an absolute and universal way:

- murder (i.e., unjustifiably killing another person)
- exploitation (i.e., taking improper advantage of people)
- inflicting pointless harm
- lying and deception for selfish advantage, betraying a trust for personal gain
- breaking promises out of sheer perversity
- misusing the institutions of one's society for one's own selfish purposes

The unacceptability (i.e., moral inappropriateness) of such actions lies in the very idea of what morality is all about. Local custom to the contrary notwithstanding, such things are morally wrong anytime, anywhere, and for anyone. Their prohibitions are moral universals, parts of morality as such. (And so they hold good not just for us humans but for all rational beings.)

Discussions of moral relativism by philosophers and social scientists alike are all too frequently vitiated by the oversimplification of seeing moral norms at all levels as being of a piece. They fail to distinguish between lower-level rules and standards, which indeed are variable and context-dependent, and higher-level values and principles, which are fixed, universal, and unchanging. Recognition of the hierarchical stratification of moral norms is essential to a proper understanding of morality. The fact that there are uniform and unchanging principles at the top of the hierarchy—principles that inhere in the very conception of morality itself—is quite compatible with plurality, variation, and even some measure of conventionality in the moral norms of the lower levels. The multilevel structure of moral norms provides the key to reconciling the inherent absolutism of morality with the "cultural relativity" of moral codes by showing how the relativistic variation of such codes is perfectly compatible with the absolutism of moral fundamentals. Plurality and variability in regard to lower-level norms is nowise at odds with an absolutistic uniformity of higher-level principles.

An absolutistic one-morality doctrine at the level of the basic (abstract or "general") principles of morality is thus perfectly compatible with a circumstantially diversified plurality of moral codes at the level of concrete rules of operation. Morality has different levels. One is a parochial matter of particular practices, of locally conditioned concrete rules of operation relating to locally established claims, entitlements, obligations, and the like.

But another is a universal matter of underlying principles that revolve about the governing factor of safeguarding people's real interests. Both are formative aspects of the overall enterprise. If one forgets about those over-arching uniformities, the moral landscape assumes a kaleidoscopic variety. But appearances are misleading. There is a single overarching framework of *moral* principles that inhere fixedly in the very notion of what morality is all about. And so the transcultural variation of moral rules does not show that morality is something merely conventional and customary in nature. It illustrates rather than destroys the many-sided bearing of the uniform, context-transcendent, universal moral principles operative at the level of fundamentals.

But if the variability of its concrete procedural rules is a fact of life in the moral domain—if different sorts of moral directives and rulings can (quite appropriately) obtain for different cultural groups—then how does one's own particular code secure its obligating hold upon oneself. Why is it that I should see myself as duty-bound to follow "our established rules" rather than some others?

The answer to this question is straightforward. In morality, as elsewhere, the universal is available to us only through mediation of the specific: one can pursue a generalized desideratum only through its particularized (and variable) concretizations. Communication is universal, language is specific; eating is universal, cookery local; morality is universal, particular concrete moral codes are variable and diversified. But such variability does not undermine or abrogate validity; it does no more than illustrate that, with morality as other things, one must pursue generalized desiderata through their specific realizations—the "married state" through a particular spouse. The universals of morality not only permit, but *require* adjustment to local conditions. The prevailing conditions and circumstances are (by hypothe-sis) those within which we have to act. And at that level we are concerned not with validation of morality as such, but with the justification of a particular moral code for a particular group in the particular circumstances at hand. The concrete code of our community is the only way in which implementation to the high-level demands of morality is available *to us*, given the realities of the particular context in which we live and labor. In transacting our moral affairs in this world—as in conducting our physi-cal movements within it—we have no choice but to go on from where we are.

To be sure, the behavioral practices of a society (ours included) are not above criticism—gift horses into whose mouths we must not presume to look. Anything that people do can be done badly, the shaping of a moral code included. Confronted by any set of purported "moral rules of behavior" we can and should ask: how well do they implement the fundamental principles that articulate the aims of the moral enterprise as we do (and must) understand it? Any system (for example) that authorizes the infliction of pain on people for no better reason than affording amusement to others deserves flat-out condemnation and rejection. It would be a decisive objection to any system of "morality" that it deems acceptable (let alone approbation-worthy) a mode of behavior which is immoral on the conscientious application of *our* fundamental standards—that it approves pointless lying, for example, or wanton cruelty, or any other practice that countervails against the legitimate interests of people. The operational code of our community can be found defective or deficient in point of morality. (Think of Nazi Germany, for example.) Socially accepted principles of action are clearly not beyond criticism. But this criticism can—if appropriate—only be developed from the vantage point of those first and fundamental principles which characterize the moral project as such. These are—unavoidably—part and parcel of any morality worthy of the name. For these fundamental standards of *morality* are, in virtue of being so, not just ours but everyone's—if they indeed are fundamental, then they must apply everywhere.

The crucial point, then, is that one can be a pluralist in matters of morality without being a relativist, let alone an indifferentist. Consider the following positions:

- MORAL PLURALISM: There are different, yet in their own context appropriate, moral codes.
- MORAL RELATIVISM: There are no fixed principles in moral matters. Everything hinges on contingent local options. Morality is wholly a matter of mores.
- MORAL INDIFFERENTISM: Moral issues are ultimately indifferent. There is no objective justification for one position rather than another, no rationale of good reasons through which a particular culture's resolution can be justified (not even for its particular conditions, let alone unconditionally).

Moral relativism is to be rejected because an absolute uniformity prevails at the level of fundamental principles and values. And moral indifferentism is to be rejected because the moral code of one's own community has a valid claim to our own allegiance. But moral pluralism does not fall with these objections; it is something we can and must accept—an absolutism of moral principles notwithstanding.

People must feed themselves and house themselves. Nature dictates no single and unique process for accomplishing such ends; we must proceed to make the best use we can of the possibilities that place and time put at our disposal. And analogously with morality's requirements of due care for the interests of people. Here too we must simply do the best we can, striving within the conditions and circumstances of our setting for practices and rules that align human interactions in a productive harmony from which everyone can benefit. But the diversity of moral codes is not at odds with the fundamental demand of moral rationality: that we pursue our own ends *appropriately*, with a due recognition of the needs, rights, and claims of others. At this level of generality, the demands of morality, like those of rationality itself, are universal. And so with morality, as with all else, the authoritativeness of rationality carries a pervasive commitment to objectivity in its wake.[19]

—ten—

MORAL OBJECTIVITY: THE RATIONALITY AND UNIVERSALITY OF MORAL PRINCIPLES

Synopsis

(1) The claims of morality purport to formulate universal duties; genuinely moral obliga-
tions are by their very nature to be seen as universally incumbent upon everyone alike. Yet
whence does morality obtain this deontic force of universal obligation? Neither utility nor
consensuality (social contract) can do the job. (2) Ultimately, the demands of morality root
in an ontological obligation of the same sort that we have already seen to be at issue with
cognitive rationality. (3) Indeed morality—seen in proper perspective—is simply an inher-
ent sector of rationality at large. The absoluteness of moral rules is part and parcel of the
absoluteness of the requisites of reason. (4) Not only are moral obligations inherently uni-
versal, moral benefits also accrue universally; everyone has a stake in morality. (5) In
consequence, a well-ordered society will strive for political arrangements that coordinate
morality with self-advantage.

1. THE CLAIMS OF MORALITY ARE UNIVERSAL

Morality transcends mere prudence. It exerts a claim going beyond the impetus to self-serving advantage, imposing other-concerning obligations
that are diffused universally, incumbent upon all of us alike. The requiredness of genuine obligation lies at the heart of morality. And so, without a
satisfactory answer to the question of the basis of obligation we lack an
adequate understanding of morality. Any acceptable account must provide
satisfactory answers to such questions as: Why *must* one be moral and heed

the interests of others in one's actions and deliberations? What is the basis of the prescriptive impetus of moral injunctions as a matter of binding *duty?* Wherein does this obligatoriness of moral obligation lie?

The core idea of morality is that someone who culpably fails to do the morally appropriate thing (wittingly and deliberately and without a good and sufficient excuse):

- does something *wrong*—not just something unwise or counter-productive or unconventional, but something actually *bad*, and accordingly
- is *blameworthy* by way of deserving of the disapproval of others and the reproach of one's own conscience

To default callously on one's moral obligations is to act in a way that by its very nature invites and deserves condemnation. And the inherent "re-quiredness" of moral comportment is something that is crucial to morality as the thing it is. Any adequate theory of morality must accordingly recognize the deontological aspect of moral judgments. It must account for the "deontic force" or duty-coordinated requiredness that is an inelimi-nable feature of such moral precepts as "Stealing is wrong." The sanctions of morality are thus stronger than anything that mere considerations of self-interest can underwrite, seeing that they must be able to ground not merely what makes people better off but what makes them better people.

In theory, one can contemplate many different sorts of bases for obli-gation, many different sorts of grounds that a must/ought contention might conceivably have: self-interest, legality, religion, social custom, and others. But *morality* is yet another, different from and irreducible to these others. Moral judgments are normative in a characteristic way with respect to good/bad and right/wrong. A deliberately performed immoral act—the wanton infliction of needless pain on someone, for example, or hurt-ing another's feelings simply for one's own pleasure—is not just foolish or antisocial or prudentially ill-advised, but *wicked*. Categories such as wise/foolish, customary/eccentric, prudent/imprudent, or lawful/illegal simply do not capture what is at issue in moral/immoral. No theory of morality can lay claim to adequacy which fails to provide for this characteristic deontic force and somehow papers over the wickedness of moral trans-gressions. It is inherent in the very idea of morality that *everyone* ought to do what is demanded here—that acting morally is a matter of duty for all rational agents because an appropriate *requirement* is at issue.

In a classic paper of pre–World War I vintage, the Oxford philosopher H. A. Prichard argued that it makes no real sense to ask "Why should I be moral?"[1] For once an act is recognized as being the morally appropriate thing to do, there is really no room for any *further* question about why it should be done. "Because it's the moral thing to do" is automatically, by its very nature, a satisfactorily reason-presenting response. The question "Why *do* the *right* thing?" is akin to the question "Why *believe* the *true* thing?" On both sides the answer is simply: "Exactly because what is at issue is, by hypothesis, something that is right/true." When rightness or truth have once been conceded, the matter is closed. According to Prichard, then, the question "Why should one's duty be done?" is simply obtuse—or perverse. For duty as such constitutes a cogent moral imperative to action—automatically, as it were, of itself and by its very nature. To grant that it is one's duty to do something and then go on to ask why one should do it is simply to manifest one's failure to understand what the conception of "duty" involves. Duty as such constitutes a reason for action, albeit a *moral* reason.

But, clearly, this line of reflection, though quite correct, is probatively unhelpful. Self-support has its limitations as a justificatory rationale. The questions still remain: "What makes reasons of moral appropriateness into good reasons?" "Why should I be the sort of person who accepts moral grounds as validly compelling for his own deliberations?" If being moral indeed is the appropriate thing to do, there must be some sort of reason for it, that is, there must be some line of consideration, not *wholly* internal to morality itself, that renders it reasonable for people to be moral. We must probe yet further for a fully satisfactory resolution to the question, "Why be moral?" And we need to improve on the true but unhelpful answer, "Because it is the (morally) right thing to do." There has to be more to it than that. But where are we to look?

When it comes to accounting for the obligatory requiredness of morality, a resort to prudence will leave us in the lurch. Even granted that we have a prudential stake in morality—individually and collectively—this matter of mere interest cannot transmute into one of actual *obligation*. Doing the self-advantageous thing may well be natural, but there is nothing obligatory about it.

At this point, someone might offer the following objection:

You are quite right to insist that a prudential rationale for morality does not provide for the deontic force of moral claims. But what it *can* (and presumably *does*) accomplish is to establish that we are rationally well advised to *deem* ourselves (and others) to be morally obligated in the full-blooded duty-oriented sense of the term. That is, it can show that we are prudentially bound *to believe in the deontic force of morality*.

By this sort of strategy, a prudentialist could maintain a mixed position that enjoins prudence and deontology through a recourse to (prudentially) rational belief.

However, this tactic still cannot provide a satisfactory rationale for authentic morality. It yields no more than a sham morality, because it does not go to show that we ever actually *are* obligated to moral action, only that we are prudentially well-advised to *think* ourselves (and others) to be so obligated. Accordingly, it does not provide for a real morality of actual obligation, but only for a play-acting morality of "as if." (To be sure, its play-acting morality is that of the "method actor" who endeavors to "live the role," but it remains play-acting all the same.) Such a prudential impetus may perhaps take a step in the direction of morality, but it certainly does not reach morality itself. No explanation, analysis, or interpretation that conjures away the deontic, duty-bound aspect of *morality* can be adequate to this conception as we actually have it.

And this sort of argumentation also tells against a utilitarian morality that locates the impetus to moral conduct in considerations not of personal but of general advantage. Such a position has no difficulty with the question why we are communally well-advised to support morality. That is obvious enough, seeing that our own personal interest is in general inextricably interconnected with the general good. But when asked why we *ought* to do so—why this should be seen as a matter of actual *obligation*—the utilitarian runs into embarrassing difficulties. Seeing morality as a matter of interest alone, he has no satisfactory way to bring obligation into it. Utilitarianism lacks the machinery for building a bridge from social demand to personal obligation. Morality cannot be reduced to social utility. (Punishing the group for the transgressions of individuals may, in some circumstances, be a policy of great social utility—and thus be urged plausibly on *political* grounds—but it cannot appropriately be recommended on *moral* grounds. The urgings of Leviathan are one thing, those of morality another; utilitarian politics makes sense in a way that utilitarian morality cannot.)

A reductionist moral theoretician, whether of utilitarian or egoistic persuasion, may perhaps insist: "I am quite prepared to let moral deliberations rest on an appeal to values other than utilitarian (or egoistic) ones, provided those values are themselves in turn legitimated by utilitarian (or egoistic) considerations. My theory calls for the two-step approach of first adopting morality *en gros* as a general program that itself pivots ultimately on reasons of utility (or self-interest), and then proceeding to address all concrete issues on classical moral principles." But this line of approach will simply not do. It is like saying "I'll sell my allegiance to the highest bidder and from there on out I'll be a loyal follower." No *real* loyalty (or *real* morality) is to be had along these lines. Where the foundations are unsatisfactory, the whole enterprise is vitiated. A validation of morality that rests its ultimate justificatory appeal upon any inherently amoral factor such as social solidarity or personal advantage cannot achieve a fully satisfactory result because its justificatory basis is insufficiently linked to the value system of morality itself. Accounting for the deontic force of moral judgments is a job that must be accomplished by different means.

On this basis, a variant approach to the validation of morality—one based on the idea of consensuality—might be attempted along the following lines:

> Admittedly, a prudential validation of morality does not establish the deontic force of moral *obligation* all by itself. However, that duty itself inheres in a "social contract" or public agreement of some sort (presumably of an implicit or tacit nature). The prudential argument goes no further than to show that we are well advised to enter into this contract. But actual obligatoriness stems from the contract itself—the consideration that once we have entered into it, then we must see ourselves as bound by it, since this is what such entry consists in.

In this vein, one recent theorist maintains that "morality arises when a group of people reach an implicit agreement or come to a tacit understanding about their relations with one another."[2] Now this may well be part of the story, and perhaps even an important part, but it certainly cannot be the whole of it. For an "agreement" or an "understanding" (however tacit or implicit) cannot come to exist *in vacuo*, in a context where people have as yet no morality in place. It is the sort of commitment that by its very nature is possible only in a preexisting moral framework. Anything worthy of the name of "agreement" (compact, mutual understanding) can subsist only within a preexisting morality, where the morally binding force of agreements is an already established fact. The very idea of an "agreement" involves a deontological relationship that cannot exist in a moral vacuum: "making an *agreement*," in the standard sense of the term, is *already* a moral act that can be performed only in a setting where "agreements should be honored" is an operative principle. A mere alignment or coordination of action is no *agreement* in the absence of an acceptance of actual obligation by the parties involved: an "agreement" in which there is no acknowledgment (at least tacit) of the undertaking of an obligation is not even so much as an agreement in name only. The reach of a moral code can indeed be *expanded* by agreement, but its specifically *moral* aspect cannot altogether *originate* therein, because "agreement" as such already has a moral status.

The long and short of it is that the proposed shifting of the burden of obligatoriness to a contract does not really solve the problem of explanation. It merely focuses the overall difficulty on one particular point, reducing the obligatoriness of morality in general to that of contracts (agreements, compacts, promises, and the like). The fundamental issue thus remains unresolved. For the question now arises as to just why we *ought* always to honor such agreements, as opposed to merely finding it prudentially advantageous to abide by them much of the time. The question has in fact been begged. What is so special about *contracts?* Why not just break an agreement in those particular cases where, all considered, it meets our selfish purposes to do so? In the context of the particular matter of agreements we are now still left with just that initial problem of accounting for the obligatoriness of morality.

And so, even if it is supplemented by the postscript of a "social contract," the prudential validation of morality cannot account satisfactorily for the deontic force of moral obligation. The Hobbes-Rousseau approach of basing morality on a social contract—seeing it as rooted in agreements or acquiescences based solely on mutual advantage for the interests of the parties involved[3] —has the crippling defect that it affords no way to explain why people should ever be *obligated* to be moral. For even if we are eminently *well-advised* to honor contracts and agreements in this prudential mode, this does not show that we are *obliged* to do so. Morality as such accordingly cannot be validated on this basis either.[4]

2. ONTOLOGICAL OBLIGATION AS THE SOURCE OF THE DEONTIC FORCE OF MORALITY

Can morality be grounded in human nature, in some special facet or feature of our condition as rational beings? Clearly, morality does *not* inhere in the realization of human potential as such. For every person has a potential for *both* good and evil—in principle, each has it in him to become a saint or a sinner. Discerning our specifically *good* potentialities requires more than a knowledge of human nature as such; it requires taking a view of the good of man—a normative philosophical anthropology. Of course, other things being anything like equal, it is better to be healthy, to be happy, to understand what goes on, and the like. But this still leaves untouched the pivotal question of what endows life with worth and value: what are the conditions that make for a rewarding and worthwhile life? This issue of human flourishing will inevitably involve such things as: using one's intelligence, developing (some of) one's productive talents and abilities, making a constructive contribution to the world's work, fostering the good potential of others, achieving and diffusing happiness, and taking heed for the interests of others. The good potentialities, in sum, are exactly those in whose cultivation and development a rational agent can take reflective self-satisfaction, those which help us most fully to realize ourselves as the sort of being we should ideally aspire to be. And it is here that morality's insistence on a concern for the legitimate interests of others can find a grip. The crux is simply the matter of cultivating legitimate interests. And we cannot do this for ourselves without due care for cultivating our specifically positive potentialities—those things which are inherently worthwhile.

This approach to deontology thus ultimately grounds the obligatoriness of moral injunctions in *axiology*—in considerations of value. For it is the metaphysics of value—and not moral theory per se—that teaches us that knowledge is better, other things equal, than ignorance, or pleasure than pain, or compassion than needless indifference. And what ultimately validates our moral concern for the interests of others is just exactly this ontological commitment to the enhancement of value, a commitment that is inseparably linked to our own value as free rational agents. We are embarked here on a broadly economic approach—but one that proceeds in terms of a value theory that envisions a generalized "economy of values," and from whose standpoint the traditional economic values (the standard economic costs and benefits) are merely a rather special case. Such an axiological approach sees moral rationality as an integral component of that wider rationality that calls for the effective deployment of limited resources. (Observe that such a deontological approach contrasts starkly with a utilitarian morality, in that the latter pivots morality on *happiness* or "utility," but the former on *value-enhancement*.)

Heeding the strictures of morality is part and parcel of a rational being's cultivation of the good. For us rational creatures morality (the due care for the interests of rational beings) is an integral component of reason's com-

mitment to the enhancement of value. Reason's commitment to the value
of rationality accordingly carries in its wake a commitment to morality.
The obligatoriness of morality ultimately roots in an *ontological* imperative
to value realization with respect to self and world that is incumbent on free
agents as such. On this ontological perspective, the ultimate basis of moral
duty roots in the obligation we have as rational agents (towards ourselves
and the world at large) to make the most and best of our opportunities for
self-development. Moral obligation ultimately inheres in this ontological obligation to the realization of values in one's own life. (Q. Why cultivate the things of value? A. Because it is the rational thing to do.) At this
point duty and self-interest enter into confluence.

And so, in the final analysis, one ought to be moral for the same sort of
reason for which one ought to make use of life's opportunities in general—one's intelligence, for example, or one's other constructive talents.
For in failing to do this we throw away chances to make something of
ourselves by way of contributing to the world's good, thereby failing to
realize our potential. The violation of moral principles thus stands coordinate with the sanctions attaching to wanton wastefulness of any sort. The
crux is not so much self-realization as self-optimization. And what is at
issue with failure is throughout not merely a loss but a violation of duty as
well. For to recognize something as valuable will, with the rational person,
be to enter into certain obligations in its regard (such as favoring it over
contrary alternatives, other things equal).

To be sure, it deserves stress that the obligation to morality—to conduct
our interpersonal affairs appropriately by heeding the interests of others—
is our only ontological obligation. The epistemic obligation to conduct
our cognitive affairs appropriately—to inquire, to broaden our knowledge,
to pursue the truth by believing only those things which *ought* (epistemically deserve) to be believed in the circumstances—is another example; the
Kantian duty to develop (at least some of) one's talents is yet another. The
scope of ontological obligation is thus substantially broader than that of
morality alone.

The obligation to morality, like the obligation to rationality, accordingly
roots in considerations of ontology, of our condition as the sorts of rational beings we are (or at any rate see ourselves as being). If one is in a
position to see oneself as in fact rational, then once one recognizes the
value of this rationality one must also acknowledge the obligation to make
use of one's rationality. And if one is a rational free agent who recognizes
and prizes this very fact, then one ought for that very reason to behave

morally by taking the interests of other such agents into account. For if I am (rationally) to pride myself on being a rational agent, then I must stand ready to value in other rational agents what I value in myself, that is, I must deem them *worthy* of respect, care, etc., in virtue of their status as rational agents. What is at issue is not so much a matter of *reciprocity* as one of *rational coherence* with claims that one does—or, rather, should—stake for oneself. For to see myself in a certain normative light I must, if rational, stand ready to view others in the same light. If we indeed are the sort of intelligent creature whose worth in our own sight is a matter of prizing something (reflective self-respect, for example), then this item by virtue of this very fact assumes the status of something we are bound to recognize as valuable, as deserving of being valued. In seeing ourselves as *persons*—as free and responsible rational agents—we thereby rationally bind ourselves to a care for one another's interests insofar as those others too are seen as having this status.[5]

I may *desire* respect (be it self-respect or the respect of others) for all sorts of reasons, good, bad, or indifferent. But if I am to *deserve* respect, this has to be so for good reasons. Respect will certainly not come to me just because I am I, but only because I have a certain sort of respect-evoking feature (for example, being a free rational agent) whose possession (by me or, for that matter, anyone) provides a warrant for respect. And this means that *all* who have this feature (all rational agents) merit respect. Our self-worth hinges on the worth we attach to others-like-us: we can only have worth by virtue of possessing worth-engendering features that operate in the same way when others are at issue. To claim respect-worthiness for myself I must concede it to all suitably constituted others as well. The first-person plural idea of "we" and "us" that projects one's own identity into a wider affinity-community of rational beings is a crucial basis of our sense of worth and self-esteem. In degrading other *persons* in thought or in treatment, we would automatically degrade ourselves, while in doing them honor we thereby honor ourselves.

When someone acts immorally towards me—cheats me or deceives me or the like—I am not merely angry and upset because my personal interests have been impaired but am also "righteously indignant." Not only has the offender failed to acknowledge me as a person (a fellow rational being with rights and interests of his own), but he has, by his very act, marked himself as someone who, though (to my mind) a congener of mine as a rational agent, nevertheless does not give us rational agents their proper due, thereby degrading the entire group to which I too belong. He has added insult to injury. And this holds more generally. One is also indignant at witnessing someone act immorally towards a third party, being disturbed in a way akin to the annoyance one feels when some gaffe is committed by a member of one's own family. For one's own sense of self and self-worth is mediated by membership in such a group and thus is something that can become compromised by *their* behavior. As rational agents, we are entitled and committed to be indignant at the wicked actions of our fellows who do not act as rational agents ought, because our own self-respect is inextricably bound up with their behavior. They have "let down the side."

The upshot of such considerations is that to fail to be moral is to defeat our own proper purposes and to lose out on our ontological opportunities. It is only by acknowledging the worth of others—and thus the appropriateness of a due heed of *their* interests—that we ourselves can maintain our own claims to self-respect and self-worth. We realize that we *should* act morally in each and every case, even where deviations are otherwise advantageous, because insofar as we do not, we can no longer look upon ourselves in a certain sort of light—one that is crucial to our own self-respect in the most fundamental way. Moral agency is an essential requisite for the proper self-esteem of a rational being. To fail in this regard is to injure oneself where it does and should hurt the most—in one's own sight.

The ontological imperative to capitalize on our opportunities for the good carries us back to the salient issue of philosophical anthropology—the visualization of what man can and should be. "Be an authentic human being!" comes down to this: Do your utmost to become the sort of rational and responsible creature that a human person, at best or most, is capable of being.[6] The moral project of treating of other people as we ourselves would be treated is part and parcel of this. What we have here is in fact an evaluative metaphysic of morals.

3. MORALITY AND RATIONALITY

It deserves to be recognized and stressed that when one's commitment to morality is emplaced within an ontological obligation to achieve one's greatest potential as a free rational agent, then morality is also rendered consistent with (though, to be sure, not based upon) a rational concern for one's prudential advantage, at any rate at the level of *real* or *best* interests.

Being moral is an integral part of self-optimization. To bring this out more clearly, it is necessary to consider the inherently ramified nature of rational action.

Every free act of an intelligent agent has wider ramifications. The issue with which we are confronted in our action choices is never *just* a matter of deciding what I want to do in this case: it is always also in part a matter of deciding *what sort of person I am to be*. The salient fact about a situation of apparent conflict between duty and advantage is that in deciding how to act here and now we effectively also decide—in some measure, at least—what sort of person we are to be. Consider an illustration. In deliberately acting immorally—in deciding, say, to betray a trust merely for my own financial gain—I produce two sorts of results: (1) the *proximate*, local result of my action in the particular case at hand—whatever immediate gains and advantages it would secure for me; and (2) the *ulterior*, large-scale result of so acting as to make myself into a person of a certain sort—someone who would do *that* sort of thing to realize *that* sort of benefit. This second, more far-reaching and systemic aspect is crucial—and unavoidable. For even if no one else knows it, the fact still remains that I myself am aware of what I deliberately do. And my self-respect is (or *ought* to be) of such great value to me that the advantages I could secure by immoral action cannot countervail against the loss that would be involved in this larger regard. For in acting in a way that I recognize to be wrong, I sustain a grave moral injury exactly where it should count the most—in my own sight.

In setting morality aside for the sake of selfish personal advantage, for example, we would shift our guiding principle of action in the case at hand from "Always do the morally appropriate thing," to "Always do the morally appropriate thing unless it is more beneficial in the prevailing circumstances for you not to do so." But in making this shift in the determinative rationale of our action we ipso facto affect a change in our very nature, transforming ourselves from type (1) to type (2) agents. Such a shift is obviously not justifiable on *moral* grounds whenever a violation of moral principles is at issue. Moreover—more surprisingly—it is, in general, not even justifiable on *prudential* grounds. For in becoming type (2) agents, we would exchange a limited and temporary advantage for a large and perduring loss. For the long and short of it is that we have a paramount stake (a *real* interest) in being moral agents, because this is needed to maintain proper self-respect. In this regard, morality is eminently rational and prudent, geared to the efficient achievement of appropriate ends. For it is quintessentially rational to seek to provide for one's own best and real interests.

And the commitment to rationality is itself an integral part of our best and true interests. No gain in goods or pleasures can outweigh its value for us rational beings. (The "happiness pill" hypothesis suffices to show that it is not pleasure or happiness as such that ultimately matters for us, but rationally authorized pleasure of happiness.) The goods we gain through deception (or other sorts of immoral conduct) afford us a hollow benefit. This is so not because we are too high-minded to be able to "enjoy" illicit gains, but because inasmuch as we are rational thinking beings—creatures committed by their very nature to strive for reflective contentment (as opposed to merely affective pleasure)—it is only by "doing the right thing" that we can maintain our reflectively based sense of self-worth or *deserved* merit.

The imperative "Act as a rational agent ought" does not come from without (from parents or from society or even from God). It roots in our own self-purported nature as rational beings. (In Kant's words it is a *dictamen rationis*, a part of the "innere Gesetzgebung der Vernunft"). Its status as being rationally appropriate roots simply and directly in the fact of its being an integral part of what our reason demands of us. And because being moral is a part of being reasonable, morality too is part of this demand.

Morality is accordingly geared to rationality in a dual way: (1) morality is a matter *of* rationality—of acting for good reasons of a certain (characteristically moral) sort, and (2) morality is an enterprise that exists *for* rationality—for the sake of protecting the legitimate interests of rational agents. And it is precisely this gearing of morality to the interests of rational agents that renders an ontological validation of morality, in terms of the inherent requisites of rational agency, thoroughly consonant with the value structure of morality itself.

But what of the person who is indifferent to the matter of real interests, the person for whom the only acceptable rationale is that of selfish advantage—someone who simply refuses to be moved by impersonal reasons and will respond to motives of selfish advantage alone? Such a person will say: "But I just don't accept that purported ontological obligation at issue in morality. I propose to assert myself as a free rational agent by rejecting the validity of moral claims." So be it, if that is what you want. The acknowledgment of a claim is up to you. However, its *appropriateness* does not lie in its being accepted—any more than the validity of an argument does—but lies in the fact that it *ought* to be accepted. No obligation—be it moral or rational—is undermined by the fact that people are disinclined to accept it. The crux of the issue of moral appropriateness is not what we want or desire but what is in our best interest—not *motivation* but *rationalization*. "Even if being moral is in my best *real* interests, that means nothing to me. I don't care about my real interests—for me these just don't matter, wants are what counts." Given the inherent connection of rationality with enlightened self-interest, such a view—however widespread—is simply irrational. A position of this perverse sort may indeed *explain* why someone acts immorally, but it cannot even begin to *justify* him in doing so. For it is the quintessence of irrationality to fail, wittingly and deliberately, to value things at their true worth.

Morality is thus not at odds with rationality but is part and parcel of it. Only someone who mistakenly thinks that selfish reasons alone can qualify as good reasons can see an irreconcilable conflict between morality and rationality. And this would indeed be a gross mistake. For a rational commitment to morality inheres in the (ontologically mediated) circumstance that other-concerned reasons for action constitute perfectly good *rational* reasons because of their unseverable link to the real interests of the agent himself. The consonance of morality with rationality is established through the fact that the *intelligent* thing to do and the *right* thing to do will ultimately agree because acting morally *is* the intelligent thing to do for those who have a proper concern for their real self-interest. There is nothing irrational about being moral, and there is nothing imprudent about it either, as long as we understand "*true prudence*" aright. (Though to say this is emphatically *not* to say that it is in its consonance with prudence that the *validation* of morality should be sought.)[7]

4. ARE THERE ABSOLUTE MORAL RULES? THE UNIVERSALITY OF MORAL OBLIGATIONS

Morality demands our conformity with a categorical stringency. It issues commands on the order of: "You must not inflict needless pain on people." Morality insists upon what should be done with an urgency and an authority that transcend the requirements of conformity to locally established practices—the mere custom of the tribe. The requirements of morality are universal and absolute: what morality asks of us is something which it would, in similar conditions, demand of anyone and everyone.

Indeed, as Kant rightly insisted, if a principle is to qualify as a moral one, it must hold not for humans alone but for rational agents in general.

All the same, the controversy about absolute moral rules has been bedeviled—like many another philosophical controversy—by the absence of agreement about what its salient term actually means. For "absolute" is a highly equivocal word, used by different discussants in rather different ways. In particular, it has been used in the discussion of moral rules to mean that such a rule:

(1) is of unrestricted and altogether universal application with respect to (potential) obligatees. (For example, honoring one's promise is a practice incumbent on everybody.)

(2) is of unrestricted and altogether universal application with respect to (potential) beneficiaries. (For example, not hurting people's feelings needlessly is a practice from which everyone gains.)

(3) is objectively valid (as a moral rule); holding good as a matter of objectively determinable fact that can be established as such by impersonal standards.

(4) is categorical in form and devoid of any hypothetical or conditional qualifications of the sort present in "Keep promises," that is, "Whenever you have made a commitment, honor it."

(5) is overriding and all-decisive in being of a weight that sweeps all other considerations aside, overruling and outweighing all other factors.

Our deliberations here have arrived at rather mixed results in this regard. Absoluteness in senses (1)–(3) has been maintained for morality: it lies in the nature of the case that any appropriate *moral* rule must, as such, be both obligatee-universal and beneficiary-universal, and that its inherent rationale (in terms of the protection of people's interests) is such that its validity as a valid moral rule represents a genuinely objective issue. But, on the other hand, we have rejected flatly claims to absoluteness in senses (4) and (5). As regards (4), we have insisted on the conditional character of all lower-level moral rules (even as "Help others in need" comes to "When someone needs your help, and you are so circumstanced as to be able to give it, then do so"). And as regards (5), we have noted that lower-level moral rules are never totally decisive because their violation may be unavoidable, in context, to avert some yet greater misfortune. The upshot is that while moral rules are indeed *absolute* in some pertinent senses, they are not so in others.

On this perspective, then, the question of moral absolutism is an equivocal one. All the same, the cardinal point for present purposes is that a cogent case can be built up for a moral realism that sees appropriate moral judgments as deontically universal and objectively valid, thus placing morality squarely within the domain of rationally cogent endeavors.

Valid moral principles are *obligation*-universal—binding (in principle, at least) upon all persons alike. It lies in the very conception of a moral rule that such a rule must be universal in its potential obligatees. Addressed to sea captains and airplane pilots, the imperative "Care for the safety of your passengers" is not as such a moral principle, save insofar as it can be subsumed under "Care for the safety of those for whose well-being you have assumed responsibility," which clearly encapsulates a duty incumbent on *everyone*. Universality is crucial to morality. If there are no absolute moral principles of this universalistic stamp, then there is no valid *morality* at all. (This alone prevents moral values—unlike political values—from rooting altogether in a "social contract.")

Consider: "John ought to repay Henry (because he promised to do so)." This obligation is as particular as can be. But it bears moral weight only because it subsumptively concretizes the strictly universal principle "*Everyone* ought to honor a freely undertaken commitment." A valid moral obligation must always inhere in a universal principle in this sort of way. It lies in the nature of the concept at issue that one can have a *moral* obligation to entitlement only insofar as it transpires that, in the particular circumstances at issue, *anyone* would have this obligation or entitlement. If there are to be any valid obligations at all, there must be some universal ones that bind all rational agents. For subsumption under such a universal higher-level principle that applies to everyone is the only way in which moral obligations can be validated as such.

For there to be morality, it is not enough for there to be *people* (members of the biological species *Homo sapiens.*) There must also be *persons*—intelligent creatures who see themselves as rational free agents, able to choose among alternatives in the light of a reasoned evaluation of their merits. Purposeful behavior as an individual agent is the crux. Initially in the history of the race, people doubtless fell short of attaining the individuality needed for actual personhood. They saw themselves in terms of their roles in a group, acting and interacting with others through the mediation of their environing group and its structures. Who they were—what they and others saw them as being—hinged on their place in a clan or tribe. Morality was not yet upon the scene, because the crucial factor of personhood was lacking, and with it the idea of a responsibility for people as people.

To be a person is to be an *individual*, to see oneself as an intelligent free agent, to be in some substantial degree independent and autonomous (a "law unto oneself"). Personhood in this special sense requires the capacity to define one's own projects (rather than derive them from a preexisting group structure) and to make one's own choices about some important matters in life, or at any rate to *purport* to do so. It involves a sense of self-identity and self-autonomy, planning one's own activities to at least some extent and assuming responsibility for them. It is to see oneself as a free rational agent acting for reasons one accepts as valid and claiming certain rights for oneself. In effect one becomes a person by viewing oneself as such, being prepared to treat others as such, and demanding like treatment by them in return. Much more than simply being a member of *Homo sapiens* is involved.

To be sure, the obligation-universality of moral principles is generally conditional. "*Everyone* ought always to keep valid promises" has the conditional form, "Whoever makes a valid promise, ought to keep it." In this regard, Kurt Baier's analysis goes amiss. He writes:

> Even very general precepts, such as "Stealing is wrong," "Adultery is wrong," "Promise breaking is wrong," "Neglecting your duties is wrong," "Failing to discharge your obligations is wrong," cannot be part of absolute morality, for these refer to specific ways of misusing specific social institutions. Within a given society there might be no institution of property or marriage, no such thing as promising or having duties or obligations. . . . [8]

It is quite correct that in a society without property one cannot steal (improperly take for oneself the property belonging to others) or that in a society of immortals one cannot murder (unjustifiably take another's life), or that in a society without marriage one cannot commit adultery (betray one's pledge of marital fidelity to a spouse). But such observations—however true—simply miss the point, which pivots on the *conditional* thesis: *If* someone steals something from another, *then* he commits a morally wrong act. The fact that some agents may be so circumstanced that stealing is impossible for them in the prevailing conditions is quite irrelevant. (The truth of "Two-headed people have an even number of heads" is not vitiated by the circumstance that people happen to have one head; it turns wholly on the conditional fact that *if* we—or anyone!—had two heads, *then* they would have an even number of heads.) The moral universality of injunctions like "Don't break promises" and "Don't steal" does not hinge on the absolute universality of promising or ownership, but merely on the relativized universality of the principles themselves: where there are genuine promises they should be kept, and where there is proper ownership it should be respected. Moral universality is thus a *conditional* universality. This conditionality abrogates the inherent universality of such principles no more than the laws of biology are abrogated in a region of nature which, like the interior of the sun, lacks organic creatures.

Its conditionality does, however, limit the effective range of a moral rule's immediate application. To say that "lying is wrong" is certainly true. Nevertheless, it may sometimes be morally excusable to lie—to prevent an enraged madman intent on murder from finding his victim, for example. Lying as such can sometimes be the lesser of two evils. One can thus conditionalize the application of the rule. But the matter is very different if we formulate the rule in a suitably qualified form: "Wanton lying is wrong," "Malicious lying is wrong," "Merely convenient lying is wrong," "Pointless lying is wrong," and so on. Once the injunction at issue is itself suitably conditionalized—qualified to preclude the presence of defeating excuses—the moral rules we arrive at are indeed exceptionless and absolute. "Killing is morally wrong" has its difficulties, but since "murder" is tantamount to "*unjustified* killing," the rule "Murder is wrong" is in the clear. When formulated in a duly qualified form, moral rules admit of no exceptions. "Never mislead another" is one thing; "Never mislead another merely for your own advantage" is something quite different.

This aspect of the present account is thoroughly Kantian. The governing idea of Kant's moral theory is that of *universality;* that when an action is wrong or right it is so always and for everyone. The objection urged by various philosophers from Kant's own day to ours is that this overlooked the issue of *circumstances;* that a certain morally improper act, albeit inherently wrong, may in the prevailing conditions serve to avert a yet greater evil. But what people forget (Kant himself occasionally included) is that this very circumstance changes the descriptive *nature* of the act—that telling a falsehood to protect someone's feelings is not adequately described as "lying" but needs to be characterized as "telling a white lie," or that a policeman's shooting someone to avert his killing others is not adequately described as "murder" but rather as "justifiable homicide." The crux is getting the characteristics of that universalizable act right. Those purported counterexamples that critics offer against a Kantian view do not really go to show that lying or murder (that is, what is *properly* characterized as such) are not always wrong. From the moral point of view, the matter of *motivation* is crucial: not every instance of telling a falsehood is a lie nor is every killing a murder.

Its obligation-universality—its inherent claim to binding stringency on all alike—is thus part of the very conception of a moral principle. Morality is inherently absolutistic in imposing its demand. If there indeed are any valid moral principles at all, then they will have to stipulate obligations or entitlements for everyone alike. If it is wrong for *me* to betray the trust of another for my own selfish advantage, then this is wrong for you also, and for anyone else as well. Morality binds everyone. And its benefits are universal as well. A moral rule is appropriate as such only when the mode of action it enjoins is something that is in everyone's interest, even as not being lied to by others is something from which everyone benefits.

Morality is inherently universal not only as regards those whom it obligates but also as regards the scope of its beneficiaries; the range of its proper concern includes *all* of us. If stealing is indeed morally wrong, then it is wrong *for anyone* to steal *from anyone*. The "others" at issue in morality's inherent concern for "the interest of others" must be *people in general*. The "discovery" that women, say, or people of another society ("outsiders," "barbarians") are also *moral* agents—that differences of gender or skin pigmentation or culture are irrelevant from a moral point of view—lies at the very heart of the matter. The operative principle regarding recognition as moral agents is: "When in doubt, don't rule them out." When it is *only* "one's own" family, clan, or class that is involved, then we are dealing with a parochial tribalism and not with *morality*. Morality is not only obligation-universal, it is beneficiary-universal as well.

However, morality does *not* demand that we "treat everyone alike" unqualifiedly. It permits and indeed requires a special duty and responsibility to care for those with whom one has linkages of affection or affinity or dependency. Morality is quite prepared to recognize that our special conditionalized responsibilities towards some—one's children for a parent, one's employees for an industrialist, one's passengers for a sea captain—may *outweigh* one's generic responsibility towards people at large. The point is simply—and crucially—that our moral obligations towards particular people (our own children) or groups (the handicapped) are always inherent in and derivative from strictly universal obligations. ("Discharge your obligations towards those for whom you are responsible is a patently universal principle.")

What renders morality *beneficiary*-universal is accordingly the combination of two circumstances: that the crux of the moral enterprise lies in protecting or enhancing the valid interests of persons, and that validity in this context turns on universality. For example, *everyone* has an interest in: not being physically harmed, not being lied to or deceived, not being unjustly discriminated against, not being deprived of opportunities for self-development. Such universal desiderata through this very fact represent morally valid interests. And this illustrates the general situation. The demands of morality are inherently beneficiary-universal because in heeding them we commit ourselves to benefiting people indiscriminately, seeing that such demands appertain to universal interests that all *persons*—indeed all rational beings—share alike.[9]

5. MORALITY'S LINK TO SELF-INTEREST: THE SOCIAL IMPERATIVE

The contention that if one acts so as to advance the general welfare of the social group one thereby furthers one's personal advantage is simply not a descriptive truth—it is not a statement of actual fact. But if the thesis of a reciprocal coordination of personal and social advantage is not an inescapable fact (and it is not), it is at any rate a regulative ideal. What is asserted may not actually be so, but this is indeed how things *ought* to be arranged, and how, in a morally well-ordered society, they actually *would* be. In an *ideal* state of affairs, it would indeed serve the self-interest of people to promote the general good: someone who exerts himself for the welfare of his fellows ought not to find his own abridged thereby, and someone who consults his own best interests ought to find that in serving them he advances those of others as well.

We thus arrive at a socially oriented demand of individual morality, an injunction to act so as to realize a social order in which action for prudential self-advantage is—at least by and large—also coincidental with action for the common good. From the moral point of view we ought to strive individually to realize a morally well-ordered society. And in a morally well-ordered society the correlation of action for individual advantage and for the social good *ought* to obtain; that is, the society ought to be so organized that this coordinative principle is operative.

We must recognize the social-engineering aspect of shaping a social order that has an "adequate moral economy" in this sense of coordination between action for personal advantage and the general good. The particular circumstances of a society will shape the nature of the customs and practices that make the channels of life flow smoothly (keeping an orderly queue versus a free-for-all, to take a very simple example). But the general direction of the task is clear: the weaving of a fabric of social incentives and sanctions (rewards and punishments) to assure balance between individual and general advantage by rendering socially benign action personally rewarding and antisocial action personally counterproductive. The development of institutions that both conduce toward the socially advantageous and deter individuals from socially deleterious behavior is a crucial desideratum. And on this basis so is the coordination of the demands of other-concerned morality with personal self-interest.

Its merits stress that the nonutilitarian morality underlying this position shares the characteristically attractive feature of utilitarian morality that sees moral obligation not simply in the negative terms of avoidance of wrongdoing (the essentially negative morality of the Old Testament injunction "Thou shalt not . . .") but also as enjoining the creative effort needed to forge the conditions of an adequate moral economy. A properly ordered society has not only the *right* but also the *duty* to foster a socially minded modus operandi by which its individuals are motivationally constrained to act for the common good.[10]

Thus while there is unquestionably a significant gap between individual and general advantage, there is a moral imperative to work toward narrowing it as much as possible so as to create a public order that ensures an adequate moral economy: a coordination of individual and social advantage within the framework of a calculus of interests. The forging of an adequate moral economy is also a crucial social desideratum. It is in everyone's interest to create a social system in which it is in everyone's interest to act morally in a manner advantageous to the social benefit. Thus a relationship between interest and morality indeed exists, not at the first level but at the second remove: *Everyone has a personal interest in so arranging matters that it comes to be in everyone's interest to act as morality demands.* It thus it emerges as a duty—albeit one seldom stressed by moralists—to work for a society in which both moral virtues and the virtuous themselves can thrive.

The dictates of morality demand that the private interest be harnessed to the general interest, so that the motive powers of individual action become productively conducive to the public weal. But the arrangements that can assure this linkage are not automatic, natural, and inevitable; they can only be a social creation, an *artifact*. Indeed, at the aggregative level needed to establish a moral economy, only society can foster the interests of the general good. The individual agent is impotent to do more than contribute his minute bit toward shifting society in this direction. Yet doing so remains part of his moral obligation.

The circumstances of the present case are such, however, that the philosopher's penchant for connections of necessity cannot be implemented here. The actual existence of a linkage between self-interested prudential advantage and the common good is a matter of the purely contingent and empirical circumstances of particular cases. Only if conditions happen to be appropriately arranged, through the creation of a social environment of a suitable sort—an "adequate moral economy"—can there be proper coordination between the *in principle discordant* factors at issue. Only in an idealized, utopian social order will personal advantage and public good be automatically coordinated. Objectivity's characteristic harmonization of the personal and the universal should be brought to realization here.

Accordingly, the moralist should not condemn self-interest but should recognize a duty to ennoble it—a duty, that is, to foster circumstances in which personal advantage is brought into coordination with the public interest, so that actions from these two very different ethical motivations should come to the same thing in practical effect.

At this point, that is, in the final accounting, morality and personal advantage come into coordination. Morality calls for working toward a social order where moral comportment is advantageous. And in the operative setting of a really well-ordered society, self-advantage—even brute, crass self-advantage—will call for working toward exactly the same end.[11]

— eleven —

VALUE OBJECTIVITY

Synopsis

(1) The pursuit of objectivity in evaluative matters does emphatically not *require putting one's own values aside—which would in any case be humanly impossible. Rather, the issue of value objectivity comes down to the question of whether rational deliberation about value is possible. (2) Thinkers in the Humean tradition hold that it is not, that all valuation is simply a matter of desires—of people's wants and preferences. But this view is very doubtful indeed. For being the sorts of creatures we humans are, we have interests which, as such, control the validity of our wants and preferences. Valuation is clearly something subject to reason once the matter of what is necessary for or advantageous to human well-being enters upon the scene. (3) The appropriateness of reasoning about values means that evaluation is not a matter of mere subjectivity. (4) And seeing that values do not simply "lie in the mind of the evaluator," a value realism of sorts is warranted. The sort of rational appraisal at issue with value objectivity is emphatically possible.*

1. OBJECTIVITY AND VALUES

Does objectivity demand that one put one's values aside? That very much depends on how the matter of what is at issue with values is going to be understood. Values, so it is often said, are mere matters of taste, mere personal predilections. If this were true, then objectivity would indeed require them to be sidelined. But is it so? The question comes down to whether normatively cogent accounts are ever available with evaluative matters. Some philosophers despair on this issue.[1] But their despair is hardly justifiable.

Tastes, as usually understood, represent unreasoned preferences and predilections, and there is consequently no disputing about them. If I prefer *X* to *Y* then that's that. But values are something quite different. They relate not to what we prefer but to what we deem preferable—that is, *worthy* of preference. And preference *worthiness* is something that is always discussible and disputable. To claim—in a manner that is sensible and reasonable—that X is preferable to Y, I must be in a position to back my claim with reasons. And this reason-boundedness of sensible evaluations carries them outside the range of mere matters of taste. The person who is not prepared to back an option of X over Y by reasons is merely evincing a preference and not actually making an evaluation at all. Value claims by their very nature as such fall within the domain of reason.

With a subjective response—matters of taste as a prominent example—the particular individual is indeed the final arbiter. Whether you *like* or *enjoy* or *approve of* a particular experience or a particular sort of thing is up to you. In such matters of personal inclination and reaction, subjectivity reigns. But whether something *deserves* being liked (or enjoyed or approved of), whether a sensible person *ought* to like it (or enjoy or approve of it) is certainly not such a matter of taste. It is an objective matter, a matter of reasonableness and rationality. For if something is indeed enjoyable (or likable or tragic or comic) there must be some sort of cogent account for why sensible people ought to find it so.

Rationality and its accompanying objectivity, accordingly, do not require putting values aside. Objectivity is not a matter of value disconnection; it is a matter of evaluative appropriateness. It calls for proceeding in such a way that the values appropriate to the context at hand are taken account of in a rationally defensible way. And as long as there are good reasons to support the evaluations that we make—as indeed there should and must be—objectivity will have to play a crucial part in the value domain.

Given the nature of the human situation, we are impelled (insofar as rational) to align our values and our needs. Like various beliefs, some evaluations will be palpably crazy. Reason, after all, is not just a matter of the compatibility or consistency of pre-given commitments, but of the warrant that there is for undertaking certain commitments in the first place. An *evaluative* rationality that informs us that certain preferences are absurd—preferences that wantonly violate our nature, impair our being, or diminish our opportunities—fortunately lies within the human repertoire. And it will not do to limit the bearing of reason to the strictly factual issue of felt needs and wants as interdistinguished from the normative issue of best interests. Our wants are certainly no gift horses into whose mouths it is inappropriate to look. For people can clearly have desires (for harm to rivals) or needs (for "recreational" drugs on which they have come to depend) that can go against their real interests.

It is thus a grave mistake to think that one cannot reason about values, that values are simply a matter of taste and thereby beyond the reach of reason, since "there's no reasoning about tastes." The fact that valid values implement and pivot upon our legitimate needs and our appropriate interests means that a rational critique of values is not only possible but necessary. Values that impede the realization of a person's best interests are clearly inappropriate.

Accordingly, people cannot—must not—refrain from making evaluations. For with reasonableness and its consequent objectivity the cardinal principle is: *To proceed as any rational / reasonable person would in the circumstances.* And so objectivity does not elbow values aside. If values were no more than mere personal tastes and preferences, then objectivity would indeed call for leaving them out of account. But this is simply not the case. To be objective in evaluative contexts is not to suppress one's evaluations but rather to conform them to the requirements of reason. There is no reason why evaluative judgments cannot be impersonally context appropriate, that is, freed from the distorting impetus of bias, prejudice, etc. In matters of evaluation, or elsewhere, rationality is a critical factor and objectivity is something that comes along in its wake.

The fact is that values are at bottom not an elective matter. They pivot not on wants but on authentic needs—or on what is necessary or desirable for us. For we humans, being the sorts of creatures we are, have interests which as such should (insofar as we are rational) control the validation of our wants and preferences. For us humans, the validation of evaluations is not and cannot be a matter of mere subjectivity. The projects into which our nature impels us—the medical project, say, or the alimentary project, or the cognitive—thus in turn carry certain value commitments in their wake. We come here to the matter of what is necessary to or advantageous for human well-being. A priority scheme that sets mere wants above real needs or sets important objectives aside to avert trivial inconveniences is thereby deeply flawed. Even great values will have to yield to the yet greater. (Some things are rightly dearer to us than life itself.)

Specifically in the cognitive case there are two categories of values, those at work in rational inquiry at large as contrasted with the differential desires, wishes, or preferences of particular individuals and groups.

Generic Values at Work in Rational Inquiry	Self-Promoting Values that Influence Individuals and Groups
truth	influence
accuracy	power
due care	reputation
verifiability	personal enrichment
rational economy	

The crux of objectivity is that it calls for a commitment to values of the former (performance enhancing) as contrasted with the latter (status enhancing) sort, although by and large the ethos of the scientific community tends to bring the two together by coordinating status with contributions. The issue is not one of dedication to values as such, but rather one of the kind of values one dedicates oneself to. After all, objectivity itself can and should serve as an important cognitive value.

In an oft-cited passage in Book III of the *Nicomachean Ethics*, Aristotle wrote:

> We deliberate not about ends but about means. For a doctor does not deliberate whether he shall heal, nor an orator whether he shall persuade, nor a statesman whether he shall produce law and order, nor does anyone else deliberate about his end. They assume the end and consider how and by what means it is to be attained; and if it seems to be produced by several means they consider by which it is most easily and best produced, while if it is achieved by one only they consider how it will be achieved by this and by what means *this* will be achieved, till they come to the first cause, which in the order of discovery is last. (*N.E.*1112b12–20)

The sort of thinking that Aristotle has in view here—deliberation about efficient means for realizing preestablished ends—is unquestionably important in human affairs. "I need a bed; to make a bed I need a hammer and saw; I can borrow a hammer; so I shall go and buy a saw." Aristotle's own examples of practical reasoning are exactly of this common and familiar sort, and are plausible enough in their way.[2] However, not *all* deliberative reasoning is means-end reasoning. Admittedly, the doctor does not deliberate about treating people's illness—that choice is already settled, included as part of one's decision to become a doctor. But a young person may well deliberate about whether to become a doctor in the first place, reflecting on whether this would be something good for her, given her abilities, skills, interests, options, and so on. And this sort of deliberation is not a question of means to preestablished ends at all. The long and short of it is that there are two very different sorts of deliberations: cognitive deliberations regarding matters of *information* (encompassing the issue of the efficiency of means), and evaluative deliberations regarding matters of *value* (encompassing the issue of the merit of ends). Whether certain means are appropriate to given ends is a question whose resolution must be addressed in the former, informational order of deliberation. But whether the ends we have are appropriate as such, whether they *merit* adoption, is an issue which can and must be addressed in the latter, evaluative order of deliberation.

Rationality plays a crucial role here. For our human situation is such as to impose certain needs upon us and rationality requires their recognition. Moreover, a rational agent certainly cannot say: " I adopt G as a goal of mine, but am indifferent regarding the efficiency and effectiveness of means towards this goal." But no more can a rational person say: "I adopt G as a goal of mine, but am indifferent regarding its validity; I just don't care about the larger issue of its appropriateness as such." Both matters—the efficacy of means and the validity of goals—are essential aspects of practical rationality. And here, as elsewhere, rationality will carry objectivity in its wake.

2. EVALUATIVE RATIONALITY AND APPROPRIATE ENDS: AGAINST THE HUMEAN CONCEPTION OF REASON

Given that value objectivity pivots on the rational defensibility of values, the issue of value objectivity is intertwined with the question of whether rational deliberation about value matters is indeed possible.

David Hume drew a sharp contrast between a (narrowly construed) "reason" that is concerned only with means and is wholly inert as to ends and a very different, reason-detached faculty of motivation that does concern itself with ends, namely, the passions. And he considered these motivating passions as autonomous forces operating outside the realm of reason proper; reason has nothing to do with them, they lie outside its prominence. He regarded an impetus toward or away from some object—a desire or aversion—as simply the wrong sort of thing to be rational or sensible; as lying outside the rational domain altogether.

As Hume saw it, the formal issues of logic and mathematics apart, reason merely deals in descriptive information about the world's states of affairs and relationships of cause and effect. Accordingly, reason is strictly instrumental: it can inform me about what I must do *if* I wish to arrive at a certain destination, but only "passion"—desire or aversion—can make something into a destination for me. When one asks what is to be done, reason as such has no instructions—it is wholly a matter of what one happens to want. Reason is thus a "slave of the passions." Its modus operandi is strictly conditional: it dictates hypothetically that if you accept this, then you cannot (in all consistency) fail to accept that. But, all this is a matter of the hypothetical if-then. The categorical "Accept this!" is never a mandate of reason, but of that extra-rational faculty of "the passions," which dictates the bestowal of one's *unconditional* allegiances. Reason herself is inherently conditionalized: she says not what one must (or must not) opt for, but only what one is consequentially committed to if one *already* stands committed to something else.

Hume insisted:

It is not contrary to reason to prefer the destruction of the whole world to the scratching of my finger. It is not contrary to reason for me to choose my total ruin. . . . It is as little contrary to reason to prefer even my own acknowledged lesser good to my greater, and to have a more ardent affection for the former than the latter.[3]

But this is clearly strange stuff. A "rationality" that precludes the prospect of irrational affections and devises is no rationality at all. If this is indeed how Hume's reason works, then few of us are sending on the same wavelength.[4] On any plausible view of the matter, reason cannot simply beg off from considering the validity of ends. Our motivating "passions" can surely themselves be rational or otherwise: those that impel us towards things that are bad for us or away from things that are good for us go against reason, those that impel us away from things that are bad for us and towards things that are good for us are altogether rational.

We cannot divorce rationality from a concern for people's best (i.e., "real" or "true") interests. Reason can and should deliberate not only about what it is ill-advised to believe (because it is probably at odds with the truth), but also about what it is ill-advised to esteem (because it is probably at odds with our interests). Rationality is not just a matter of keeping our

beliefs consistent among themselves and compatible with what we acknowledge as true, but also one of keeping our evaluative judgments
consistent among themselves and compatible with what we can appropriately recognize as being in our genuinely best interest.

Evaluative contentions along the lines of "Smith is selfish, inconsiderate,
and boorish" thus do not lie outside the sphere of rational inquiry—nor
for that matter do contentions like "Behavior that is selfish / inconsiderate / boorish is against the best interest of people." The issue of *appropriate*
action in the circumstances in which we find ourselves is pivotal for rationality. Be it in matters of belief, action, or evaluation, we want—that is,
often do and always *should* want—to do the best we can. For, one cannot
be rational without due care for the desirability of what one desires—the
issue of its alignment with our *real*, as distinguished from our *putative*, or
merely seeming, interests.

Hume's profound error lay in his taking a part of *reason* to be the *whole*
of it. For, reason at large must care for ends as well as means. If our ends
(our goals and values) are themselves inappropriate—if they run counter
to our real and legitimate interests—then no matter how sagaciously we
cultivate them, we are not being fully rational. (A voyage to a foolish destination, no matter how efficiently conducted, is a foolish enterprise.)
Hume mistakenly effected a total divorce between reason and choice: "I
have prov'd that reason is perfectly inert, and can never either prevent or
produce any action or affection."[5] But, while reason indeed cannot of itself
"prevent or produce" action, the fact remains that it can justify and thereby
motivate action through providing good reasons for it. When rational inquiry indicates to me that doing act *A* is beneficial, then—insofar as I am
rational—it impels me towards this action. Alternatively, if it indicates
that the action is detrimental, it impels me away from it. Reason's task
in relation to action is to provide *grounds* for or against. Of course, the
consideration that something is the rational thing for her to do in the circumstances will not move an agent to do so unless she also takes the stance
"I shall heed the instructions of reason—be it by explicit intent ot tactit
habit." But just this, of course, is the stance which is routinely mandatory
for all those of us who see ourselves as rational agents and set ourselves to
act accordingly. And this means that any disconnection of reason from
action is quite mistaken. To see reason as irrelevant to the validation of
choice and action over and above matters of efficiency is to misrepresent
it to the point of caricature.

Evaluation lies at the very heart of rationality. For rationality is a matter
of balancing costs and benefits, of best serving our overall interests. The

question of worth is thus never far removed from the thoughts of a rational mind. The rationality of ends is an indispensable component of rationality at large. The rationality of our actions hinges critically both on the appropriateness of our ends *and* on the suitability of the means by which we pursue their cultivation. Both of these components—the *cogently cognitive* ("*intelligent* pursuit") and the *normatively purposive* ("*appropriate* ends")—are alike essential to full-fledged rationality.

The rationality of ends is an indispensable component of rationality at large for two reasons. (1) Rationally valued ends must be evaluatively appropriate ones: if we adopt inappropriate ends we are not being rational, no matter how efficiently and effectively we pursue them. (2) We cannot proceed rationally without considering the ends-relative value of our means, inquiring whether the cost of those means (the resources we are expending through them) is consonant with the values supposedly being realized through the ends, by asking: "If *those* costs are involved in the means, then are the ends really worth it?" Without rational evaluation, practical rationality becomes infeasible as a meaningful project, with fatal consequences for rationality as a whole, given the systematic unity of reason.

Action in pursuit of what we ourselves desire is not automatically rendered rational by this fact. The crucial issue is one of evaluating that desire itself, of determining whether the desired object is actually desirable, something *worthy* of desire. (Desire may be enough to *explain* an action, but it is not thereby enough to qualify it as rational.) Other things being equal, it is rational to pursue one's wants. But generally other things are not equal. In the main, the point is not what we do want but what we *ought to* want, not what we desire but "what's good for us." And when these differ, rationality and desire part ways. (From the rational point of view it is *counterproductive* to pursue wants at the expense of needs and real interests.) Being desired does not automatically make something desirable, or being valued make it valuable. The pivot is how matters *ought* to be.

Economists, decision theorists, and utilitarian philosophers generally hold that rationality turns on the intelligent cultivation of one's *preferences*. But this is problematic in the extreme (as the preceding chapter argued). Such a formula would only begin to be tenable if one happened to have sufficiently enlightened preferences. And this of course is not necessarily so. What I want or merely may think to be good for me is one thing; what I need and what actually is good for me is another. To move from preferences and perceived interests to genuine benefits and real interests I must be prepared to get involved in a rational critique of ends, to examine in the light of objective standards whether what I desire is desirable, whether my actual ends are rational ends, whether my putative interests are real interests. The genuinely rational person is the one who proceeds in situations of choice by asking himself not the introspective question "What do I prefer?" but the objective question "What is to be deemed preferable? What *ought* I to prefer on the basis of my best interests?"[6] Rational comportment does not just call for desire satisfaction, it demands desire management as well. The question of *appropriateness* is crucial. And this is an issue about which people can be—and often are—irrational; not just careless but even perverse, self-destructive, and crazy.

But just what is it that is in a person's real or best interests? Partly, this is indeed a matter of meeting the needs that people universally have in common: health, satisfactory functioning of body and mind, adequate resources, human companionship and affection, and so on.[7] Partly, it is a matter of the particular role one plays: cooperative children are in the interests of a parent, customer loyalty in those of a shopkeeper. Partly, it is a matter of what one simply happens to want. (If John loves Mary, then engaging Mary's attention and affections are in John's interests—some things are in a person's interests simply because he takes an interest in them.) But these want-related interests are valid only by virtue of their relation to universal interests. Mary's approbation is in John's interest only because "having the approbation of someone we love" is in *anyone's* interest. Any valid *specific* interest must fall within the validating scope of an appropriate *universal* covering principle of interest legitimation. (The development of my stamp collection is in my interest only because it is part of a hobby that constitutes an avocation for me and "securing adequate relaxation and diversion from the stress of one's daily cares" is something that is in *anyone's* interests.) A specific (concrete, particular) interest of a person is valid as such only if it can be subordinated to a universal interest by way of having a basis in people's legitimate needs.

To proceed rationally we must care not just for the efficacy of means but for the worth of ends. Man is not only *homo sapiens* but *homo aestimans*. The most fundamental judgment we make regarding even merely hypothetical developments is whether they are or are not "a good thing." Being rational involves endeavoring to do well (intelligently) what we must by nature do, and evaluation is, emphatically, a part of this.

Consider the contrast between:

- *professed wants*: what I say or declare that I want or prefer;
- *felt wants*: what I (actually) do want or prefer;

- *real (or appropriate) wants*: what the reasonable (impartial, well-informed, well-intentioned, understanding) bystander would think that I ought to want on the basis of what is "in my best interests."

It is this last item that is decisive for rationality, namely, what is in my "real" or "best" interests. Rationality is not just a matter of doing what we *want* (if this were so, it would be far simpler to attain!), it is a matter of doing what we (rationally) *ought*, given the situation in which we find ourselves. Those initial two steps are indeed subjective. But with that third, rationality-geared item, objectivity comes into operation. For wants are rational just exactly insofar as they inhere in one's needs and harmonize with them overall.

Values are purposive instrumentalities. They are functional objects that have a natural teleology, that of aiding us to lead lives that satisfy (meet our individual needs) and are communally productive (facilitate the realization of constructive goals for the community at large). The rationality of ends inheres in the simple fact that we humans have various valid *needs*, that we require not only nourishment and protection against the elements for the maintenance of health but also information ("cognitive orientation"), affection, freedom of action, and much else besides. Without such varied goods we cannot thrive as human beings, we cannot achieve the condition of human well-being that Aristotle called "flourishing." The person who does not give these manifold desiderata their due—who may even set out to frustrate their realization—is clearly not being rational.

These various "goods" are not simply instrumental means to other goods; they are aspects or components of what is in itself a quintessentially good end in its relation to us—human flourishing. What that involves and how it is particularized in the concrete situation of specific individuals is something complex and internally variegated. But it is this overarching desideratum that validates the rest. Flourishing as *humans*, as the sorts of creatures we are, patently is *for us* an intrinsic good (though not, to be sure, necessarily the supreme good). We are so situated that from our vantage point (and who else's can be decisive for us?) it is clearly something that must be seen as good. We need not deliberate about it, need not endeavor to excogitate it from other premises; for us, it comes direct—as an inevitable "given."

But what of "mere whims and fancies." If I have a yen for eating crabgrass, is my doing so not a perfectly appropriate "interest" of mine? Yes it is. But only because it is covered by perfectly cogent universal interest, that of "Doing what I feel like doing in circumstances where neither injury to me nor harm to others is involved." It is these higher-level principles that are the controlling factors from the standpoint of reason and provide the fulcrum for objectivity's generality.

Accordingly, a person's "appropriate interests" will have a substantial element of personal relativity. Only at the most abstract and generic level will my need be exactly the same as yours. One person's self-ideal, as shaped and concretized in the light of his own value structure, will thus—quite appropriately—be different from that of another. And what sorts of interests a person has will hinge in significant measure on the particular circumstances and conditions in which he finds himself—including his wishes and desires. (In the *absence* of any countervailing considerations, getting what I want is in my best interests.) All the same, there is also a large body of real interests that people share in common, for example, as regards standard of living (health and resources) and quality of life (opportunities and conditions), and it is these factors of life sustainment and enrichment that are ultimately determinative of the validity of individualized interests. Both sorts of interests—the idiosyncratic and the generic—play a determinative role in the operations of rationality.

There is nothing automatically appropriate, let alone sacred, about our own ends, objectives, and preferences. We can be every bit as irrational in the adoption of ends as in any other choice. Apparent interests are not automatically real, getting what one wants is not necessarily to one's benefit, goals are not rendered valid by their mere adoption. People's ends can be self-destructive, self-defeating impediments to the realization of their true needs. For rationality, the crucial question is that of the true value of the item at issue. What counts is not preference but preferability—not what people do want, but what they *ought* to want; not what *people* actually want, but what *sensible* or *right-thinking* people would want under the circumstances. The normative aspect is inescapable. Rationality calls for objective judgment, for an assessment of preferability rather than for a mere expression of preference. The rationality of ends, their rational appropriateness and legitimacy, is accordingly a crucial aspect of rationality. More is at issue with rationality than a matter of strict instrumentality— mere effectiveness in the pursuit of ends no matter how inappropriate they may be. When we impute to our ends a weight and value they do not in fact have, we pursue mere will-o'-the-wisps. There is an indissoluble connection between the true value of something (its being good or right or useful) and the rationality of choosing or preferring this thing. And so, the crucial question for rationality is not that of what we prefer but of what is in our best interests; not simply what we may happen to desire but what is good for us in the sense of contributing to the realization of our true interests. The pursuit of what we want is rational only insofar as we have objectively *sound* reasons for deeming this to be want-deserving. The question of whether what we prefer is preferable, in the sense of *deserving* this preference, is always relevant. Ends can and (in the context of rationality) *must* be evaluated. It is not just beliefs that can be stupid, ill-advised, and inappropriate—that is to say, *irrational*—but ends as well.

The crucial fact is that there is not only inferential ("logical") reason but also evaluative ("axiological") reason. Just as rational people believe only what is belief-worthy for someone in the circumstances, so they value only what is value-worthy—*deserving* of being valued. And the determination of value-worthiness requires the sensible application of appropriate standards—in short, reasoning. For it is quintessentially the work of reasoning to determine what sorts of commitments are rational (reason-conforming) and what sorts are not. (And this is so whether the "commitments" at issue be beliefs or evaluations.)[8] Only when we make an evaluative commitment contrary to the requirements of reason do we thereby enter into the realm of the strictly subjective.[9]

As this perspective indicates, rationality involves two sorts of issues—means and ends. The rationality of means is a matter of factual information alone—of what sorts of moves and measures lead efficiently to objectives. But the rationality of ends is a matter not of *information* but of *legitimation*. It is not settled just by factual inquiry, but involves appraisal and evaluative judgment. And in the larger scheme of things both aspects are needed: ends without requisite means are frustrating, means without suitable ends are unproductive and pointless. Accordingly, rationality has two sides: an *axiological* (evaluative) concern for the appropriateness of ends and an *instrumental* (cognitive) concern for effectiveness and efficiency in their cultivation. The conception of rationality fuses these two elements into one integral and unified whole.

The sensible attunement of means to ends that is characteristic of rationality calls for an appropriate balancing of costs and benefits in our choice among alternative ways of resolving our cognitive, practical, and evaluative problems. Reason accordingly demands determination of the true value of things. Even as cognitive reason requires that in determining what we are to accept we should assess the evidential grounds for theses at their true worth, so evaluative reason requires us to appraise the values of our practical options at their true worth in determining what we are to choose or prefer. And this calls for an objectively cogent cost-benefit analysis. Values must be managed as an overall "economy" in a rational way to achieve overall harmonization and optimization. (Economic rationality is not the only sort of rationality there is, but it is an important aspect of overall rationality.) Someone who rejects such economic considerations—who, in the absence of any envisioned compensating advantages, deliberately purchases for millions benefits he recognizes as being worth a few pennies—is simply not rational. It is just as irrational to let one's efforts in the pursuit of chosen objectives incur costs that outrun their true worth as it is to let one's beliefs run afoul of the evidence.

3. VALUE OBJECTIVITY

Some writers (J.-P. Sartre, for example) see reason-providing considerations in the practical sphere as locked into a potentially infinite regress that can be broken only by an ultimate appeal to unreasoned "reasons" that lie in the domain of judgmental decisions and acts of will. But this is just not how things go in the explanation and the validation of actions. Here, the regress of reasons (*A* because *B* because *C*) will and must terminate automatically and naturally with any normatively valid universal reason—an interest which it is only proper and appropriate for *anyone* to have when other things are anything like equal. I want *this* sandwich because I am hungry, and I want to stop feeling hungry (i.e., relieve those hunger pangs) because it is painful. But there is just no point in going further—and no need for it. When such a universal is reached, no further elaboration is called for. (It is this circumstance that endows the matter of the rational validation of ends with its importance.) The regress of reason ends not in individual wants but in universal needs, not in idiosyncratic acts of will but in the recognition of objective requirements.

The rationality of ends is essential to rationality as such; there is no point in running—however swiftly—to a destination whose attainment conveys no benefit. It is useless to maintain "rational consonance" relative to what we believe or do or value if those items with respect to which we relativize are not rational in the first place. Principles of relative rationality are pointless in the absence of principles of categorical rationality.

Wants per se (wants unexamined and unevaluated) may well provide impelling *motives* for action, but will not thereby constitute good *reasons* for action. To be sure, it is among our needs to have some of our wants satisfied. But, it is needs that are determinative for interests, and not wants as such. A person's *true* interests are not those he *does have* but those he *would have* if he conducted his investigative business and his evaluative business properly (sensibly, appropriately). A person's *welfare* is often ill-served by his *wishes*—which may be altogether irrational, perverse, or pathological.[10] This distinction of appropriateness—of *real*, as opposed to *merely seeming*, wants and interests—is crucial for evaluative rationality. The latter turns on what we merely happen to want at the time, the former on what we *should* want, and thus on "what we would want if"—if we were all those things that "being intelligent" about the conduct of one's life requires: prudent, sensible, conscientious, well-considered, and the like.[11] And so here, as elsewhere, rationality carries objectivity in its wake.

What makes evaluation a rational enterprise is the fact that values are *objective* in at least one of the various senses of that term, namely, in that evaluation is subject to *standards* of appropriateness/inappropriateness or correctness/incorrectness. For only through standards can we reach that impersonality and generality of application which is crucial to objectivity. What separates evaluations from mere preferences is that the former involves standards. In evaluating we bring criteria to bear on whose basis the ideas in question are rated as good or bad, superior or inferior, just or unjust, etc. Evaluations will, as such, have to be backed by reason articulated in terms of the relevant norms—norms which ultimately inhere in the architecture of our generalizable needs.

To get beyond the level of means–evaluation (i.e., of assessment of efficiency in the realization of otherwise unevaluated ends), then, we must also have criteria of inherent positivity that constitute standards for evaluation of ends. And in the case of us humans these must, in the final analysis, pivot on whether the items at issue somehow manage to serve a genuine interest of ours, that is, function universally in some way conducive to enabling us to flourish as human beings. The objectivity of rational evaluation ultimately roots in the nature of our real interests. To be sure, this issue of real interests is itself in part normative. But this fact does not establish a vicious circularity: it simply reflects the fact that the value domain is probatively self-contained, that it lies in the very nature of things that in cogent reasoning about values we cannot reach evaluative conclusions without evaluative inputs—exactly in parallel with the case of factual issues. (To be sure, those inputs can be "mere truisms.")

The lesson for the question of value objectivity is clear. Once the issue of the rationality of ends is accepted as meaningful, the objectivity of evaluation is something that follows immediately in its wake. What thus matters for our present concern with objectivity is that evaluations can be validly supportable by rational considerations, that a sensible case can be made from endorsing them (as *justified*, not necessarily as *true*), that they can be supported by sensible considerations and convincing arguments. What counts is that we should be able to reason about evaluative issues by cogent reasoning that (fully) rational people are bound to accept as such and that all people in consequence should accept.

4. CIRCULARITY AND CLOSURE: THE SYSTEMIC UNITY OF REASON

Rationality is a matter of the intelligent pursuit of appropriate ends. And here "intelligence" bespeaks knowledge, "pursuit" indicates action, and "appropriate ends" calls for evaluation. A seeming circularity is at work. Value legitimation turns on rationally appropriate interests and interest legitimation turns on a process of rational evaluation.

This sort of circularity is not, however, anything vicious and self-defeating. For it is clear that all sectors of reason must be invoked and coordinated in any formula that adequately characterizes the overall nature of rationality. To serve its function as a guide to human actions and inter-actions, reason must eliminate disorder and dissonance and similar impediments to well-coordinated thought, and accordingly she strives—always and everywhere—for consistency, uniformity, generality, and orderly harmony of all sorts. Rationality demands that our beliefs, evaluations, and actions should "make sense." And this means that the whole fabric of rationality must be seamless; cognition, evaluation, and action must form a cohesive unit. Under the aegis of rationality, these three domains form part of a single, uniform, and coordinated whole. If our acts are based on inappropriate beliefs, they lack rational justification; if our beliefs do not admit of implementation in practice, they too suffer a defect of rationality; if our values are inappropriate they clearly go against reason. In no such case would a *rational* agent be able to muster the confidence necessary for effectual thought and action.

It is this holistic unity of reason that serves to secure our analysis against a charge of circularity. For someone might object "How can you say that

A presupposes *B* and *C*, and yet that *B* presupposes *A* and *C*?" The response is, that this is *not* what has been said. We have spoken in terms of involvement, not *pre*-supposition; of mutual connection, not of preliminary requirement. What is at issue in relating the three modes of rationality is a matter not of sequential priority but of systematic coordination, of reciprocal consonance rather than linear order. The only "circularity" that is relevant is the fact that there must be evaluative inputs into the rational evaluation/validation of values, and that is not vicious. It is simply part of the self-supportiveness of reason.

A skeptical objection yet remains:

> All this emphasis on the role of reason is problematic. For surely our own intellectual tradition—with its heavily rational orientation—is not the only viable one. Consider such alternatives as the mysticism of the Zen Buddhist, the otherworldly religiosity of monasticism, the aestheticism of the bohemian, the utopianism of the political visionary. Rationality does not occupy a high place in such alternative value-hierarchies, since various other values (desirelessness, self-control, godliness, attunement to the march of history, or the like) would take a superior place. How then can you ultimately justify a determinative role for the value commitments of *your own* particular rationalistic tradition (with its emphasis on cognitive truth and pragmatic success), in contrast to the variant values of such reason-subordinating traditions?

But, this line has its difficulties. Questions about the rational appropriateness of an appeal to reason are analogous in character to the question "Can I ever pose meaningful questions?" By the time one poses *this* question, it is already too late to ask. The point of no return has been passed; the issue has become academic. One has *already* reached a juncture where no further observations on the issue can reasonably be demanded. If it is a *rational* justification for valuing reason that the objector demands of us, then this consideration gives rationality a special standing of (context-relative) preeminence from the very outset.

After all, how can someone who is prepared to join the mystic or the bohemian in subordinating reason to other values sensibly proceed? How can one cogently defend such priorities save by reasoned argumentation? And how can one intelligently implement them save by thinking their implications through? One can certainly live a life that does not grant prominent value to reason. (No doubt about that—instances abound on every side.) But, given reason's nature, one cannot do so intelligently. A mode of life can indeed be advocated by people from the standpoint of an a-rational tradition—mystical, or aesthetic, or hedonistic. But such a "justification" can be *cogent* only insofar as it is rational.

Reason's autonomy from "external" pressures means that there just is no "greater" or "higher" authority to which she answers, no court of higher jurisdiction to which appeal from the decrees of reason can *reasonably* be made. But, to say this is not, of course, to say that man lives by reasoning alone. To see reason as autonomous is certainly not to deny that there are important human goods and goals outside the domain of ratiocination. Rather, it is simply to say that insofar as other human enterprises have valid claims upon us reason is in a position to discern this and to value them for it. Reason, then, is the arbiter of value albeit not an external arbiter but a complex quality-control resource that itself contains an evaluative sector.

And it is the ultimate arbiter. For it lies in the nature of things that "the rational thing to do" cannot be rationally overridden; it is just exactly what must win out in rational deliberation. It is *never* sensible to proceed unintelligently. Rationality is (rationally) indefeasible. One can certainly reject or neglect reason. But, one cannot do so in a sensible, rationally defensible way. To produce an argument against reason is already to do it homage. Reason is autonomous: no wholly alien authority is in a position to lord it over her. Rational justification—including the rational justification of placing reliance on reason—admits of no court of appeal whose authority is not endorsed by reason herself.

5. VALUE REALISM

But what of the other mode of objectivity/subjectivity than one concerned with the ontological dimension of the matter. Do our values have an ontological standing—is value realism of some sort in order?

Three distinctively different sorts of value realism can be envisioned:

- *Alethic realism.* Do evaluative contentions fall into the range of assertions characterizable as true or false?
- *Property realism.* Does the ascription of value to things of a certain sort (acts of artifacts, say) attribute objective (and thus evidentiable, perhaps even "observable") properties to those items?
- *Warrant realism.* Can evaluative contentions be supported by objective, rationally cogent considerations that, when duly legitimated, can justify people in maintaining them?

Let us begin with the alethic case: the controversy over the question whether evaluative claims are to be categorized as having a truth status, as being true or false.[12] This mode of realism turns on the issue of whether evaluations can be assimilated to statements (assertions or propositions) in the specific regard that the particular appraisal categories true-false are applicable to them as well. This issue seemingly arises in the present context because it might seem that in regarding certain evaluative claims as "trivial and truistic," our present discussion is predicated on an affirmative, realism-endorsing stance on this issue. But this is not actually the case.

For present purposes, nothing substantial hinges on the specific appraisal categories true-false. All that matters for our deliberations concerning the issue of objectivity is that some evaluative claims can be fitted out with a suitably straightforward legitimating rational warrant. Appraisal in the range of validatable-nonvalidatable, warranted-unwarranted, correct-incorrect, appropriate-inappropriate, right-wrong is altogether sufficient, and the *truth* issue as such need not arise.[13] Where values are concerned, the issue of alethic realism is immaterial to the issue of objectivity.

To judge by the literature on the subject, many philosophers are under the impression that alethic value realism is the only way to avert a corrosive subjectivism of the it's-all-a-matter-of-taste variety. The idea seems to be abroad that evaluations must either lie in the catchment area of the true-false characterization or be empty expressions of subjective inclinations. But this is surely nonsense. One can evaluate the credentials of appropriateness for questions, commands, hypotheses, and so forth, each in their own truth-noncommittal way, so why not evaluations? The appraisal categories for different sorts of utterances differ, as per true/false with respect to statements, sensible/absurd with respect to questions, probable/improbable with respect to claims, appropriate/inappropriate with respect to commands, and correct/incorrect with respect to evaluations. Why then should evaluations be destroyed as rationally cogent objects if it were to turn out that the appropriate appraisal categories are not true-false but something like (say) well grounded or ill grounded?

In the end, the issue of alethic value realism is really not terribly interesting or significant, despite the great pool of ink that has been expended on it. Only those who labor under a mistaken impression that determination as true or false is the only conceivably appropriate pathway to rational legitimation can think that by addressing alethic realism they are getting at something crucial for the objective validity of evaluations. Even as regards statements, there are many other sorts of categories of rational appraisal than true/false: foolish/shrewd, correct/incorrect, plausible/implausible, and so on. There simply is no good reason to think that an alethic realism oriented to true-false with respect to values is the only way to prevent a value subjectivism that submerges the whole field of evaluation in a corrosive sea of subjective taste. Alethic realism is not the only kind there is: value realism figures on the scene as well.

Yet how can one be a warrant realist if one abandons the idea that evaluations can be derived from facts? If the relevant facts of the matter do not sustain and substantiate our evaluations, then what can possibly do so?

The answer here lies in recognizing that evaluations do indeed supervene on facts, but they do so only in view of "appropriate considerations" that are themselves evaluative, even though they may verge on triviality. The following argumentation with regard to *moral* evaluation is paradigmatic:

- In doing action A, Jones deliberately hurt Smith's feelings. [Fact]
- Neither in fact nor in Jones's thought on the matter was any constructive ulterior purpose served by Jones's doing A. [Fact]
- It is morally wrong to hurt people's feelings when doing so has no compensating positivities in other respects. [Evaluative truism]
- Therefore: Jones acted (morally) wrongly in deliberately hurting Smith's feelings.

The given facts of the case do indeed sustain that evaluative conclusion, but of course they do so only in the presence of the enthymematic evaluation. The value conclusion follows from the facts all right, but does so in view of trivial or truistic considerations that are themselves evaluative— albeit on the side of warrant. For once we look to the particular domain of evaluation at issue (be it cognitive, or moral, or whatever), its inherent teleology will—as we have seen above—provide a rational basis for some determinations of appropriateness.

Finally, what of property realism? Do value ascriptions attribute actual properties to the items at issue? Well, properties perhaps (the term is surely a very broad one), but certainly not properties of the usual sort. For the "properties" at issue in value appraisals exhibit three salient characteristics. They are dispositional, mind-involving relational, and not perceptually observational but judgmentally evaluational. Such properties are not instances of the familiar types: they are not "primary" properties (object descriptive), nor yet "secondary" ones (characterizing what sort of perceptual reaction the object evokes from a normal observer under standard conditions of sensory observations), but something rather different.

If we are going to discuss whether or not their value features represent *properties* of objects, we first of all have to get clear about what sorts of properties there are. And here the philosophers' traditional conception of properties must undergo some broadening from the very outset. For the English empiricists have managed to focus the attention of philosophers on properties or qualities of two sorts:

Primary properties that represent *descriptive* features of the physical makeup of a thing. (The weight of an apple, for example, or its shape or size.)

Secondary properties that represent *sensory perceptible* features. (The color of the apple, for example, or its taste.)

Primary properties—shape, for example—are supposed to characterize the physical makeup of the object in itself; secondary properties, such as (phenomenal) colors correspond to causal dispositions to involve certain sensory responses in normal observers.

But what this listing patently ignores is that there are also:

Tertiary properties that represent *cognitively discernible* features—characteristics that (only) a suitably informed mind reflecting on the object and its context can—and standardly will—come to recognize.

Such tertiary properties represent causal dispositions to evoke certain judgmental responses in duly cognizant respondents.

The "uniqueness" of an occurrence, for example, its being the only one of its kind, is certainly a property of it. But it is neither an integral aspect of its internal makeup nor a sense-discernible feature of it. Again, a man's "(physical) similarity to Napoleon" is undoubtedly a property of his but represents neither a primary quality nor a sensory disposition. Or again, consider the ink configuration: &. Its property of representing the conjunction "and" is certainly not something discernible by observation alone, apparent as such to a perceptive Chinese, for example. Secondary qualities are supposed to be something that any physiologically normal person can observe. Tertiary properties, by contrast, are features that only a suitably informed intelligent *thinker* can recognize. There is nothing mysterious about them, they are just something conceptually different from and more complex than secondary properties. An object's secondary properties pivot on its disposition to evoke characteristic *affective* responses in an observer's suitably responsive senses. Its tertiary properties pivot on its disposition to evoke characteristic *reflective* responses in a suitably informed mind in standard conditions, relating to judgmental rather than sensory responses. When a Greek vase is (truly) said to be "a typical second-century B.C. Cretan amphora," it is undoubtedly the case that an empirical property of some sort is ascribed to it. But that property is clearly neither primary nor yet secondary in the classic sense of that distinction, which was nowise designed to capture issues relating to features whose nature is dispositional, relational, context-bound, and attributively inferential.

Now if we are going to see the value features as *properties* of things, then it is clearly at the level of tertiary properties that we shall want to proceed. And there is no good reason to expect any undue difficulties here. The "beauty" of a vase is something that, unlike its shape, is not going to be detectable by bare, straightforward observation. Like its being "a typical product of its era," the validation of its attribution is going to require a great deal of peripheral information and principled reflection. Rational valuation calls for value ascriptions rooted in the thought of an intelligent, unbiased mind that adequately reflects on the nature and ramifications of items at issue. A value of this sort inheres neither in the object as such nor "in the minds-eyes of the beholder" pure and simple. It is a matter of how duly informed, unbiased, and sensible individuals normally respond to objects in standardized conditions. Values are indeed a part of "the furniture of the world," J. L. Mackie notwithstanding.[14] But the world at issue will include not objects alone but also minds as well as the interactions between them.[15]

The dispositional status of secondary properties loosens their connection with the actual responses of actual observers: the issue is merely that if there were observers and if their observations were properly constituted, then what sort of response would the item evoke? And similarly with tertiary properties, where the issue is if these observers were duly appraised and if their evaluative endorsements were properly constituted, then what sort of response would the item evoke? The dispositional properties at issue thus relate to the item's response-evoking capacities and do not simply "lie in the eye of the beholder." Value thus lies in the object, not just in the response to it; it is an inherent feature *of an object* that it manifests in certain transactions in which it is "evoked" in appropriately endowed intelligent beings.

While value contentions, accordingly, bring persons and their reactions onto the stage of consideration, evaluations are clearly not themselves secondary properties that turn on sensory responses. For tertiary properties carry us into the new region of a mind-correlative realism. We ascribe secondary properties on essentially causal grounds but tertiary properties on essentially judgmental ones. Here thought is pivotal, and reasons come into it. And while secondary properties are specifically linked to the makeup of our human sensibility (our sense organs), nothing inherently species-bound need be involved in the reflectivity at issue with tertiary properties.

There is nothing "subjective" here, nothing that impedes objectivity. That a transaction of a certain *physical* nature affecting creatures of a certain physical constitution results in a sour taste or a painful sensation is certainly as much a fact about the world as anything else. But that a transaction of a certain *conceptual* nature (the witnessing of needless pain, for example) results in a judgment of a certain character—one of distress and disapproval—is equally natural for creatures of a certain intellectual constitution. The one is every bit as objective as the other.

In principle there are three sorts of issues:

(1) those that have no connection with minds (as apart, perhaps, from being knowable by them) and whose resolution lies with the makeup of nature alone. (How many moons has Jupiter?)

(2) those that deal with what is wholly mind-constructed and which depend wholly in the operation of minds. (What are you thinking about at the moment?)

(3) those that deal with mind-nature interactions and whose resolution turns on the interactive contributions for both parties—nature and the mind itself.

And this third category itself has two sectors:

(a) those issues that deal with their interactions between nature and minds operating in certain standard, communally generic ways. (What is the phenomenal color of this piece of fruit?)

(b) those issues that deal with the interactions between nature and the minds operating in idiosyncratic, individual-characteristics ways. (What do those ink-blots remind you of?)

By anyone's standards (1) represents objective issues and (2) represents subjective ones. The problem is what to do with (3). And the—surely plausible—stance we take here is to split the difference: to class (3a) with the objective issues and (3b) with the subjective ones.

Two sorts of evaluative doctrines are generally distinguished:

- *Value absolutism*: evaluative distinctions (good/bad, right/wrong, etc.) operate independently of the inclinations of intelligent beings to approve or disapprove of things.
- *Value subjectivism*: evaluative distinctions operate wholly and solely through the natural inclinations of duly sensitive intelligent beings to approve or disapprove of things.

But intermediate between these is the position of the present discussion, a *normative value personalism* which on the one hand sees values as rooted in the tendencies of intelligent beings to approve and disapprove, but on the other hand insists that for appropriate evaluations these evaluative capacities must be exercised rightly, in line with normatively appropriate standards (i.e., in their proper or natural way). This normative position, in sum, insists that these tertiary value properties be apprehended rightly. There is nothing ineluctably subjective here: tertiary properties—value properties included—can be just as objective as the rest. There is nothing subjective about the judgment that Amadeus Mozart is a greater composer than Ignaz Stumblebum.

The concept of *supervenience* has been invoked by R. M. Hare with respect to the relation between values and natural facts. Tracing out ideas of G. E. Moore's, he writes "Let us take that characteristic of 'good' which has been called its supervenience. Suppose that we say 'St. Francis was a good man.' It is logically impossible [Hare surely means *incoherent*] to say this and to maintain at the same time that there might have been another man placed exactly in the same [descriptive] circumstances as St. Francis, and who behaved in exactly the same way but who differed from St. Francis in this respect only, that he was not a good man."[16] But of course the "logical impossibility" at issue is not a matter of pure logic but rather a matter of those evaluative principles built into the use of evaluative terms like the ethical epithet "good man." The crucial role of such meaning-expository principles governing the use of value terms means that the "supervenient" dependency of evaluating on the "natural facts" is totally compatible with a rejection of a value naturalism that sees evaluative as derivable from matters of pure fact alone. Those tertiary morally evaluative properties are no doubt "supervenient" on an item's factual situation and context, encompassing its descriptive makeup and its descriptive embedding in the wider setting in which it figures. If an item's primary and secondary qualities were different, its tertiary qualities would differ as well. But the judgment-dispositional nature of what is at stake means that this supervenience proceeds in a way in which evaluative considerations are also involved. Our concrete evaluations are—when appropriate—indeed rationally constrained by the underlying facts, but constrained in ways that involve the operation of judgmental value principles.

G. E. Moore did not serve the interests of philosophical clarity at all well in adopting the contrast terms "natural-nonnatural" to characterize a distinction for which, on his own principles, the less question-begging contrasts of sensory-nonsensory or perceptual-nonperceptual would have been far more suitable.[17] For, in the final analysis, all that Moore means by calling the value characteristics of things "nonnatural" is that they do not represent observationally discernible features of their putative bearers; that they are, in their nature, not sensible. (However, to call them "supersensible" would introduce the wrong connotations here—what has "higher" or "lower" to do with it?) But to characterize the evaluative features of things as nonnatural, as Moore unfortunately did, strongly suggests that something rather strange and mysterious is going on, that the purported condition of things is somehow extra- or super-natural. And invoking this mystery invites the misguided response that just as we have inner and outer senses to observe the natural properties of things, occurrences, or situations (the taste of an apple or the painfulness of a wound), so there must be some special sense-analogous faculty to determine their evaluative aspects. Forgetting the good Kantian point that evaluation is a matter of judgment on the basis of principles, much of Anglo-American moral theory thus followed Moorean inspirations down the primrose path of a value-insight empiricism that looked to some sort of perceptual or quasi-perceptual access to value, thereby stumbling once more into the blind alley of the older British theorists of moral sense or sensibility. This approach launched philosophers on the vain quest for a value sensibility—with all of its inherent insolubilia, including the prospect of evaluative color blindness and the intractable problem of how value perception (of any sort) can *justify* rather than merely *explain* evaluations.

The fundamental contrast, of course, should simply be that between what can be observed or inferred from observational data and that which cannot. The value of an item is no more accessible to perception than is the ownership of a piece of property. In neither case can mere *inspection* suffice to determine the issue. But that of course does not make it something mysterious and "nonnatural"—the special object of a peculiar detection-faculty, a value intuition. The crucial fact is that value is not sense-perceptible but mind-judgmental: something to be determined not simply by observation of some sort but by reflective thought duly sustained by background information and suitably equipped with an awareness of principles.

· · ·

Our deliberation regarding the ontological aspect of value realism has distinguished three main versions of the doctrine: alethic realism, property realism, and warrant realism.

As regards alethic realism, our discussion has taken no definite position, having found no pressing need to do so, because the significance of this issue for the problem of objectivity that is at stake here has been greatly exaggerated.

As regards property realism, we have dismissed *primary* properties from our range of concern (since their evaluative features are clearly not inherent, nondispositional characteristics of things). And we have also dismissed *secondary* properties from our range of concern (since value is not a matter of disposition to affect a normal observer's sensory repertoire in a certain way). Instead, we have adopted a realism of *tertiary* properties, since the issue of appropriate evaluation is indeed one of an item's disposition to figure in a certain sort of way in the thought processes of duly informed and enlightened reflective appraisers.

Finally, as regards the justificational realism of rational warrant, our position has been that it is exactly this issue that lies at the heart of the value realism controversy. As the preceding discussion has sought to show, there is good reason for believing that evaluations can indeed be rationally substantiated as cogent, notwithstanding the circumstance that values cannot be derived simply and solely from facts. And so it emerges from every relevant perspective that the sort of rational appraisal at issue with value objectivity is emphatically possible.[18]

twelve

HERMENEUTIC OBJECTIVITY: AGAINST DECONSTRUCTIONISM

Synopsis

(1) Deconstructionism maintains an indifferentist relativism with regard to textual interpretation that sees all the alternatives as equally justified and appropriate. In its unwillingness to draw evaluative distinctions with respect to rational cogency, such a subjective to-each-their-own approach is the diametric opposite of objectivism in this domain. (2) However, this relativistic indifferentism badly misapprehends and underestimates the crucial role that context plays in the sphere of text interpretation. For it is in fact coherence with the resources of context (in the widest sense of this term) that is at once the appropriate instrument of text interpretation and the impetus to objectivity in this domain. (3) The ramifications of systemic coherence preclude an indifferentist egalitarianism of textual interpretation and provide the materials for an interpretative objectivism. (4) In communicative settings there are purposive constraints to objectivity that differentiate between appropriate and inappropriate interpretations. (5) Only where people are concerned merely and solely with using text interpretation as a training ground for the unfettered imagination—rather than as a venture in information transmission—does that free-floating deconstructionist approach to texts make any sense.

1. THE PROJECT OF DECONSTRUCTION

Chapter 6 considered the importance of objectivity in matters of communication in general. However, one particularly prominent sector of this domain relates to the interpretation of textual and, above all, written material. And there are few areas where the contemporary denial of objectivity been more prominent than in the study of language and the texts that we produce by its means. The "deconstructionism" associated with the name of Jacques Derrida is Exhibit No. 1 here.[1]

Deconstructionism is a theory regarding the interpretation of texts that denies any prospect of objectivity in this domain. Initially projected with regard to *literary* texts, the enthusiasm of its more ambitious exponents soon led them to expand the theory's application to texts in general—historical, biographical, philosophical, what have you. The doctrinal core of the position involves two theses: first, that a text always allows many alternative interpretative constructions whose elaboration is the proper mission of the interpretative enterprise, and, second, that all these various interpretations are effectively coequal in merit—that none can be rejected without much ado as unsuitable, inappropriate, incompetent. At the core of this doctrinal stance lies a view of textual plasticity; that as the enterprise of text interpretation proceeds, it brings to view an ever-increasing range of viable and more or less equivalent alternative interpretations. As deconstructionism sees the matter, the enterprise of text interpretation accordingly confronts us with an inevitable plethora of coequal alternative possibilities. On this basis, the partisans of deconstructionism condemn with the dismissive epithet of "textualism" the view that a given text has "a meaning" in such a stable and objective way as to favor one particular interpretation over the rest. They insist upon the relativistic stance that there is no room for objectivity here: interpretation is a matter of "to each his own."

Insofar as deconstructionist theory represents a *doctrine* rather than a methodological *attitude* about text interpretation, it is a position based on a group of hermeneutical views or contentions which may be sketched roughly as follows: In the domain of text interpretation we face a situation of:

(1) *Omnitextuality:* Any proposed interpretation of a text must itself take the form of simply another text. In the hermeneutical sphere there is no way of exiting from the textual domain.

(2) *Plasticity:* Every text has multiple interpretations—it admits a plurality of diverse constructions.

(3) *Equivalency:* Every interpretation is as good as any other. These various interpretative constructions of a text are all of equal or roughly equal merit: none is definitive, canonical, discriminatively appropriate—indeed none is substantially more cogent or tenable than the others.

It follows from these theses that in interpreting texts we always confront a plurality of (roughly co-meritorious) variants. Text interpretation admits of no rational validation or invalidation for one resolution over against another. It is always simply an exercise of free imagination: a project in which we can do no more than to explore interesting possibilities and cannot hope to validate a particular result as optimal in a cogent and stable way. Where issues of interpretation are concerned, we can only explore alternatives and cannot substantiate particular resolutions; we can project possibilities but cannot reduce them by eliminative processes of plausibility assessment. Accordingly, we should never ask what a text *does* mean, but only what it *can or might* mean. In the realm of text interpretation there are no forced choices: it is an inherently indecisive enterprise, a fact that, happily, manages to "liberate us from the prison-house of language."[2] Deconstructionism is, in sum, a doctrine of indifferentist relativism with respect to textual interpretation. In its refusal to let those restrictive considerations of rational cogency come into play, it is the diametric opposite of objectivism in this domain.

How can a more discriminating rationalism come to grips with such an anarchical position? Clearly, there is little point in quarreling with premisses (1) and (2) of the preceding argumentation, seeing that the former is an obvious and evident truth, and that the latter a fact amply substantiated by historical evidence. And it follows from these two theses that any interpretation itself admits of variant interpretations. The problematic crux of deconstructionism's argument for a relativistic indifferentiation of text interpretation is thus premiss (3), with its assertion of merit equivalency. But is this premiss tenable? Is the hermeneutic realm indeed a free-for-all ruled by the idea that all interpretations are created equal? Is the textual interpreter indeed wandering through a hall of mirrors, wholly unable to implement the distinction between appearance and reality?

2. THE IMPORTANCE OF CONTEXT: THE FLY IN DECONSTRUCTIONISM'S OINTMENT

The idea that a merit-annihilating indifferentism holds reign in the sphere of textual interpretation is willfully blind to a crucial reality. The fact is that interpretations—and the texts through which they are conveyed— are emphatically *not* created equal: Some make sense, some only nonsense; some are ambiguous (have many plausible interpretations), others are more definite; some convey much information, others little; some state truths, some falsehoods. For what the fallacy of indifferentist relativism of text interpretation overlooks, to its own decisive detriment, is the crucial matter of *context*.

While it is indeed true that every text interpretation is itself a text, some nevertheless have a better systemic fit than others. They harmonize more smoothly and adequately both into the larger context of texts in general, and into the circumambient context of the extratextual realm of thought and action. And it is exactly here that we come to the crux of the issue of interpretative adequacy. The context at issue has three distinguishable levels:

- *Immediate:* Other parts of the same text.
- *Nearby:* Other cognate discussions by the same author; other cognate discussions of the same genre or in the writings to which the author is responding by way of development or opposition.
- *Distant or Peripheral:* General aspects of the state of information and opinion of the time; general linguistic and philological considerations, etc.[3]

Considerations at all these levels stand in the way of our equating the merits of all those different constructions and interpretations of a text by circumscribing the range of acceptable understandings that a text is able to bear. For text interpretation is clearly an evidential exercise where one has to make the best possible use of the relevant data over a wide range of information because a wide variety of hermeneutical factors must come into play:

- What the text itself explicitly affirms.
- Other relevant discussions by the author bearing on the issues that the text addresses.
- Biographical evidence regarding the author's education, interests, contacts, relevant interactions with contemporaries, and the like.
- Considerations of "intellectual history" regarding the state of knowledge and opinion in the author's place and time, and the cultural translation within which the text originated.
- Philological data regarding the use of terms and expressions in the time and place where the text was produced.

Moreover, it must never be forgotten that these texts themselves are human artifacts produced by flesh-and-blood individuals along with innumerable other artifacts (buildings, utensils, etc.) not as an idle game but in an effort to achieve certain determinate purposes. And so we also come to yet another crucial hermeneutical factor in addition to the five listed above:

- The setting of a nonverbal modus operandi within which texts take their place and play their purposive role.

The crucial point, then, is that any text has an envisioning historical and cultural *context* and that the context of a text is itself not simply textual—not something that can be played out solely and wholly in the textual domain. This context of the texts that concern us constrains and delimits the viable interpretations that these texts are able to bear.

The process of *deconstruction*—of interpretatively dissolving any and every text into a plurality of supposedly merit-equivalent constructions—can and should be offset by the process of *reconstruction* which calls for viewing texts within their larger contexts. After all, texts inevitably have a setting—historical, cultural, authorial—on which their actual meaning is critically dependent. And this contextual setting projects beyond the textual realm itself in comprising both processes (know-how) and products (artifacts) relating to human action in relevant regards. In particular, this context encompasses both noncommunicative (behavioral) and communicative practices, including the processes, procedures, and methods that characterize people's life-styles. To the extent that we do not understand the ways and means of a people's mode of living—what they are concerned to do with their energies, resources, and time—we will have great difficulty in understanding their texts.

The crucial point that has to be urged against deconstructionism's hermeneutical egalitarianism is that not every reality is virtual. The textual realm is *not* closed, because texts often as not concern themselves with the real world. They can and do bear upon noncommunicative processes and interactions with artifacts of a text-external realm. There are not only tennis rulebooks and tennis manuals but also tennis courts and players and games. Texts interconnect with reality through the mediation of intelligent agents. In sum, texts have a wider functional context. And this means that text interpretation is not a matter of free-floating imagination—it is a matter of scholarship.

Neglect of this crucial contextual dimension leads to what is perhaps the most severe shortcoming of deconstructionism, betokening its deeply problematic commitment to the idea that the textual realm is self-sufficient and autonomous. Such a stance reflects the bias of academics committed

to a logocentrism that sees the world in terms of discourse and forgets that
it is not the case that everything is a matter of language through and
through. Our texts and our use of words are, for the most part, no more
than just one other instrumentality by which we function in a nontextual
world—in this instance preeminently the social world of human interaction. To see texts and the libraries that warehouse them as self-contained
is akin to contemplating the molehills without the mole.[4]

3. COHERENCE AS AN INTERPRETATIVE STANDARD

To be sure, all of the various interpretations of a text that are not totally
bizarre have (by assumption) some sort of merit; there is almost always
something to be said for them. But to affirm this is not, of course, to say
that all those different (nonabsurd) interpretations are thereby *equally*
meritorious. To concede the prospect of a hermeneutical underdetermination that allows for a plurality of alternative nonabsurd interpretations
is certainly *not* to say that any such interpretation is every bit as viable as
any other. The situation here is akin to the old story that trades on the
Talmudic belief that each passage of the Torah contains forty-nine possible meanings. The story has it that once a student offered an interpretation of a passage to the rabbi who was giving him instruction. "No,
you are quite wrong," the rabbi proclaimed. "How can you say that?"
protested the student. "Didn't you say there are forty-nine meanings
for each passage?" "Yes," replied the rabbi, "but yours isn't one of them."
Given the often underdeterminative impetus of our contextual resources,
the interpretation of texts is sometimes somewhat flexible. But there are
definite limits to the elasticity that is available here.

Any viable approach to the theory of text interpretation must accordingly be *normative:* it must be predicated on standards and criteria that
provide for the evaluation of better and worse, of sensible and foolish, of
responsible and irresponsible. Sensible text interpretation is not a matter
of anything-goes imaginative flights into the never-never world of free-
floating fancy; it is tethered to the down-to-earth realities of the case
imposed by rational standards of validity and appropriateness.

The idea that any and every construal of a text—any bending or twist-
ing of its message—is as good as any other is particularly dubious with any
text that has a how-to aspect, whether this be small-scale (recipes for
baking bread, instructions for cleaning a rifle) or large-scale (prescriptions

for successful salesmanship, guidelines to scanning Spanish poetry). In such matters there is no anything-goes plasticity; the simple fact is that some ways of interpreting that text and implementing the lessons of such an interpretation are materially better than others. The merit of deconstructionism lies in its stress on the importance of texts in humanistic studies and on the pluralism of interesting, discussible, and attention-worthy interpretations. But its defect lies in the idea that interpretations are created equal, that issues of quality and cogency are out of place in this domain.

The crucial task of text interpretation is one of not merely *examining* possibilities but of *evaluating* them. One must go beyond the survey of *possible* interpretations to assess which of them are *plausible* and—going even beyond this—to endeavor to decide which (if any) among them is *optimal*. But how to implement this project?

It is a profound error to see the textual sector as closed—to take the line that it is all a matter of texts "all the way through." Texts come into contact with contexts. The cardinal instrumentality of text interpretation is represented by the principle of *hermeneutical optimization* according to a standard of merit provided by the coherence of the proposed interpretation of a text with its overall context. Whatever interpretation best harmonizes with a text's overall context is ipso facto a superior interpretation which thereby has greater claims on our acceptance. In the light of such contextual considerations, text interpretations are emphatically not created equal.

The most sensible approach to the existence of a variety of alternative text interpretations is what might be called the *coherence theory* of interpretation. This theory is predicated on two main theses:

- The ultimate object of the interpretative enterprise is *optimization*. Its goal is not just to survey possible interpretations but to assess their respective merits and—above all—wherever possible to determine which one is the best.
- The optimal interpretation of a text is that which can best achieve a *systemic unification* of the whole range of the hermeneutical factors previously enumerated (context, authorship, philology, intellectual history, and the rest). The determinative issue is that of the best overall fit, leaving the least overall residue of residual questions, problems, difficulties, loose ends, or the like.

Whatever can be said against a coherence theory of *truth*, a coherence theory of *interpretation* is eminently sensible. The fact that there is a context that conditions the text—that the situation we face in dealing with information-conveying texts is not a matter of an unfettered, imaginative, free-wheeling word-spinning—brings rationality on the scene once more. Text interpretation is a practice that can be more or less adequate in the light of the need for *systematization*: for fitting texts into its larger setting. Not only can a text have a *subtext* of implicit but inarticulated messages but it also—and more usually—has a *supertext*—a wider contextual environment within which its own message must be construed. It is in fact coherence with the resources of context (in the widest sense of this term) that is at once the appropriate instrument of text interpretation and the impetus to objectivity in this domain.

But who makes the rules of appropriateness? The answer is that they are not *made by* but *given to* us, not something invented but rather something to be discovered by anyone who examines the range of relevant phenomena with sufficient care. They are implicit and inherent in the broader context, revolving both about the text itself and the purposive tradition within which the interpretation proceeds. A text interpreter no more makes up the rules of the process on which he/she is engaged than a speaker makes up the meanings of the words he/she uses. (To be sure, both emerge from a tradition of human praxis and are not legislated from on high by a deus ex machina.) It is—to reemphasize—a matter of *reconstruction* rather than *deconstruction*.

It is thus necessary for a sensible venture in text interpretation to reject the mistaken idea that we can afford to forget about the existence of an extratextual world with which we humans interrelate on the basis of texts. The use of words is not something free-wheeling that stands disconnected from the verbal and behavioral environment in which they figure. The textual realm is not disconnected from the realm of human praxis. (Indeed even moving into and through that textual realm is a matter of praxis; producing and consuming texts is a matter of *doing* things.) The context of a text is set not only by other related texts but also by the artifacts that constitute its material environment and by the common elements of experience that we ourselves share with that text's author in virtue of the fact of sharing a common experiential framework in a shared human setting in a common world. And this endows texts with an objective aspect.

With textual interpretation as with all other branches of rational endeavor we can obtain no categorical guarantees. Here, as in any other "inductive" situations, all that rationality can do for us is to offer the best available prospect of successful goal-realization. But insofar as we are reasonable this circumstance should also satisfy us, seeing that it is absurd to ask for more than can possibly be had.

4. AGAINST TEXTUAL EGALITARIANISM IN COMMUNICATIVE CONTEXTS

Jacques Derrida complains in his *Speech and Phenomena* that Western scholarship has privileged "voice" (authorial thought and intention) over "writing" (the resultant objective text)—process over product.[5] But this involves a profound misconception. It overlooks the import of the hermeneutic circle: the lesson that in the endeavor to understand texts, issues of process and product are coordinate; that neither can be subordinated to the other, let alone consigned to oblivion. To agree with Derrida in subordinating process ("voice") to product (the textual product in "writing") would be to ignore the crucial lesson that what a text *is* depends on its function, on what it sets out to do. And that at this point the author's own position is dominant. The texts being of the author's making, we need to take the contexts of its production into account to determine what it actually is as a product.

The reason why interpretations are not created equal lies in the circumstance of their contextual embedding in "voice"-related matters. For texts are produced with a view to their communicative mission; they are instruments of communication—of conveying information and inciting to action—even where the only "action" at issue is one of deliberation or discussion. Even merely belletristic texts can guide people towards implementation of beliefs and values in ways that can be pointless and meretricious—or the reverse. Texts can be veridical or mendacious, helpful or hurtful. They are not disconnected from life: they can be life-enhancing or life-degrading, impelling us to views that conduce to self-enhancement or to self-loathing.

Medical texts influence the medications we take. Engineering texts influence the projects we construct. Literary texts influence the values we maintain and the lives we lead on their basis. Philosophical texts influence our priorities and the way we conduct our intellectual affairs. Texts have a bearing not only upon what we think but upon what we do: our actions and activities, our experiments and observations, our predictions and ventures at control. And insofar as texts are elements of a wider teleological domain, their adequate interpretation will pivot on this fact. The textual world is *not* self-contained, it is inextricably interconnected with the realm of action, activity, and living. And actions (even intellectual actions like understanding) can be more or less successful. Accordingly, we can evaluate our texts (representations) because they have a pragmatic dimension in the communicative domain.

One cannot, of course, leave "writing" out of it. The public dimension is uneliminable. In using language to produce his text, the author avails himself of a public instrumentality. What words mean is a matter of convention—of the social and, as it were, decisional modus operandi of human linguistic and symbolic arrangements. And of course what can *appropriately* (warrentedly, correctly) be said once those controversial arrangements are in place is something that is itself no longer free-floating and decisional. Once we decide what "cat" and "mat" mean, the question of whether one can appropriately assert "The cat is on the mat" is not an issue open for *decisional* resolution: our contribution has come to an end and the rest lies with the nature of things. What our words stand for— what we *mean* by "cat" or "mat" or "dog" is entirely a matter of human arrangements—of the "decision" of linguistic communities. But once these matters are fixed, the question of whether and where and how frequently dogs and cats are to be encountered in nature—and in the proximity of one another and of mats—is something that only nature can resolve; the conventional arrangements of language-using communities has nothing further to do with it; the world's concrete realities now gain the upper hand. Here text interpretation once more requires an objective and, as it were, contextual dimension.

The critical flaw of a deconstructionist relativism of texts and their interpretations lies in the fact that rational evaluation is possible also in this interpretative sphere. For texts can and should be evaluated in terms of their contextual ramifications. The appropriateness of thought and assertion in matters of communication will generally depend on objective factors outside the domain of individual wishes or acts. It simply is not the case that everything in the textual realm is created equal—as deconstructionist relativism would have us believe. The resources of systemic coherence within an overall purposive context preclude an indifferentist egalitarianism of textual interpretation and provide for an interpretative objectivism.

5. IRENIC CONCLUDING OBSERVATIONS

There is, of course, always the prospect of a halfway house between personal subjectivity and impersonal objectivity that goes with the inter-personal agreement that can obtain within particular communities.[6] But this halfway house does not afford a really habitable space in the present context. Communities and their practices and traditions are almost as fickle and fallible as individuals. They too can overlook and neglect crucial considerations. Even when we know how the community *does* comport itself we can still ask how it *should* comport itself. And this is something we can do—though admittedly only within limits—with respect to the community to which we ourselves belong. Objectivity is an ideal towards which we can and should strive. But no one says that the process is easy. The prospect of different questions looms before us. "What *does* the text mean?" is one sort of issue, and "What *might* the text mean?" is another. Here as elsewhere the answer pivots on what the question at issue is.

The situation is not, however, entirely one-sided. There is something, after all, that can be said for the deconstructionist perspective. But interestingly enough, this something falls wholly outside the sphere of meaning-oriented hermeneutics. For when we speak of "interpreting" a literary text, two distinctly different things can be at issue. It is crucial to distinguish between:

- *exegetical interpretation*—the endeavor to elucidate the meaning of a text in relation to the intentions of its producer vis-à-vis the intended audience then and there.
- *imaginative (re-) interpretation*—the re-casting or re-presentation of a text in an endeavor to evoke aesthetic responses and affective resonances in a current (present-day) recipient.

In doing actual (exegetical) interpretation we operate in the domain of scholarship. Here issues of context become centrally important because the pivotal question is "What did *the author* mean by the text?" The point of concern is with the original message and purport of the text. The issue of historical authenticity is paramount. But a text—and not only a text but any artifact that has an "esthetic" such as a painting or sculpture—can also be regarded abstractly, in a context-independent way. Here the issue is not one of producer-centrality but one of consumer-centrality, and the question is not "What *does* the text mean for its author?" but rather "What *can*

the text mean for us?" "Interpretation" here is not a matter of the
hermeneutical interpretation of meaning explanation, but rather the sort
of thing at issue when we speak of a performer's "interpretation" of a musical composition or the director's "interpretation" of a play. What we do
here is not so much *interpret* the text as to creatively *reinterpret* it or endeavor to endow it with current relevance and interest. Producing a play
or performing a musical composition affords a paradigm example. Here
we are (usually) not trying for historical authenticity but for the enlistment
of interest. We are not addressing issues of scholarship but issues of edifi-
cation or entertainment. Here authorship (and with it context) becomes
of subsidiary importance; instead, imaginative creativity comes to the forefront. Where this sort of enterprise is at issue, the free-wheeling inven-
tiveness envisioned by deconstructionism has something to be said for it.
But the hermeneutical commerce with texts geared to the enterprise of
understanding their actual *meaning* as concrete historical artifacts is of
course something quite different.

The crux, then, is the contrast between text interpretation as conscientious scholarly exegesis as against an imaginative de- (or perhaps better
re-) construction of texts freed from the constraint of considerations of
historical context—and thus with issues of scholarly exegesis held in suspension. And behind this duality of approach looms a far-reaching quarrel
in the area of educational approach and policy. The question is, who owns
the texts—by whose ground rules of textual "interpretation" is the game
to be played? Are we to deal in scholarly exegesis or in imaginative edifi-
cation? Are the text-consumers expected to bring scholarly industry to
bear or are they being invited to indulge in imaginative flights of fancy?
And, in particular, in conjuring with texts in the educational process,
are we to advantage the philologically and historically well-informed, or
are we to create a more level playing field of imaginative sensibility where
anyone can play?

In sum then, the fact has to be recognized that texts come into being in
relation to rather different sorts of aims and purposes. In particular, they
can be made either for the transmission of information and ideas or for
thought-provocation and the stimulation of the inventive imagination.
And therefore two quite different "interpretative" enterprises can be at
issue. Only where we put substantive (let alone scholarly) concerns aside
and use text interpretation as a means to thought-provocation—as a training ground for the free-ranging imagination—does a free-floating deconstructionist approach to texts make any sense. The prospect of a *theoretical*

reconciliation is thus at hand: "It's all a matter of how you understand interpretation. Different things can be at stake. Scholarly exegesis is one, deconstructively imaginative innovation is another."

In the communicative use of texts, where the transmission of information is the paramount factor, the impetus to objectivity is paramount. And this holds even for "literary" texts, given that the authors of such works generally desire and endeavor to be understood in their own terms. Ultimately it is a matter of ownership. Hermeneuticists recognize the ownership rights of authors and of the scholars who address their products. Deconstructionists think that the text belongs to interpreters to do with as they wish in using texts as springboards for ventures in the imaginative expansion of sensibility.

To be sure, life is not there for toil alone. "All work and no play makes Jack a dull boy." There will be time for serious thought and a time for imaginative fancy. But it is only when intellectual endeavor takes a playful turn that deconstructionism comes into play. When it is the informative aspect in any of its dimensions that is at issue in the texts with which we deal, then our interpretative efforts will have to take the more scholarly road where objectivity once again comes to the fore.[7]

— conclusion —

IS OBJECTIVITY SUBJECT TO LIMITS?

Synopsis

Human life as we prize it undoubtedly requires room for a "private space" where subjectivity reigns supreme—where we can indulge our biases, prejudices, idiosyncrasies, and individual peculiarities. But this very fact is itself an objective fact about our condition as best rational inquiry reveals it to us. Thus objectivity, properly understood, knows no limits—or at any rate none apart from those that it itself acknowledges as appropriate.

Is objectivity subject to limits? Is there ever a time when objectivity is out of place? At first sight it seems that the answer will be a clear affirmative. For are there not various things that we do not—should not—want to be objective about? Surely, parents should not be objective in judging their own children, nor would one expect the fortunate heir to be objective in assessing the value of his beloved grandfather's favorite watch fob. Surely, there is a "personal space" where we can properly indulge our idiosyncratic fancies and give free play to our personal biases, allegiances, prejudices, idiosyncrasies, and individual peculiarities without feeling called upon to be objective—a region where we can "be ourselves" as idiosyncratic individuals or groups of like-minded kindred spirits, however eccentric in their judgments or evaluations.

Now all this is well and good as far at it goes. But it does not really go against the claims of objectivity. For one thing, such a view of the matter becomes problematic through its neglect of the all–important feature of context. Of course the parent will be partial to the child. Of course the loyal grandson will attach a special ("sentimental") value to his grandfather's bequest. When the issue is one of harmonious relations with our children or our spouses, emotion, sentiment, feelings, instinct, etc., are bound to play a prominent role. Who would want to put subjective personal involvements and idiosyncratic predilections aside and be objective in forming friendships, or in selecting one's spare-time reading? Why should I expend my efforts and resources in the same way that other people would? Why should I not indulge my personal tastes in matters of dress, say, or of music. Surely with works of the creative imagination (fiction or poetry, for example), or when cultivating the elective affinities of personal friendship, objectivity's concern for "what another would do in one's place" becomes irrelevant. But of course these themselves are altogether reasonable—perfectly objective—truths.

And so the objection to objectivity runs into difficulty through its neglect of the crucial factor of *contextuality*. What objectivity-tropism would have one do is not what someone else would, but rather what someone else would do *in my place*. Of course there is a place in our lives for idiosyncrasies that requires a room of one's own where we can be ourselves and need not bother all that much about what others would say or do. All of us are entitled to a personal and private sector of being where matters stand on an altogether different footing and where it is perfectly appropriate to indulge our predilections and prejudices. But all the same, one must take note of that element of universality inherent in that "all of us are entitled. . . ." It has a far-reaching significance. For it means that what is at issue here is not in fact a violation of objectivity, however much appearances may look to the contrary. Giving scope to our personal idiosyncrasies in certain contexts is perfectly natural, perfectly understandable, perfectly reasonable and rational. What we have here is not *departure* from objective cogency and universality, but rather a particular *instance* of it.

But a deeper objection yet looms: "Why should we always be objective? Why do what abstract reason demands? After all, humans do not live by reason alone. And, in particular, the traditional aims of science (understanding how things work in the world, acquiring predictive foresight, and achieving effective control over at least some major aspects of our environment) do not represent the be-all and end-all of human existence. Surely not *every* humanly appropriate cultivation-domain involves a commitment to cold, passionless objectivity." In particular, it would be inhuman to be entirely objective with respect to those with whom we do— or ought—to stand in a relationship of affective involvement: our friends, relatives, kindred spirits, and the like. So goes the objection.

Now in dealing with this objection one must begin by acknowledging that it is certainly in order and that it merits the acknowledgment that, in a way, objectivity has its limits. Many rewarding human activities—family life, social interaction, sports and recreations, "light" reading, films, and other entertainment—make little or no use of reason or reasoning. But this concession does not settle the main point. For reason itself can and does recognize as wholly proper and legitimate a whole host of useful activities in whose conduct it itself plays little if any part. Reason itself is altogether willing and able to give them its stamp of approval, recognizing their value and usefulness. What is at issue, after all, is a matter of recognizing various objective facts about our human situation.

Of course there is more to humanity than rationality. Our natural makeup is complex and many-sided—a thing of many strains and aspects. We have interests over and above those at issue in the cultivation of reason. But there is no reason whatever why our reason should not be able to recognize this fact. To fail to do so would be simply unintelligent and thus contrary to the very nature of rationality. The very fact that man is the rational *animal* means that there is a good deal more to us than reason alone, and nothing prevents reason from recognizing that this is so and respecting the affective and passionate side of our nature for what it is—a crucial component of what makes us into the individuals we are. The point is that while subjectivity does indeed have an appropriate place in our lives, it is a place assigned to it by considerations of objective cogency. For of course reason is capable of recognizing all this. That man does not live by reason alone is a contention for whose acknowledgment there is very good reason indeed.

Accordingly, one cannot be too rationally objective for one's own good. If, contrary to fact, there were such a defect—if this could be established at all—then objective reason herself could bring this circumstance to light. Intelligence does not stand as one limited faculty over against others (emotion, affection, and the like). It is an all-pervasive light that can shine through to every endeavor, even those in which reason herself is not involved. Whatever human undertaking is valid and appropriate can be shown to be sound by the use of reason. It is the exercise of objectivizing rationality that informs us about priorities. And for that very reason it itself takes top priority.

Yet, does objectivity not undermine the emotional and affective side of people, the uncalculating, unselfish, friendly, open, easygoing side that is no less significant in the overall scheme of human affairs than the sterner enterprise of "pursuing our ends"? Is objective rationality not deficient in one-sidedly emphasizing the "calculating" aspect of human nature? Not at all! There are good grounds for reason *not* to deny the claims of our emotional and affective side. For life is infinitely fuller and richer that way! Reason, after all, is not our sole directrix. Emotion, sentiment, and the affective side of our nature have a perfectly proper and highly important place in the human scheme of things—no less important than the active striving for ends and goals. Insofar as other valid human enterprises exist, there is good reason why reason can (and should) recognize and acknowledge them. To insist on reasoning as the sole and all-comprising agency in human affairs is not rationalism but a hyper-rationalism that offends against rationality as such.

The fact to be emphasized here is that it is eminently rational—and thus objectively appropriate—to recognize that we do not live by and for reason alone. There are many contexts in life where it is perfectly appropriate to let one's hair down and to give full play to one's personal predilections and prejudices. Not every department of life—personal relationships and diversions included—needs to be dedicated to the pursuit of reason. We must and should preserve a region of personal space for the cultivation of our idiosyncratic wants. It is a cogent fact that we cannot and need not always proceed objectively. But this, of course, is itself a need of ours. And it is a perfectly true and objective fact about our situation. The circumstance that objectivity has its limits represents a perfectly objective fact with which reason can and should come to terms. What is at issue is not a defect of objectivity but a perfectly objective recognition that objectivity has certain limits.

The salient point, then, is that within all those various characteristic purposive/functional ranges that characterize human endeavor—science, morality, and "the pursuit of happiness" included—objectivity will reign supreme. To whatever extent we are seriously dedicated to achieving such ends, it is by the established ground rules of rational procedure as traditionally conceived—objectivity included—that we must proceed. To *this* particular goal there is no other, more effective route that leaves objectivity aside. It is indeed the case that there is a strictly personal sector that is of prime importance in human life. Clearly, objective rationality is no substitute for personalized sensibility. But, for one thing, rationality itself recognizes this. And, for another, the reverse is equally true.

NOTES

INTRODUCTION

1. Recent influential philosophical discussions of objectivity include Richard J. Bernstein, *Beyond Objectivism and Relativism* (Philadelphia: University of Pennsylvania Press, 1983); Hilary Putnam, *Realism with a Human Face*, ed. James Conant (Cambridge, Mass.: Harvard University Press, 1990); and Richard Rorty, *Objectivity, Relativism, and Truth* (Cambridge: Cambridge University Press, 1991).

1. OBJECTIVITY AND RATIONALITY

1. Note that such probative or epistemic objectivity is something generic that can obtain in very different areas (for example, in politics or in ethics). The term *cognitive objectivity*, by contrast, will here be used specifically for (epistemic) objectivity in matters relating to knowledge.

2. The objective/subjective distinction has undergone a curious inversion in the history of thought. In pre-Kantian days—from the time of Scholastics such as Suarez to that of Descartes, Spinoza, and Berkeley—for something to obtain *objectively* was for it to exist as an object of thought (as an idea or other item of mental representation), while for it to obtain *subjectively* or *formally* was for it to exist as an actual subject in the real world, independently of whatever mental representation might be connected to it. Descartes in the seventeenth century thus spoke of the subjective as "the reality that philosophers call actual or formal" (*Meditations* III, sec. ii). For Descartes "objective" meant being an object to a thinking mind, and "subjective" meant being a mind-independent subject of thought. However, Immanuel Kant reversed this situation. For him subjectivity involves a correlativity to thinkers—to subjects who carry on an inquiry—and objectivity implies a thinker-independent, self-sustaining object of possible consideration. Regarding Kant's treatment of objectivity, see Henry E. Allison, *Kant's Transcendental Idealism* (New Haven: Yale University Press, 1983), esp. chap. 7, "Objective Validity and Objective Reality," pp. 133–72.

3. William James, *Talks to Teachers on Psychology* (New York: Henry Holt, 1899), p. 4.

4. For an elaborate development of this position, see the author's *Rationality: A Philosophical Inquiry into the Nature and the Rationale of Reason* (Oxford: Clarendon Press, 1988).

5. To be sure, this does not hold for a "personally appropriate goal"—as opposed to one that is unqualifiedly appropriate. For, clearly, given your skills, a certain goal (competing in the Olympics, say) may be appropriate for you but absurd for me. But this very fact is, of course, rationally inherent in the objective circumstances of our differential situation.

6. On our duty towards the cultivation of rationality, see also pp. 204–9 of the author's *Rationality*.

7. There is also a significant contrast between a speaker-selected, antecedently constituted FPP group ("we lawyers") or one whose self-relation is left as an exercise to the recipients ("we kindred spirits"). The constitution of that FPP group is not something that is clear in and of itself without further ado.

8. Compare the position of Immanuel Kant's *Critique of Pure Reason*.

9. Compare Derek Parfit, "Providence, Morality, and Prisoner's Dilemma," *Proceedings of the British Academy* 65 (1979): 555ff.

10. This of course comes to "what rationality *as we understand it* is." For the inquiry and the questions that give rise to it are ours.

11. Note, too, that different top-level finalities can lead to priority conflicts through competing demands on resources. Health and knowledge, or family life and professional life, may certainly conflict—not, to be sure, as abstract desiderata but in the competing demands that arise in the course of their practical implementation. Insofar as such conflicts are rationally resolvable at all, still other finalities must be involved as arbiters. And there need be no absolute uniqueness here. Resolutions can, in principle, always be accomplished in distinct yet still appropriate ways.

12. K. R. Popper, *Objective Knowledge* (Oxford: Clarendon Press, 1972), pp. 106–52 (see p. 109).

13. Some of the issues discussed in the present chapter are also touched upon in the author's *Rationality*, especially in chap. 10, "The Universality of the Rational."

2. CRITICS OF OBJECTIVITY

1. See Allan Megill, ed., *Rethinking Objectivity* (Durham: Duke University Press, 1994) for an anthology of instructive discussions bearing on the topics of the present chapter.

2. This view has become axiomatic for the entire "sociology of knowledge." See, for example, Peter Berger and Thomas Luckmann, *The Social Construction of Reality: A Treatise on the Sociology of Knowledge* (Harmondsworth: Penguin Books, 1967), and David Bloor, *Knowledge and Social Imagery* (London: Routledge, 1976).

3. Peter Winch, "Understanding a Primitive Society," *American Philosophical Quarterly* 1 (1964): 307–24, reprinted in B. R. Wilson, ed., *Rationality* (Oxford: Oxford University Press, 1970), and also in Michael Hollis and Steven Lukes, eds., *Rationality and Relativism* (Cambridge, Mass.: MIT Press, 1982).

4. Lucien Lévy-Bruhl, *Primitive Mentality* (London: Macmillan, 1923; first pub. in French, Paris, 1921).

5. E. E. Evans-Pritchard, *Witchcraft, Oracles and Magic Among the Azandi* (Oxford: Clarendon Press, 1937); *Nuer Religion* (Oxford: Clarendon Press, 1956).

6. The relevant issues are interestingly treated in John Kekes's book, *A Justification of Rationality* (Albany: SUNY Press, 1976), 137–49.

7. On "alternative standards of rationality," see Peter Winch, "Understanding a Primitive Society," pp. 307–24.

8. See the informative examination of this issue in Peter Novick, *That Noble Dream: The "Objectivity Question" and the American Historical Association* (Cambridge: Cambridge University Press, 1988).

9. The concluding chapter will return to this theme.

10. Contemporary feminism has given rise to a sizable literature of discussions of feminist epistemology in general and the nature of women's work in science in particular. See, for example: Sandra Harding, *The Science Question in Feminism* (Ithaca: Cornell University Press, 1986); Margaret Eistler, *The Double Standard: A Feminist Critique of Social Science* (New York: St. Martin's Press, 1980); Evelyn Fox Keller, *Reflections on Gender and Science* (New Haven: Yale University Press, 1985); Helen Longino, *Science as Social Knowledge: Values and Objectivity in Scientific Inquiry* (Princeton: Princeton University Press, 1990).

11. Susan Bordo, *The Flight to Objectivity: Essays on Cartesianism and Culture* (Albany: SUNY Press, 1987).

12. One prime shortcoming of feminist science studies lies in their neglect of the question/answer distinction at issue here. Thus Evelyn Keller envisions a "science [that] is divorced from nature and married instead to culture" ("The Gender's Science System: Or, Is Sex to Gender What Nature is to Science?" *Hypatia* 2 (1987): 34–49 (see p. 45). Compare also Keller's *Reflections on Gender and Science* (New Haven: Yale University Press, 1986); Jane Duran, *Towards a Feminist Epistemology* (Savage, Md.: Rowman and Littlefield, 1991); Sandra Harding, *Whose Science? Whose Knowledge?* (Buckingham: Open University Press, 1991); Sandra Harding and Jean F. O'Barr, eds., *Sex and Scientific Inquiry* (Chicago: University of Chicago Press, 1987).

13. Compare Susan Bordo, *The Flight to Objectivity*.

14. See Barry Barnes and David Bloor, "Relativism, Rationalism, and the Sociology of Knowledge," in Hollis and Lukes, *Rationality and Relativism,* pp. 11–47.

15. Regarding this perspective and its problems, see Frank Cunningham, *Objectivity in Social Science* (Toronto: University of Toronto Press, 1973).

3. OBJECTIVITY AND CONSENSUS

1. Sextus Empiricus, *Outlines of Pyrrhonism (Pyrrhôneiôn Hypotypôseôn)*, Book I, 145ff.

2. G. S. Kirk, J. E. Raven, and M. Schofield, *The Presocratic Philosophers*, 2d ed. (Cambridge: Cambridge University Press, 1983).

3. Cf. Duncan Black, *The Theory of Committees and Elections* (Cambridge: Cambridge University Press, 1958), for an examination of various problems of this sort.

4. The lottery paradox was originally formulated by H. E. Kyburg, *Probability and the Logic of Rational Relief* (Middletown, Conn.: Wesleyan University Press, 1961). For an analysis of its wider implications for inductive logic, see R. Hilpinen, *Rules of Acceptance and Inductive Logic, Acta Philosophica Fennica*, fasc. 22 (Amsterdam: North-Holland, 1968), pp. 39–49.

5. For a philosophically informed account of the relevant issues, see Alfred F. MacKay, *Arrow's Theorem: The Paradox of Social Choice* (New Haven: Yale University Press, 1980).

6. See Ludvik Fleck, *Genesis and Development of a Scientific Fact* (Chicago: University of Chicago Press, 1979), originally written in German in the 1930s and published in Switzerland in the 1940s.

7. An informative discussion of cognitive issues is presented in Keith Lehrer and Carl Wagner, *Rational Consensus in Science and Society* (Dordrecht: D. Reidel, 1981); see esp. pp. 7–8. On the relation of recent philosophical discussions of objectvity to issues in the philosophy of science, see Helen E. Longino, *Science as Social Knowledge: Values and Objectivity in Scientific Inquiry.*

8. Some of the issues touched on here are developed further in the author's *Pluralism* (Oxford: Clarendon Press, 1993).

4. AGAINST COGNITIVE RELATIVISM

1. For a conspectus of recent discussions of relativism, as well as references to the literature, see: Michael Krausz and Jack Meiland, eds., *Relativism: Cognitive and Moral* (Notre Dame: University of Notre Dame Press, 1982); Hollis and Lukes, *Rationality and Relativism*; Joseph Margolis, ed., *Is Relativism Defensible?*, special issue of *The Monist* 67, no. 3 (July 1984).

2. William James, *Pragmatism* (New York, 1907), p. 171. The basic line of thought goes back to the ancient skeptics. Compare Sextus Empiricus, *Outlines of Pyrrhonism*, I, 54, 59–60, 97, and passim.

3. This position is often attributed to Thomas Kuhn on grounds of his classic *The Structure of Scientific Revolutions* (Chicago: University of Chicago Press, 1962; 2d ed. 1970).

4. Richard J. Bernstein, *Beyond Objectivism and Relativism* (Philadelphia: University of Pennsylvania Press, 1983), p. 8.

5. The author has told this story in his own way as regards the standard epistemology of "the scientific method" in *Methodological Pragmatism* (Oxford: Blackwell, 1977).

6. To be sure, someone could convince me that my understanding of the implications of my standards is incomplete and leads me to an *internally* motivated revision of my rational proceedings, amending those standards from within with a view to greater systemic coherence.

7. Alasdair MacIntyre, *Whose Justice? Which Rationality?* (Notre Dame: University of Notre Dame Press, 1988).

8. "Reste von christlicher Theologie innerhalb der philosophischen Problematik" (Martin Heidegger, *Sein und Zeit* [Leipzig, 1923], p. 230).

9. William James, "Pragmatism and Humanism," in *The Writings of William James*, ed. John J. McDermott (New York: Random House, 1967), p. 450.

10. Compare Hilary Putnam, "Why Can't Reason be Naturalized?" *Synthèse* 52 (1982): 3–23 (see pp. 12–13).

11. Some of the themes of this chapter are also touched upon in chap. 9 of the author's *Rationality* and in chap. 10 of his *Satisfying Reason* (Boston: Kluwer, 1995).

5. OBJECTIVITY AND QUANTIFICATION

1. A collection of particularly fine articles on the subject is Harry Woolf, ed., *Quantification: A History of the Meaning of Measurement in the Natural and Social Sciences* (Indianapolis: Bobbs-Merrill, 1961). See also Brian Ellis, *Basic Concepts of Measurement* (Cambridge: Cambridge University Press, 1966).

2. See, for example, the introduction to David R. Kranz et al., *Foundations of Measurement*, vol. 1 (New York: Academic Press, 1971).

3. S. S. Stevens, "Measurement, Psychophysics, and Utility," in *Measurement: Definition and Theories*, ed. C. W. Churchman and P. Ratoosh (New York: Wiley, 1959), pp. 18–63 (see p. 19).

4. M. R. Cohen and Ernest Nagel, *An Introduction to Logic and Scientific Method* (New York: Harcourt Brace, 1934), p. 294. Compare Norman R. Campbell: "Measurement is the process of assigning numbers to represent qualities," *Foundations of Science* (New York: Dover, 1957).

5. The rationale for the fashionable idea of a "system" is to play just exactly this role.

6. Herbert Dingle, "A Theory of Measurement," *British Journal for the Philosophy of Science* 1 (1950): 5–26.

7. The issues are closely parallel because a measured feature of something can be looked upon as constituting a parametrized quality of it. As my Pittsburgh colleague Nuel Belnap has noted in discussion, all of the seven factors singled out in the previous quantity-oriented discussion have close analogies in the qualitative case in relation to the natural kind vs. random assemblage distinction. The difficulty of maintaining natural kindhood in the face of *logical* combinations (such as conjunction) exactly parallels the difficulty of taking mathematical combinations (such as multiplication) as automatically continuing to constitute actual measurements.

8. Sir William Thomson, "Electrical Units of Measurement," *Popular Lectures and Addresses*, 3 vols. (London, 1889–91), vol. 1, p. 73.

9. See Peter Skrabanek and James McCormick, *Follies and Fallacies in Medicine* (New York, 1990), p. 27.

10. On these issues, see Theodore M. Parker, *Trust in Numbers: The Pursuit of Objectivity in Science and Public Life* (Princeton: Princeton University Press, 1995).

11. Topics related to this chapter's themes are treated in chap. 7, "Meaningless Numbers," of the author's *Satisfying Reason.*

6. OBJECTIVITY AND COMMUNICATION

1. William James, *Principles of Psychology,* 2 vols. (New York: Henry Holt, 1890); reissued in 3 vols. in *The Works of William James* (Cambridge, Mass.: Harvard University Press, 1981); vol. 2, p. 401 of the latter edition.

2. The ideas at issue here are developed more fully in chap. 3, "Economic Aspects of Communication," of the author's *Cognitive Economy* (Pittsburgh: University of Pittsburgh Press, 1989).

3. Usefully relevant discussions can be found in David Lewis, *Convention: A Philosophical Study* (Cambridge, Mass.: Harvard University Press, 1969). But contrast Angus Ross, "Why Do We Believe What We Are Told?" *Ratio* 28 (1986): 69–88.

4. Compare F. H. Bradley's thesis: "Error *is* truth, that is, false only because partial and left incomplete." *Appearance and Reality* (Oxford: Clarendon Press, 1893), p. 169.

5. The justification of imputations of this general nature is treated more fully in chap. 9 of the author's *Induction* (Oxford: Blackwell, 1980).

6. Compare Charles S. Peirce, *Collected Papers,* vol. 5 (Cambridge, Mass.: Harvard University Press, 1934), sec. 5.383.

7. Some of the themes of this chapter are also treated in chap. 5 of the author's *Empirical Inquiry* (Totowa, N. J.: Rowman and Littlefield, 1982).

7. ONTOLOGICAL OBJECTIVITY GROUNDS COGNITIVE OBJECTIVITY

1. One possible misunderstanding must be blocked at this point. To *learn* about nature, we must *interact* with it. And so, to *determine* a feature of a physical object, we may have to make some impact upon it that would perturb its otherwise obtaining condition. (The indeterminacy principle of quantum mechanics affords a well-known reminder of this.) It should be clear that this matter of physical interaction for date-acquisition is not contested in the ontological indifference thesis here at issue.

2. To be sure, *abstract* things, such as colors or numbers, will not have dispositional properties; being divisible by four is not a *disposition* of sixteen. Plato got the matter right in Book VII of the *Republic.* In the realm of *abstracta,* such as those of mathematics, there are no genuine *processes*—and process is a requisite of dispositions. Of course, there may be dispositional truths in which numbers (or colors, etc.) figure that do not issue in any dispositional properties of these numbers (or colors, etc.) themselves—a truth, for example, such as my predilection for prime numbers. But if a truth (or supposed truth) does no more than to convey how someone *thinks* about a

thing, then it does not indicate any property of the thing itself. In any case, however, the subsequent discussion will focus on *realia* in contrast to *fictionalia* and *concreta* in contrast to *abstracta*. (Fictional things, however, *can* have dispositions: Sherlock Holmes was addicted to cocaine, for example. Their difference from *realia* is dealt with below.)

3. This aspect of objectivity was justly stressed in the Second Analogy of Kant's *Critique of Pure Reason*, though his discussion rests on ideas already contemplated by Leibniz, *Philosophische Schriften*, ed. C. I. Gerhardt, vol. 7 (Berlin: Wiedmann, 1890), pp. 319ff.

4. See C. I. Lewis, *An Analysis of Knowledge and Valuation* (La Salle, Ill.: Open Court, 1962), pp. 180–81.

5. Immanuel Kant, *Critique of Pure Reason*, A250.

6. For variations on this theme, see the author's *Satisfying Reason*.

7. C. S. Peirce, *Collected Papers*, vol. 5, sec. 5.64–67. Compare also vol. 2, sec. 2.138, and: "Whenever I've come to know a fact, it is by its resisting us. A man may walk down Wall Street debating within himself the existence of an external world; but in his brown study he jostles against somebody who angrily draws off and knocks him down. The sceptic is unlikely to carry his scepticism so far as to doubt whether anything besides the Ego was concerned in that phenomenon. The resistance shows that something independent of him is there. When anything strikes upon the senses the mind's train of thought is interrupted, for if it were not, nothing would distinguish the new observation from a fancy" (ibid., vol. 1, sec. 1.431).

8. René Descartes, *Meditations*, no. 6 in *Philosophical Works*, ed. E. S. Haldane and G. R. T. Ross, vol. 1 (Cambridge: Cambridge University Press, 1911), pp. 187–89.

9. See his essay on "The Rational Imperatives" in C. I. Lewis, *Values and Imperatives: Stakes in Ethics,* ed. John Lang (Stanford: Stanford University Press, 1969), pp. 156–77.

10. Kant held that we cannot experientially learn through perception about the objectivity of outer things, because we can only recognize our perceptions as perceptions (i.e., representations of outer things) if these outer things are taken as such from the first (rather than being learned or inferred). As he summarizes in the "Refutation of Idealism": "Idealism assumed that the only immediate experience is inner experience, and that from it we can only *infer* outer things—and this, moreover, only in an untrustworthy manner. . . . But in the above proof it has been shown that outer experience is really immediate . . ." (*Critique of Pure Reason*, B276). On these issues, see J. N. Findlay, *Kant and the Transcendental Object, A Hermeneutic Study* (Oxford: Clarendon Press, 1981).

11. Moses Maimonides, *The Guide of the Perplexed*, I, 71, 96a.

12. On this issue, recall the ideas of C. S. Peirce on truth as the ultimate product of an eventually perfected inquiry. For the details of the line of thought at work here, see the author's discussion of truth as an idealization in chap. 12 of his *Human Knowledge in Idealistic Perspectives* (Princeton: Princeton University Press, 1992).

13. Some of the themes of this chapter are also touched upon in chaps. 10 and 11 of the author's *Scientific Realism* (Dordrecht: D. Reidel, 1987).

8. THE PRAGMATIC RATIONALE OF
COGNITIVE OBJECTIVITY

1. This is why it seems mistaken to characterize objectivity as a *fundamental* epistemic value as Brian Ellis does in his *Truth and Objectivity* (Oxford: Basil Blackwell, 1990), pp. 228–31. The value of objectivity is not *fundamental* but *instrumental* and lies in its capacity to facilitate the achievement of other, ulterior goals.

2. Some of the themes of this chapter are also touched upon in chap. 3 ("The Rationale of Rationality") of the author's *Rationality*.

9. MORAL OBJECTIVITY:
AGAINST MORAL RELATIVISM

1. The most notable modern exponent of the position was David Hume. See his *A Treatise of Human Nature* (London: A. Millar, 1738), and sec. 1 of Appendix I of *An Inquiry Concerning the Principles of Morals* (London: A. Millar, 1752).

2. See Charles L. Stevenson, "The Emotive Meaning of Ethical Terms," in his *Facts and Values* (New Haven: Yale University Press, 1963), and also his earlier *Ethics and Language* (New Haven: Yale University Press, 1944). Two works particularly useful on the "emotive theory" are G. J. Warnock, *Contemporary Moral Philosophy* (London: Allen and Unwyn, 1967), and J. O. Urmson, *The Emotive Theory of Ethics* (Oxford: Oxford University Press, 1968). The "norm expressivism" of Alan Gibbard's *Wise Choices, Apt Feelings* (Cambridge, Mass.: Harvard University Press, 1993), affords a more recent example.

3. Stevenson, *Facts and Values,* p. 16.

4. A. J. Ayer, *Language, Truth and Logic* (New York: Dover, 1952), p. 108.

5. Compare R. M. Hare, *The Language of Morals* (Oxford: Clarendon Press, 1952).

6. It is to the credit of the utilitarian tradition that it has stressed this gearing of morality to the benefit of people, for this clearly establishes the issues as subject to rational deliberation. But it is to its discredit that it has generally seen these benefits in terms of pleasure and mere personal preference alone, so that the veneer of rationality is very thin indeed.

7. Compare J. N. Findlay, *Language, Mind and Value* (London: Allen and Unwyn, 1963), chaps. 9 and 10.

8. Though their choices do affect how these interests operate. Once you have chosen Helen to be your future wife, her attitude towards you becomes a matter of substantial interest for you.

9. W. D. Ross, *The Right and the Good* (Oxford: Clarendon Press, 1930), p. 89.

10. An interesting discussion on objectivity in ethics—albeit one that proceeds along lines rather different from those that figure in the present deliberations—is

found in Thomas Nagel's *The View from Nowhere* (Oxford and New York: Oxford University Press, 1986).

11. Only by turning his back upon morality altogether can an existentialist maintain, with Sartre, "that freedom is the unique foundation of values and that *nothing*, absolutely nothing, justifies one in adopting this or that particular value, this or that particular scale of values" (*Being and Nothingness*, trans. H. E. Barnes [New York: Philosophical Library, 1953], p. 46). For morality is, as we have seen, inextricably bound up with rationality since moral validity calls for a justification of a certain sort (in terms of protecting the interests of people). A "value" whose adoption one cannot justify with reference to cogent principles is no real *value* at all but merely an arbitrary preference.

12. These issues are also treated more fully in the author's *Moral Absolutes* (New York and Bern: Peter Lang, 1989).

13. Does this way of viewing the issue put subrational beings outside the pale of moral concern? By no means. For it matters deeply to rational agents how they themselves treat animals, or for that matter any other sorts of beings that have interests capable of being injured. We have a substantial interest in how others comport themselves who also belong to the type to which we see ourselves as belonging.

14. But just who are the "we" at issue? Clearly, those who are members of our linguistic community—those able to realize that when we speak of "morality" we mean *morality* (with the various things involved therein) and not, say, basket weaving.

15. The analogy of natural law is helpful: "Theft, murder, adultery and all injuries are forbidden by the laws of nature; but what is to be called theft, what murder, what adultery, what injury in a citizen, this is not to be determined by the natural but by the civil law" (Thomas Hobbes, *De Cive*, chap. 4, sec. 16). This follows St. Thomas's earlier thesis that appropriate human law must be subordinate to the natural law by way of "particular determination," with different human laws, varying from place to place, nevertheless representing appropriate concretizations of the same underlying principle of natural law (see *Summa Theologica*, IaIIae, q. 95–96).

16. Aspects of these issues are helpfully discussed in Susan Wolf, "Two Levels of Pluralism," *Ethics* 102 (1992): 785–98.

17. After all, "the actual variations in the moral code (of different groups) are more readily explained by the hypothesis that they reflect different ways of life than by the hypothesis that they express perceptions, most of them seriously inadequate and badly distorted, of objective values" (J. L. Mackie, *Ethics: Inventing Right and Wrong* [Harmondsworth: Penguin Books, 1977], p. 37).

18. See Clyde Kluckhohn, *Culture and Behavior* (Glencoe, Ill.: The Free Press, 1962); idem, "Ethical Relativity; Sic et Non," *The Journal of Philosophy* 52 (1955): 663–77; R. Redfield, "The Universally Human and the Culturally Variable," *The Journal of General Education* 10 (1967): 150–60; Ralph Linton, "Universal Ethical Principles: An Anthropological View," in R. N. Anshen, ed., *Moral Principles of Action* (New York:

Harper, 1952); idem, "The Problem of Universal Values," in R. F. Spencer, ed., *Method and Perspective in Anthropology* (Minneapolis: University of Minnesota Press, 1954).

19. Some of the issues of this chapter are elaborated more fully in the author's *Moral Absolutes*.

10. MORAL OBJECTIVITY: THE RATIONALITY AND UNIVERSALITY OF MORAL PRINCIPLES

1. H. A. Prichard, "Does Moral Philosophy Rest on a Mistake?" *Mind* 21 (1912): 21–37.

2. Gilbert Harman, "Moral Relativism Defended," *The Philosophical Review* 84 (1975): 3–22 (see p. 3). See also his *The Nature of Morality* (New York: Oxford University Press, 1977).

3. The most recent and cogent articulation of this position is David Gauthier's *Morals by Agreement* (Oxford: Oxford University Press, 1985).

4. One can develop the idea of a hypothetical contact that it would (in idealized circumstances) be sensible to enter into as a device for assessing what is morally appropriate. This may indeed provide a way of invoking morality (as inherent in *altogether* sensible contracts) to validate social appropriateness. But it does not afford a way of using wholly nonmoral factors (such as "prudentially advantageous contracts") to determine morality, let alone to validate it. Even a compact that advantages *all* participants (but only, say, to the deteriment of their eventual descendants) is not ipso facto a morally appropriate one.

5. Someone may ask: "Why think of ourselves in this way—why see ourselves as free rational agents?" But to ask this is to ask for a good rational reason and is thus already to take a stance within the framework of rationality. In theory, we can "resign" from the community of rational beings, abandoning all claims to being more than "mere animals." But this is a step one cannot *justify*—there are no satisfactory rational grounds for taking it. And this is something most of us realize instinctively. The appropriateness of acknowledging others as responsible agents whenever possible holds in our own case as well.

6. Immanuel Kant portrayed the obligation at issue in the following terms:

> First, it is one's duty to raise himself out of the crudity of his nature—out of his animality (*quoad actum*) more and more to humanity, by which alone he is capable of setting himself ends. It is man's [paramount] duty to . . . supply by instruction what is lacking in his knowledge, and to correct his mistakes. . . . [T]his end [is] his duty in order that he may . . . be worthy of the humanity dwelling within him. (*Metaphysics of Morals*, p. 387, *Akad.*)

7. The general line of these deliberations has been to ground morality in rationality, while at the same time denying that it is appropriate to ground morality in

prudence. In simple self-consistency then, a validation of rationality that proceeds wholly in terms of prudential self-interest alone is automatically denied us. Instead, consonance and consistency require a validation of rationality that is itself ultimately ontological and axiological (value-oriented), validating rationality too in terms of its ontological fitness. And this is indeed the line of the author's book, *Rationality*. Relevant considerations are also presented in the author's *Moral Absolutes*.

8. Kurt Baier, *The Moral Point of View* (Ithaca: Cornell University Press, 1958), p. 115.

9. Some of the themes of this discussion are also touched upon in chap. 12, "Moral Rationality," of the author's *The Validity of Values* (Princeton: Princeton University Press, 1993).

10. Of course, an "adequate moral economy" in which people will do the right thing, if only for prudential reasons of self-interest, is not yet a "morally superlative order" in which they do the right thing *for morally cogent reasons* (e.g., from a Kantian "sense of duty"). And, of course, we must recognize an obligation to work to *this* sort of system as well (by fostering moral education, etc.). But this (perfectly valid) point transcends the scope of our present concerns.

11. The ideas of this section are elaborated more fully in chap. 6 ("The Social Rationale of Benevolence") of the author's *Unselfishness* (Pittsburgh: University of Pittsburgh Press, 1975).

11. VALUE OBJECTIVITY

1. Compare Crispin Wright's discussion of the comic/amusing in his *Truth and Objectivity* (Cambridge, Mass.: Harvard University Press, 1992), pp. 7–12.

2. Aristotle, *Metaphysics*, 1032b17–22; *De Motu Animalium*, 701a18–20. A helpful guide to Aristotle's theory of practical reasoning is Norman O. Dahl, *Practical Reason, Aristotle, and Weakness of the Will* (Minneapolis: University of Minnesota Press, 1984).

3. David Hume, *A Treatise on Human Nature*, Bk. II, Pt. iii, sec. 3. For Hume, the only inappropriate desires are those that depend on irrational beliefs.

4. For strict consistency, a rigorous Humean should, by analogy, hold that cognitive reason, too, is only hypothetical; that it only tells us that certain beliefs must be abandoned *if* we hold certain others, and that no beliefs are contrary to reason as such, so that "it is not contrary to reason to think one's finger larger than the entire earth."

5. David Hume, *A Treatise on Human Nature*, ed. L. A. Selby Bigge (Oxford: Clarendon Press, 1964), p. 458.

6. A good though ultimately unconvincing exposition of the opposing position may be found in Frederick Schick, *Having Reasons: An Essay in Rationality and Sociality* (Princeton: Princeton University Press, 1984).

7. The issue goes back to the specification of the "basics" (*principia*) of the human good in the Middle Academy (Carneades)—things like the soundness and mainte-

nance of the parts of the body, health, sound senses, freedom from pain, physical vigor, and physical attractiveness. Compare Cicero, *De finibus*, V.vii.19.

8. On the matter of rational vs. irrational ends see Kurt Baier, *The Moral Point of View*, and Bernard Gert, *The Moral Rules* (New York: Harper and Row, 1973).

9. Some theorists would change the "contrary to" of this sentence to "above and beyond." But for the already indicated reasons this would be inappropriate. Reason is no self-sufficient be-all and end-all.

10. See the author's *Welfare* (Pittsburgh: University of Pittsburgh Press, 1972). Cf. John Rawls, *A Theory of Justice* (Cambridge, Mass.: Harvard University Press, 1971), p. 421. Rawls traces this line of thought back to Henry Sidgwick.

11. The contrast goes back to Aristotle's distinction between *desire* as such and *rational preference*. Many aspects of Aristotle's ethical theory bear usefully on the present discussion.

12. The current state of this discussion as regards specifically *moral* values is depicted in Geoffrey Sayre-McCord, ed., *Essays in Moral Realism* (Ithaca: Cornell University Press, 1988).

13. In this light, our previous recourse to "truistic" statement has to be glossed not through a reference to truths as such but to statements whose acceptability validation is more or less immediate.

14. J. L. Mackie, *Ethics: Inventing Right and Wrong*.

15. Some tertiary properties may be causally connected only with yet further tertiary ones. (Crispin Wright's discussion suggests that *funny* (i.e., amusing) may be an example. See his *Truth and Objectivity*.) But this circumstance, while interesting in its own right, has no negative implications for tertiary properties as such. After all, other tertiary properties will certainly be causally connectable with primary ones (intense temperature will strike intelligent people as dangerous).

16. R. M. Hare, *The Language of Morals*, p. 145; cf. also Mackie, *Ethics*, p. 41.

17. G. E. Moore, *Principia Ethica* (Cambridge: Cambridge University Press, 1903), chap. 1.

18. Some of the themes of this chapter are also touched upon in the author's *The Validity of Values*. See especially chap. 3, "The Rationality of Values and Evaluations."

12. HERMENEUTIC OBJECTIVITY: AGAINST DECONSTRUCTIONISM

1. See especially Jacques Derrida's *De la Grammatologie* (Paris: Editions de Minuit, 1967), translated as *Of Grammatology* by G. Spivak (Baltimore: Johns Hopkins University Press, 1976).

2. J. Hillis Miller, in Harold Bloom et al., eds., *Deconstruction and Criticism* (New York, Seabury Press, 1979), p. 229.

3. On the trichotomy at issue here, see the essay on "The Threefold Way" in the author's *Forbidden Knowledge* (Dordrecht: D. Reidel, 1987), pp. 83–92.

4. This apropos of the quip that a book no more shows where its author is presently located in thought than a molehill shows where its maker is presently located in nature.

5. Jacques Derrida, *Speech and Phenomena*, trans. D. Allison (Evanston: Northwestern University Press, 1973). Original: *Le Voix et le phénomène* (Paris: Presses Universitaires de France, 1973).

6. In the context of textual interpretation, the case for this halfway-house position is cogently formulated in Stanley Fish, *Is There a Text in This Class? The Anthology of Interpersonal Communities* (Cambridge, Mass.: Harvard University Press, 1980).

7. This chapter is a substantially revised and expanded version of chap. 10 of the author's *Satisfying Reason*.

NAME INDEX

Alexander, Samuel, 57
Allison, Henry E., 215n2
Anaximander of Miletus, 89, 95
Aristotle, 175, 181, 225n2, 226n11
Arrow, Kenneth J., 51
Ayer, A. J., 222n4

Baier, Kurt, 166, 225n8, 226n8
Bordo, Susan, 217n11, 217n13
Barnes, Barry, 217n14
Belnap, Nuel, 219n7
Berger, Peter, 216n2
Bergson, Henri, 57
Berkeley, George, 215n2
Bernstein, Richard J., 215n1, 218n4
Black, Duncan, 218n3
Bloom, Harold, 226n2
Bloor, David, 216n2, 217n14
Bradley, F. H., 90, 220n4
Bridgman, P. W., 76

Caesar, Julius, 98
Campbell, Norman R., 219n4
Cicero, 226n7
Cohen, M. R., 219n4
Condorcet, M. S. A. de, 50
Cunningham, Frank, 217n15

Dahl, Norman O., 225n2
Derrida, Jacques, 197, 205, 226n1,
    227n5
Descartes, René, 105, 215n2, 221n8
Dewey, John, 57
Dilthey, Wilhelm, 57
Dingle, Herbert, 76, 219n6
Duran, Jane, 217n12
Durkheim, Emile, 26

Einstein, Albert, 53
Eistler, Margaret, 217n10
Ellis, Brian, 219n1, 222n1
Euclid, 61
Evans-Pritchard, E. E., 27, 217n5

Findlay, J. N., 221n10, 222n7
Fish, Stanley, 227n6
Fleck, Ludvik, 52
Freud, Sigmund, 145

Galen, 10, 12
Gauthier, David, 224n3
Gerhardt, C. I., 221n3
Gert, Bernard, 226n8
Gibbard, Alan, 222n2
Gödel, Kurt, 102
Goethe, J. W. von, 80

Harding, Sandra, 217n10, 217n12
Hare, R. M., 194, 222n5, 226n16
Harman, Gilbert, 224n2
Hegel, G. W. F., 90
Heraclitus of Ephesus, 49
Hilpinen, R., 218n4
Hobbes, Thomas, 223n15
Hollis, Martin, 217n14, 218n1
Hume, David, 176–78, 222n1, 225n3,
    225n5

James, William, 8, 57, 69, 86, 215n3,
    218n2, 219n9, 220n1

Kalven, Harry Jr., 50
Kant, Immanuel, 101, 108, 120,
    162–63, 167, 221n3, 221n5,
    221n10, 215n2, 216n8, 224n6

ABOUT THE AUTHOR

Nicholas Rescher is Professor of Philosophy at the University of Pittsburgh. Among his many books are *Baffling Phenomena and Other Studies in the Philosophy of Knowledge and Valuation* (1990), *Human Interests: Reflections on Philosophical Anthropology* (1990), *Pluralism: Against the Demand for Consensus* (1993), and *Philosophical Standardism: An Empirical Approach to Philosophical Methodology* (1994).